CLOCKWORK

REVISED AND EXPANDED

MIKE MICHALOWICZ

CLOCKWORK

REVISED AND EXPANDED

DESIGN YOUR BUSINESS TO RUN ITSELF

PORTFOLIO / PENGUIN

Portfolio / Penguin
An imprint of Penguin Random House LLC
penguinrandomhouse.com

First published in hardcover as *Clockwork* by Portfolio / Penguin in 2018

This revised and expanded edition with new material
published by Portfolio / Penguin in 2022

Most Portfolio books are available at a discount when purchased in quantity for sales
promotions or corporate use. Special editions, which include personalized covers,
excerpts, and corporate imprints, can be created when purchased in large
quantities. For more information, please call (212) 572-2232 or e-mail
specialmarkets@penguinrandomhouse.com. Your local bookstore can also assist
with discounted bulk purchases using the Penguin Random House corporate
Business-to-Business program. For assistance in locating a participating retailer,
e-mail B2B@penguinrandomhouse.com.

Illustrations by Elizabeth Dobrinska
Photograph of Jason Barker taken of himself thanking
Mike Michalowicz used with permission.

ISBN 9780593538173 (hardcover)
ISBN 9780593541036 (ebook)

Printed in the United States of America
2nd Printing

Book design by Pauline Neuwirth

For Jason Barker. You inspired me.

CONTENTS

PHASE TWO
INTEGRATE

PHASE THREE
ACCELERATE

FOREWORD

As a rule, I very rarely write forewords. But sometimes circumstances dictate that a rule must be broken. Such is the case for *Clockwork, Revised and Expanded.*

This book will change your life. I don't say this flippantly. I say it with great pride. Mike and I share the same passion for helping entrepreneurs succeed. It's my life's passion. It's his.

What makes us a match made in business heaven is that I help entrepreneurs in stages one and three and he bridges the gap by helping entrepreneurs in stage two.

Not familiar with the entrepreneurial stages? Let me explain by first asking a question. Are you running your business or is your business running you?

If you are a typical business owner, your business is running you.

There are three stages in a business's life that every successful entrepreneur experiences. Stage one is when you are scratching your head thinking about starting a business, stage two is surviving the startup stage, and stage three is the growth stage.

To successfully launch at stage one, you must determine if entrepreneurship is right for you. This is the Entrepreneurial Leap stage (which is why I wrote *Entrepreneurial Leap*). To successfully navigate stage two, you must extract yourself from being the linchpin of the business so it can run without dependency on you. This is the Clockwork stage (which is why Mike wrote *Clockwork, Revised and Expanded*). And in stage three, you must scale with an operating system that harnesses human energy. This is the Traction stage (which is why I wrote *Traction*).

I have lived the journey myself—all three stages. I know first-hand how difficult the entrepreneurial path can be. And I've dedicated many years to the research and development of an operating system for business. I call it the Entrepreneurial Operating System (EOS).

As a company grows from ten to hundreds of employees, your business demands an operating system. You need to build a leadership team that works cohesively. You need to unify all elements of your business to work together, seamlessly and progressively, to break through and enjoy the next stage. You need disciplines and tools such as scorecards, issue lists, vision planning, people systems, and documented processes. This is the stage of growth where businesses will generate tens, even hundreds, of millions in revenue.

If you haven't started your business yet, you need to evaluate the options and prepare accordingly. You need to know the essential traits you must have to increase your odds of success. In stage one, you need to go in prepared, not just go in. Like a recipe, if you use the right ingredients, you have the potential to cook up a masterpiece. But if you don't have the correct ingredients, regardless of your efforts, you don't have a shot.

After the Entrepreneurial Leap stage and before the Traction stage there is a stumbling block. An entrepreneurial hurdle of sorts. This is where the odds are most stacked against you. It is where you, the entrepreneur, are pulled in countless directions. You are trying to do the work and have others do the work at the same time. This is when you may feel compelled to revert from having employees to just doing everything yourself. You tell yourself it would be easier. You think "no one can do what I do." You wish someone would clone you.

When you arrive at this stage, you need to stop being the only leader and let go of the reins. It is a scary, treacherous time, and sadly, most entrepreneurs never make it further. Most stay stuck in stage two forever, an entrepreneurial purgatory. Or they give up and return to the solopreneur ways and days. And that's why I believe Mike's work in *Clockwork, Revised and Expanded* and my work are a perfect match. With this book, you will breeze through stage two.

Stage two is very much a state of mind. You must transition from doing the work (or making all the decisions for others doing the work) to true delegation—the assignment of outcomes. You need to design the vision for the company and orchestrate all your resources to get there. Then you must get over yourself and let your team carry that vision to reality.

The belief that one day your business will just start running itself, by itself, is a fallacy. You won't wake up one day to find that everything in the business just clicks. You aren't one big client away from a successful business. You aren't just one more year of carrying the business on your back before it takes off. Things don't switch overnight or suddenly come together. Transitioning your business through the Clockwork stage is a process. You will slowly remove the organization's dependency on you as your business starts to run itself.

What you can change immediately is your mindset. You are building a company. Not working for a company—building it. Your company is a puzzle and your job is to put the pieces in place.

Are you ready to have your business run itself? Ask yourself this simple question: If I left my business for the next four weeks without any physical or digital connection to work, would the business survive?

In *Clockwork, Revised and Expanded,* Mike suggests that the four-week vacation is the ultimate acid test for a business that runs itself, and I concur. For more than twenty years I have taken the month of August off. It's called my "one-month sabbatical." I did it through the entire process of building EOS Worldwide from one person to two hundred people. You can do the same. And if you feel that you can't leave your company for four weeks, or even four days, we need to fix that.

Throughout this book you will discover simple techniques that ensure your business grows, breaks through, and runs on automatic. You will learn how to find, serve, and protect the heart of your organization. You and your growing team will root out Time Piles, areas where your business has bottlenecks in need of improvement.

If I may be so bold, I would like to offer some points of consideration and summarize the above. If you are considering starting your first business, then read *Entrepreneurial Leap.* You will be far better equipped to have a successful start.

If you are positioning your company to surpass ten employees, then read *Traction.*

And if you are in stage two, where the business is just you or a handful of employees—if you can't leave the business because it is constantly needing you, if a four-week vacation seems like a pipe dream—then read *Clockwork.*

Entrepreneurial Leap is where you start, *Traction* is where you finish, and *Clockwork, Revised and Expanded* is what bridges them together.

In these pages you will find the missing link that will prepare your business and your mind for the next stage of growth. You will make the transition from serving your business to it serving you. You are about to own a business that runs itself.

I wish you tremendous success. You deserve it.

Gino Wickman, author of *Traction* and *Entrepreneurial Leap*

INTRODUCTION

LEARN WHY USING CLOCKWORK IN YOUR BUSINESS IS ABOUT MORE THAN JUST YOU

One day, doing more of the same for "just one more day" may be the costliest mistake of your life. The grind stops now. The hustle is over. It's time to make your business run itself. Your company needs it. You need it. And the people in your life are starving for it. Perhaps more than you might ever know.

In the picture that business owner Jason Barker emailed to me, he holds up a sign that reads, "Thank you Mike Michalowicz!!" He's sitting in the exit aisle of a plane as he prepares to depart for an annual guys' weekend trip. Jason almost always missed the outing because he couldn't leave his business, not even for a weekend. But not this year. Jason's implementation of the Clockwork system had freed him up for a time of fun, relaxation, and friendship. The photo touched my heart. His story shifted my soul.

"This picture was taken of me on the way back home from a recent trip to Phoenix with a group of twelve friends," Jason's email began. "We all go on a trip annually to watch our Oregon

Jason Barker

State Beavers play football on the road somewhere. I don't typically get to go due to my time commitments and being shackled to my business."

Shackled to my business. I hear that phrase often from entrepreneurs.

"But about a year ago I started implementing your Clockwork plan as soon as I read the book. My branch manager of twenty-three years had just walked in and gave me his two weeks' notice. What a shocker and a turning point! It turned out to be the perfect time to implement Clockwork while I searched for a new manager."

Jason owns Fresh Start Detail in Beaverton, Oregon, a business he started in 1983. He was the friend who would tell the guys "not this year" because he was "too busy," or who would cancel on them last minute because he had to put out fires. On the few trips he made, he wasn't really there. He stressed over what was happening back at his business. Was his small team getting the work done? Were customers being served? Were customers going elsewhere and becoming permanent noncustomers?

No one starts a business with the goal of being trapped by it. Your business should be as you always intended, a platform for your freedom. Freedom to do what you want and, in Jason's case, freedom to spend precious time with his friends.

"Skip ahead a few months and I was not only able to easily make the guys' trip this year but even went a day early to spend more time with my friends," Jason's email continued. "During the trip, however, one of my friends had a heart attack and died right in the restaurant after we had finished breakfast together. So why am I thanking you? Because working your system gave me what I thought was just a cool four-day vacation, but it turned out that I was able to spend the last days of a great friend's life with him."

My soul shifted when I read that. Did yours? Or at least did your perspective? Clockwork isn't about working less as much as it is about living as you intend. When your business runs itself, you have the freedom to do what brings you joy and fulfillment. And to do it without worrying about your business being compromised.

Clockwork is not about abandoning your business, either. It's about the freedom of choice. If you love aspects of your work, you will have the freedom to lean into that without the need to do the work you aren't good at or don't enjoy. If you want to work a twenty-hour week, you can. If you want to take a sabbatical from your business, you can. If you want your business to simply run on its own, permanently, it can. Clockwork does all that for you.

For years, I'd been encouraging entrepreneurs to take vacations from their business—for sanity, but also to create the systems needed so they *can* take a vacation from their business—and I'd seen a lot of vacation photos. But Jason's email was something I never anticipated. I stared at the photo and teared up. I can't imagine how Jason would feel if he hadn't been there with his friend because the business "needed him."

As business owners, we are used to missing stuff. We long ago convinced ourselves that cancelling plans is the price of our dreams. The buck stops with us, right? So when there's work to be done or a problem to be solved, we have to do it. We can't just take the time off and stop thinking about our business for a couple of weeks. What if everything falls apart?

According to research out of Babson University, about 14 percent of the adult population in the US become entrepreneurs and business owners.[1] Which means that if your kindergarten class had thirty students in it, four of your friends went on to become entrepreneurs. But the US Bureau of Labor Statistics reports that only around one third of entrepreneurs are still around at the ten-year mark.[2] Which means, of your kindergarten class, only one person has succeeded as an entrepreneur. And it's likely that they are funky-monkey exhausted. (I was going to swear there, but we are talking about kindergarteners, and that just ain't right.)

Business owners suffer from an "I must do the work myself" problem. We do the work ourselves to save money. We do the work ourselves because we think no one can do it as well as we do. We do the work ourselves because it's "just easier" than handing it off to someone we think is too green, too inexperienced, or too incapable of acting like an owner.

We do the work, which makes us the only ones capable of doing the work. So we get trapped in an infinite loop and can't see our way out. We start to lose things—precious memories we can't get back, a good night's sleep (or any sleep, for that matter), our interests, time off, and for some of us, even the people we love.

Jason broke free from his business, but not everyone does. Another email I received made it clear how dire things can get. It came from Celeste and it started like this:

"It's two a.m. and I am writing you out of desperation. I own a preschool. We make no money. I haven't taken a salary since we started. I'm racking up debt. And tonight, I am broken. Not just financially but in my soul. I am convinced an immediate termination of my life would be the fastest resolution to my predicament."

Reading that email, I felt as if my heart had dropped into my stomach. I was terrified for Celeste. At the same time, I recognized her vulnerability.

"Please understand, I am not sending you a suicide note," Celeste went on, "and I am not at risk for such stupidity at the moment. That decision would just leave the burden to my family. But if I was single, I would be gone. You see, I have double pneumonia right now. I can't afford someone to clean our preschool, and for the last four hours, I have been scrubbing the floors and cleaning the walls. I am exhausted. I am crying and stop only because I am too exhausted to cry. I am starving for sleep. I am so ill yet I can't sleep because my worry keeps me up. The only thing I have left to give my business is my time and that is now depleted, too."

My heart broke for Celeste. I'd been in a similar state of mind a few times in my life as an entrepreneur, and I knew countless others who had been lower than low, desperate for a solution. The last lines of the email will stay with me forever:

"What has become of my dream? I am trapped. I am exhausted. I can't work more than I already do. Or maybe I can. Maybe my work is the slow suicide I am thinking of."

What has become of my dream? Does that question ring true for you? It did for me when I read her email. We work and work and work, and before we know it, the business idea we once proudly shared with our friends, the plan we outlined on a whiteboard, the vision we shared with our first employees seems like a dim memory of an unobtainable goal.

Celeste never responded to my attempts to get in touch with her. I included her story in the original *Clockwork* in part because

I hoped she'd read it and contact me, but she never did. I think of her often and I pray she's okay.

Celeste wasn't holding her business back. It was her system—and those systems can be fixed.

Perhaps you can relate to Celeste. Perhaps (I hope) you're in a less dire situation, managing to keep up the grind week after week and keep the wheels of your business turning. Whatever the case, chances are you don't ever feel like you can ease up and spend *less* time and effort on your business. Why is that?

Most entrepreneurs I know do everything. Even when we bring on help, we spend just as much time, if not more, telling the team *how* to do all the things that we are supposed to no longer worry about. We put out fires. We stay up late. We put out more fires. We work weekends and holidays, flake on commitments to family, and bail on nights out with friends. We put out even more fires. We push on, we push harder. We compromise our health in the name of building a healthy business. But we're not.

Here's the irony: even when things are going well with our business, we are still exhausted. We have to work even harder when things are good because "who knows how long this will last?" And the growth opportunities we know we should grab by the horns, the visionary work that is crucial to explosive growth, the stuff we *love* to do, is set aside day after day until that notepad with all our ideas is lost under a sea of papers and to-do lists, never to be found again.

We're blowing it. We're all blowing it.

"Work harder" is the mantra of both the growing *and* the collapsing business. "Work harder" is the mantra of every entrepreneur, every business owner, every leader, every five-star employee, and every person just struggling to keep up. Our perverted pride about working longer, faster, and harder than everyone else in our industry has taken over. Instead of running one marathon, we are trying to sprint ten. Unless something changes, those of us who buy into this way of life are headed for a breakdown. And maybe double pneumonia to boot.

I want you to know you are not the only one who is going through this. You are not the only entrepreneur who feels they must work harder, who is skipping trips with friends and time with family, who is exhausted and wondering how long they can sustain this level of work. You're not the only business owner who wonders why all your improvements haven't improved your bottom line or garnered you more clients or helped you retain good team members or simply given you back just a little bit of your precious time. You're not the only person who is reading this book because you feel stuck and you're desperate for answers—and a nap. That was me, and so many entrepreneurs I talked with over the years.

I started writing this book when I asked myself a key question: Could my business achieve the size, profitability, and impact I envisioned without me doing all, or any, of the work? This question triggered my decades-long quest for answers—for me and for the business owners and entrepreneurs I serve. *For you.*

If you're unfamiliar with my previous books, or if you've yet to hear me speak, I want you to know that my life's mission is to *eradicate entrepreneurial poverty.* I am committed to freeing entrepreneurs from lack: Lack of money. Lack of time. Lack of life. In my book *Profit First,* I sought to defeat one of the monsters that drives most entrepreneurs to despair: the lack of money. In this book, we're going to slay an even bigger beast: the lack of time.

Whatever answers you are looking for, in this book you'll find real, actionable business efficiency strategies that have worked for countless entrepreneurs, numerous business owners, and for me, too.

The goal is not to find more hours in your day. That is the

brute force approach to business operations, and even when you pull it off, you'll just fill that time with more work, anyway. The goal is organizational efficiency.

You are about to learn how to make simple but powerful shifts in your mindset and day-to-day operations that will make your business run on automatic. I'm talking predictable outcomes, my overworked friend. I'm talking real, sustained growth. I'm talking a thriving workplace. I'm talking freedom to focus on what you do best, and what you *love* to do. And that, compadre, is the only way to build a truly successful business—by freeing ourselves to do the work we do best and the work we love most.

We are also going to free you from the grind. We are going to rescue you from the constant pull on your time, your body, your mind, *and* your bank account. Yes, it is possible to feel at ease about your business. Yes, it is possible to regain the optimism you felt when you first started your company. Yes, it is possible to scale your business without doing any of the day-to-day work. In fact, it's imperative that you remove yourself.

Your business needs a vacation *from* you so it doesn't depend *on* you.

You need to stop doing everything. You need to streamline your business so it can run itself. I'm talking about your business running like a well-oiled machine. An organization of coordinated systems run by a highly efficient team aligned with your objectives and values. A business that runs like clockwork. (Slick, right?)

Apple continues without Steve Jobs. Mary Kay continues without Mary Kay. Hewlett-Packard rolls forward without Hewlett or Packard. At a certain point, each of these businesses broke free from the gravitational pull of the owner; the owner gave the company independence to run without them.

There is strength in independence. You see, the vacation is nice for you, but it's *critical* for your business. It may go against everything you think and believe about your role in your business, but when you get out of the way, that is the moment your business can truly grow.

The process you will discover in this book is simple. You will not find shortcuts, tricks, or hacks to packing more in. Instead, you will discover how to get the work done that matters most, avoid the stuff that doesn't, and have the wisdom to know the difference. Yep, I borrowed a bit from the Serenity Prayer. Serenity may seem like an impossible goal right now. Heck, you'd probably settle for sanity at this point. But by following the Clockwork phases I outline in this book, serenity is definitely back on the table, baby!

Emails from readers like Jason and Celeste—and you—drive the work I continue to do, and they are the reason I wrote this revised and expanded edition. I've "clockworked" the Clockwork process. In these pages, you'll read success stories from readers who implemented Clockwork and dramatically changed their business for the better. You'll hear about new "operation vacation" experiences—one week, two weeks, four weeks, and longer—and how those intentional disruptions helped owners improve systems and grow their businesses—just as Jason did.

In his email, he added a postscript:

"Another little thing I almost forgot to share: Due to *Clockwork*, I was able to spend the day with my wife in the ER when she had a sudden gallbladder attack last week. It happened at three p.m. during the week, a time I normally could not miss from work no matter what. But because I'm working the Clockwork system, I was able to send a quick text to my shop manager, then totally forget about my business and devote ALL attention to my wife. It not only helped me stay calm during the next several hours' emergency, but my attitude helped everyone else stay calm because I wasn't choking back my stress about missing work at the last minute.

"This is a life-changing system. Your book *Profit First* gave me money. *Clockwork* gave me something more precious: time."

Life is about impact, not hours. On my deathbed, I will be asking myself if I fulfilled my life's purpose, if I grew as an individual, if I truly served you and others, and if I deeply and actively loved my family, my friends, and humanity. If I may be so bold, I think you will be asking the same.

It's time to be an entrepreneur the way it was always intended—to be the architect of your business, not the contractor. Take a stand now, first at my website, clockwork.life,* and then at the beach or in the mountains, or both, one day soon. It's time to get back to what you love—in your life, in your work, and in your business. It's time to implement strategies with ease and joy. It's time to bring balance back to your life. This book will help you do that.

That is my wholehearted promise to you.

---

* To make it super easy for you to get all the free resources for this book, I created a site called clockwork.life. Everything you need for this book, including a Clockwork Quick Start Guide, is there. Additionally, if you want professional help, I have a small business that does just that at runlikeclockwork.com. Note that clockwork .life is not a .com, but a .life, because this is about a lifestyle. And runlikeclockwork .com is a .com because it is all about our company serving your company.

A NOTE TO EMPLOYEES

First, let me acknowledge how remarkable it is that you are reading this book. This tells me you care about the company you work for and the people you work with. In these pages, you'll learn how the Clockwork system applies to you and the company you serve. In the process, you'll get a peek into your boss's world. I hope this awareness helps you better understand their choices, challenges, and why they chose to clockwork your company. I hope you also realize that you are a big part of pulling this off. The business you work for is about to grow, and so are you.

At the end of Chapters Two through Ten, you'll find content I wrote especially to help you implement what you've learned. You play a vital role in the Clockwork system and in helping the company you work for become more efficient. Your commitment to reading this book will help you strengthen your role and your team, do more work *you* love, and help your employer realize their vision for the business.

So thank you. You are needed. You are valued. And the work you do makes a difference.

Let's do this.

CHAPTER ONE

WHY YOUR BUSINESS IS (STILL) STUCK

UNCOVER THE AREAS WHERE OWNERS AND LINCHPIN TEAM MEMBERS STRUGGLE TO BREAK FREE FROM THE BUSINESS

As is tradition for many people born and bred in the Garden State, every summer my wife, Krista, and I pack up the kids and meet my sister and her family for a week of fun at the Jersey Shore. Up until a few years ago, our summer trip went something like this: everyone would spend the day at the beach and then the adults would start happy hour around four p.m., talk a big game about hanging out until the sun rises, and then promptly fall asleep by seven p.m.

Except I hardly ever made it to happy hour or spent much time at the beach. I worked. Always. When I was not focused on completing a project, or in a meeting, I tried to sneak "a few minutes" to check emails. When I did make it outside to join everyone, I was so distracted by thoughts of work that I wasn't really there. This caused me stress and annoyed the heck out of my family.

Every year, I tried to break the "workcation" habit by using the cram-and-scramble technique. First the cram: I would get all my work done in advance so that "*this* time" I could finally enjoy my vacation and be fully present with my family. Then the scramble: When I returned from my "relaxing" vacation I thought I could easily get back up to speed with a little extra hustle. But my plan never worked out. Often, it was just the opposite of what I expected.

The last time I tried to prove that I really could work this vacation plan, it was a total disaster. A problem with a client came up the afternoon of the day before we were to leave. I can't even remember the problem, but at the time, I thought it important enough to work on the solution well into the night. Then I stayed up even later to finish the work I had to do before the client crisis.

It was nearly dawn before I made it back home from work. I slept for three hours, then headed to Long Beach Island. (If you aren't from New Jersey, I want you to know that LBI is the real Jersey Shore, *not* the old boozefest of a show that lays claim to it.) Before I went to the beach, I decided to check my email to "make sure everything was okay." It wasn't. I spent the rest of my day making calls and sending emails. When I finally made it to the beach the next day, my mind was on the business and my body was dying for sleep. Yet again, I wasn't really there. I'd compromised my family's vacation, too, because my tension spread like smoke in a bar. One person can really stink up the place and ruin everyone else's fun.

Frustrated with my workaholic ways, Krista sent me for a walk on the beach one afternoon—without my phone. As I looked at the beachfront houses, I thought, "The people who vacation at those mega-mansions have it all figured out." They had financial freedom. They could take time off and not worry about work. They could enjoy themselves and come back to a business ticking along, still growing, still making money. That's what I wanted.

But as I looked closer, I saw person after person sitting on their decks frantically plugging away on their laptops. I even saw people on the beach with laptops perched precariously on their knees, trying to shield their screens from the glare of the sun. The people I assumed had it all together weren't any different from me. We were all working on vacation. *What the F?*

At this point in my life, I had built and sold one multimillion-dollar business to private equity and another one to a Fortune 500 company, written two business books, and spent a good part of my year speaking to thousands of entrepreneurs about how to grow their companies quickly and organically. Sounds like I was living the dream, right? You would think that I had retired my workaholic badge for good. But stressing out about work on yet another vacation proved I hadn't. I wasn't even close. And it was clear: I was definitely not alone. Neither are you.

THE SOLUTION IS NOT THE SOLUTION

As is true for many business owners I've known, I thought the cure for my workaholism was better productivity. If I could just do more, faster, I could find more time for my family, for my health, for fun, and to *get back to doing the work I really loved.* The work that fed my soul.

I was wrong.

You and I both know extremely productive people who work sixteen hours a day. You and I absolutely know the "I do best when I cram" people. Maybe it's you. Once upon an embarrassingly boastful time, it was me.

In an effort to be more productive, I tried it all: Focus apps, the Pomodoro method, working in blocks. Starting my day at four a.m. Ending my day at four a.m. To-do lists. Not-to-do lists. Lists on yellow notepads. Lists on my phone. Lists of just five things. Lists of everything. Bigger lists on bigger yellow notepads. The Don't Break the Chain method, which quickly led me to the Chain Myself to My Desk method. No matter what hack or technique I tried, no matter how productive I became, I still slipped into bed at night long after I should have, and woke up the next morning way earlier than I should have, with a to-do list that seemed to have magically grown overnight. Maybe I did things faster, but I didn't work fewer hours. If anything, I worked more. Maybe I was making progress on many small projects, but many more new projects were filling up my plate. And my time was still not my own. All my years of studying productivity had given me nothing but more work. It was an epic fail.

If you haven't tried some of the productivity strategies I rattled off like failed diet plans, I'm sure you have your *own* list. An entire industry is built around the desire to do more, faster. Podcasts, articles, and books; mastermind groups and coaches; productivity challenges, calendars, journals, and software. We buy into the next productivity solution someone recommends because we're desperate. Desperate to grow our companies by getting more done, faster, and somehow managing all our work without losing our minds.

It took me about fifteen years to figure this one out. I actually wore the productivity master's badge of honor—the workaholic badge. I was a proud member. I was the fastest task-ticker-offer in the land. (What? It's a thing.)

In *Profit First*, I applied Parkinson's Law—"our consumption of a resource expands to meet its supply"—to profit. Just as we use all the time we have allocated for a project to finish it, we also spend the money we have, which is why most entrepreneurs rarely earn as much as their employees, much less turn a profit. The more money we have to spend, the more we spend. The more time we have, the more of it we spend working. You get the idea.

The fix to this behavior is ridonkulously simple: limit the resource and you limit your utilization of it. For example, when, after you collect revenue, you allocate profit first and hide it away (in a remote bank account), you have less money to spend. When you don't readily have access to all the cash flowing through your business, you are forced to find ways to run your business with less.

Whatever time you give yourself to work, you will use. Nights, weekends, vacations—if you think you need it, you'll work right through your time off. This is the root cause of the failure of productivity. The goal of productivity is to get as much done as quickly as possible. The problem is, because you've prioritized a seemingly endless amount of time to running your business, you'll continually find ways to fill up the time. The more productive you are, the more you can take on. The more you take on, the more productive you have to be.

Yes, productivity is important; we all need to make the best use of our time. To be unproductive is like sinning against the business gods. But in time, I came to understand that the real holy grail is organizational efficiency. Productivity gets you in the ballpark. Organizational efficiency gets you hitting home runs.

Organizational efficiency is when all the gears of your business mesh together in harmony. It is the ultimate in leverage because you design your company's resources to work in concert, maximizing their output. Organizational efficiency is when you access the best talents of your team (even a team of one) to do the most important work. It is about managing resources so that the important work gets done instead of always rushing to do what's most urgent. And it's about removing yourself from the day-to-day grind so you can make all that happen.

Productivity is about doing *more* to increase output. Efficiency is about doing *less* to increase output.

I have a feeling this is not news to you. So why are you still caught in the hamster wheel?

STOP GROWING, START SCALING

Growing a company is different from scaling it. Most businesses grow. Very few scale. You grow a business by doing more to get more. You scale a business by doing less to get more. They are different orientations. Extremely different.

I have no doubt you already know how to grow your business. The growth approach is easy: do more of what you are already doing. More brings more. But inherent to this approach is the limitation of resources. You only have so much time. You can only hire so many people. You only have so much money. Doing more has a ceiling. Coming up against that ceiling is probably why you're reading this now. If what was working before was still working now, why would you seek an alternative? Growth works until it doesn't.

You likely have a proven track record of growth. I bet your business is bigger now than it was then. I suspect you have had ups and downs, and you got through the downs by doubling your efforts. You've worked your ass off to make your company what it is today. All that stuff, every bit of it, is growth work. The irony is that you won't build a healthy business by growing it. By definition, the growth orientation exhausts the business. Trying to grow, ultimately, prevents it from growing.

The refrains for a growth orientation abound:

"How will I do this?"

"How do we do more things, faster?"

"Time to double down on my/our efforts."

"Push yourself."

"Work harder."

"Hustle."

"Grind."

I am not suggesting this approach isn't noble. I'm saying it's a shitty way to build a business. It's also the most common. But just because lots of people are doing things the wrong way doesn't make it right. Starting now, we will scale your business.

In the pages to come, you will learn how to do this. As you shift to scaling, your refrains will shift, too.

"Who will do this?" (Instead of "How will I do this?")

"Let's do fewer things, better." (Instead of "Let's do more things, faster.")

"How do we halve our efforts to double the output?" (Instead of "How do we double our efforts so we can double the output?")

"Master yourself." (Instead of "Push harder.")

"Work smarter." (Instead of "Work *even* harder.")

"Design." (Not "Hustle.")

"Scale." (And surely not "Grind.")

That last one, "scale," is the most noble approach of all. If you own a business, your number-one job is to create jobs, not to do them. Scale and your business will grow right.

Your "ceiling" may seem impenetrable, but it's not. We just need to shift your mind from a growth orientation to a scale orientation. Stop smashing your head against the glass and go through the opening right over there. Do you see it? Just follow the sign that reads: TAKE E*SCALE*ATOR TO NEXT FLOOR.

There's a fable that circulates within the entrepreneurial community. It is about two lumberjacks. They decided to settle a dispute on who could split more wood per day. For the next eight hours, they went to work.

The first lumberjack dove into his stack and started splitting wood immediately. The second lumberjack followed suit with the same fervor. After an hour, the second lumberjack took a break. The first lumberjack, noticing that his competition had left, doubled his efforts. After ten minutes, the second lumberjack returned from his break and started splitting wood again. After another hour, the second lumberjack again took a ten-minute break. The first lumberjack pushed on harder, knowing that he advanced his lead every time the other lumberjack took a break.

At the end of eight hours, the first lumberjack was shocked that the second had produced nearly twice as much split wood. The first lumberjack asked, "Did your regular breaks allow you to rest and recover? To produce more, do you need to work less?"

The second lumberjack responded, "No. During those breaks I worked the hardest, sharpening my axe."

Scaling a business is not about less work. It is about different work. You must put less effort into those outcomes, but more thought. The hard work is the thinking. This is not a flippant comment. Thinking, as in deep, calculated thoughtfulness, is the hardest work of all. And that is why we avoid it.

It is easier to do work than to design outcomes. It is easier to keep chopping with a dull axe than it is to stop and sharpen it. The sense of time and production loss is too much. Yes, a sharp axe will help, but I can't afford to stop chopping. The logic is obvious—we need a sharp axe. But the emotion of "just keep grinding" is what we need to overcome first.

Your job is to scale your business. Your challenge is to think accordingly. Thoughtful, calculated design work is the hardest and most important work of all. Right now. Stop growing. Start scaling.

THE "SOMEDAY SWITCH"

In November of 2013, I delivered a keynote address at INCmty in Monterrey, Mexico. Michael Gerber, author of *The E-Myth*, opened and Guy Kawasaki, author of *The Art of the Start*, closed the show on the main stage. I anchored one of the other days on the side stage and was psyched to do it.

On the last night of the conference, I went out to dinner with Michael and some other folks. We had a discussion around *The E-Myth*. If you haven't read the book, the core message is to work *on* the business, not *in* the business. We all wondered, why did so many entrepreneurs appreciate the message of his book and so few act on it? If most of them knew they needed organizational efficiency, why was it so difficult for them (ahem, me) to pull it off?

Our conversation made it clear: We think our freedom from doing the work happens magically, like a switch that suddenly flips. We think if we only work *in* the business long enough and hard enough, one day we will find ourselves working *on* the business. We think that we will get to a point where everything just clicks into place. That's the fallacy—that it happens eventually, almost as if our five-to-nine (as in five a.m. to nine p.m.) schedule can flip that "someday switch" by sheer will.

That approach didn't work for me and it won't work for you. To get to the point where you aren't the workhorse inside the business, you need to slowly and surgically extract yourself. The process to make your business run itself two months, two years, or two decades from now starts today. Deliberately. Consistently. Relentlessly.

My conversation with Michael Gerber that night partly inspired this book. Still, I knew I'd uncovered only part of the puzzle as to why we don't do what we know we need to do.

THE SURVIVAL TRAP

My first business coach, Frank Minutolo, once told me, "The clogged artery in an otherwise healthy business is inevitably the owner. In other words, you are the problem, Mike. Entrepreneurs aren't different from any other human, in that when something is familiar, it becomes comfortable. We are most comfortable working relentlessly. And while you may say you 'hate it' and 'can't take it anymore,' the truth is, you are familiar with it. And when you are familiar with something, as ugly as it is, it is easiest to keep doing it. Stop bragging about your work ethic. Stop forcing yourself to push hard. And please, oh please, stop saying you're 'getting shit done.' Because if you are getting shit done, it means you are doing shit."

Frank is not one to mince words. He's from New Jersey, too, after all. He had been president of a company that he took from zero to $100 million in revenue. He had more than street cred; everyone he mentored experienced a similar trajectory.

Entrepreneurs have become way too comfortable with the hardship, so they keep doing the things that keep them in that state. And because they keep doing these things, they end up in the Survival Trap. If you've read my previous books, you have probably heard about this black hole of a problem. I have talked about it for a long time now. And still, I'm going to return to the Survival Trap because, unfortunately, this is the state that most of us entrepreneurs end up in, and very few of us ever escape from.

The Survival Trap is what I call that never-ending cycle of reacting to whatever comes up in your business—be it a problem or an opportunity—in order to move on. It's a trap because as we respond to what is urgent rather than what is important, we get the satisfaction of fixing a problem. The adrenaline rush of saving something—the account, the order, the pitch, the entire damn day—makes us feel as though we are making progress in our business, but really, we are stuck in a reactive cycle. We jump all about, fixing this, saving that. As a result, our business careens to the right, then to the left. Then we throw it in reverse and jam it forward. Our business is a web of misdirection, and over the years it becomes a knotted mess—all because we were just trying to survive.

The Survival Trap is all about getting through today with utter disregard for tomorrow. It's about doing what is familiar, as Frank warned. We feel good that we survived the day. But then, at some distant point in the future, we wake up and realize that years and years of work didn't move us forward one iota, that merely trying to survive is a trap that results in a long, drawn-out drowning of our business and our willpower.

Sadly, you will discover that living in the Survival Trap leads to a very frightening day-to-day life of quick highs, deep lows, and doing anything to make a buck. Me? I sacrificed both business integrity and any semblance of sound fiscal responsibility to survive just one more day, and then I continued that behavior as I expanded into multiple disastrous businesses.

I convinced myself to keep at the grind because sometimes, on rare blue-sky days, everything clicked. Money came in. Employees got work done (on their own). I had cleared enough off my plate to leave by three p.m. I drove home thinking I'd finally flipped that mythical, magical switch and now everything would be okay. *Everything would be okay.*

But then the next day arrived and it was a shitstorm.

What happened? Happenstance happened. One day works well and we think we've got it. Nope. You can't grow your business out of lucky moments. You need planned execution, the creation and enforcement of systems. Every day needs to click, not one here and one there.

Time and sanity are not the only costs of staying stuck in the Survival Trap. You'll also stunt your company's growth and keep less of the money you earn.

In *Profit First*, I wrote a little section that was the seed of this book: "Sustained profitability depends on efficiency. You can't become efficient in crisis. In crisis, we justify making money at any cost, right now, even if it means skipping taxes or selling our souls. In crises, the Survival Trap becomes our modus operandi— until our survival strategies create a new, more devastating crisis that scares us straight or, more commonly, scares us right out of business."

Was Celeste, the preschool owner I mentioned in the introduction, caught in the Survival Trap? Most definitely. She was experiencing the extreme version of the trap. You may be comfortable in your trap. Maybe it's manageable. Maybe you take pride in managing it. But what does that matter if you're still in the trap?

Or maybe, just maybe, you're worried about something you are afraid to admit: becoming irrelevant. If you aren't needed in your business, what's the point? Sitting on the beach for a few weeks sounds nice, but for the rest of eternity?

The Survival Trap is what's keeping you from driving toward your vision and meeting short- and long-term goals. In some sense, we know this. We feel guilty about that five-year plan we haven't looked at in seven years. We see other businesses launching new initiatives or products in alignment with trends, and we wonder how they found the time to predict and respond to the changes in our industry. (They must have superpowers, right?) We know we're behind in terms of making the best use of innovations in technology and workplace culture. And we know that in order to take our business to the next level, we need to get back to our visionary roots—the ideas and plans and *heart* we had when we first started our business.

We need to get back to being shareholders.

YOU ARE A SHAREHOLDER

The reframe that made all the difference for me was to stop thinking of myself as the hardest-working, most-driven doer for my small business (the modern definition of entrepreneur) and start declaring myself a shareholder of the business. Simply put, a shareholder is someone who owns part of a company and influences its strategic direction with their votes. What is most important about the definition of shareholder is what it does *not* include. Shareholders don't work their asses off. Shareholders are not the ones who manage the day-to-day. Shareholders are not the best employee—or any kind of employee, worker, or doer.

To be super clear, you already are a shareholder of your company. Maybe even a majority shareholder, owning 50 percent or more. But just because you technically are a shareholder doesn't mean you are behaving like one. And we need to fix that right now.

From this moment forward, call yourself a shareholder of your business. And act like it.

I own one hundred Ford shares. I realize this is a drop in the bucket of total stock, but a critical lesson presents itself nonetheless. Every quarter I get a profit distribution from Ford. Recently I have been averaging about thirteen bucks. (Can you say pizza party—minus any good pizza?) I don't call Ford and say I am ready to head to the factory for a bit to earn the money. And when I get the check, I don't say I need to plow this back or reinvest it into the company. It is a reward I get for taking the risk of owning stock. What I do is keep the profit *and* influence the strategic direction of the company. I, along with other Ford shareholders, vote for the leadership team. We vote on corporate objectives, compensation, employment equity, mergers and acquisitions, stock splits, and policy. We, the shareholders, set the vision.

Your job as a shareholder is to set the vision and give the company strategic direction. And to share in the profit, a thank-you for investing in a small business, for contributing to the economy, and for creating jobs.

Sadly, the word "entrepreneur" has become bastardized to be all about hustle and grind. You know, the artist formerly known as workaholism. And even more tragic, a lot of prominent people promote this approach as *the* entrepreneurial path. You need to work harder. You need to hustle more. You need to give up life to build a successful business so you can live life one day.

The entrepreneur's hustle-and-grind approach is pure bull-shit. Don't fall for it.

A business owner's job is to create jobs. Your role is to produce the opportunity for people who want a good job with a good company. If you are doing the work, you are not creating jobs; you are stealing them.

To break the hustle-and-grind cycle—and to be clear, you must—don't call yourself an entrepreneur. I hate saying that be-cause I love the word "entrepreneur." At least, I love what it was always meant to be: a person who organizes a business to achieve a vision and takes financial risks because they believe in that vi-sion. But alas, "entrepreneur" has been wrongly equated with "workaholic."

Calling yourself an entrepreneur can be unhealthy. The word is too strongly (and too wrongly) associated with work more, work harder, work endlessly. Instead, starting today, call yourself a shareholder of a business. Or a major shareholder of a small business. But no matter what, use the word that speaks to the truth of your responsibility: sharing in the profit (a reward for risk) and setting the direction (navigating the growth). You are a shareholder.

When you own the fact that you are a (or the) shareholder of your business, you'll become that identity. And you will see how empowering it is for you and the people around you. As a shareholder you will focus on the strategic moves for the business. You'll empower your team to do the work that needs to be done. And if that's not possible right out of the gate—as is true for almost all early-stage business owners—you'll step in with a different hat when called upon, like a substitute teacher helping out for the day. All the while you will create systems so your team *can* do the work without you. The shareholder's responsibility is for the business to run without the shareholder.

OPERATION VACATION

In my quest to develop a simple way to make my own business run on automatic, I've met several people who took sabbaticals from their business only to come back to a more successful business than when they left it—including one person who left for two entire years! I'll share more of those stories with you throughout the book. Hearing about their adventures and successes made me realize that taking a long vacation was the best test for a streamlined business, and that committing to *taking* that vacation is the best incentive to streamline your business in preparation for that vacation.

Then I had an epiphany: committing to a four-week vacation— the length of most business cycles—is the perfect incentive to streamline your business. During a four-week period, most businesses will pay bills, market to prospects, sell to clients, manage payroll, do the accounting, take care of administrative tasks, maintain technology, deliver services, ship products, etc. Remember school fire drills? It was an intentional disruption that ensured you and your classmates would get out of the building safely. *The four-week vacation serves as a fire drill for your business.*

If we know we're going to be away for four weeks without access to our business, we'll do whatever it takes to get it ready for our absence. If we don't commit to the vacation, we'll take our own sweet time getting through the streamlining steps.

With the first edition of this book, we launched Operation Vacation. You and me and everyone, we're all in this together, and we can support one another in taking the steps we need to take to grow our businesses *and* get our lives back. *My challenge to you is to commit to taking a four-week vacation within the next eighteen months.* And when I say commit, I mean book that vacation. And to make sure you never back out of it, tell your kids, tell your mom, write it in your diary. Or make the boldest declaration of all: post it on social media so the world will be up your butt if you don't do it. You can even tell me about your plan when you email me (I'll tell you how and why to contact me in a second). Maybe we will end up on vacation at the same time in the same place. We can throw back a margarita while your business grows in your absence.

In Chapter Eleven, I give you a detailed, step-by-step timeline that will help you get your business ready for your four-week vacation. If you're a rebel or a nonbeliever, and you have already decided *not* to take a four-week vacation at some point in the next couple of years, please read the chapter anyway. The timeline provides a framework for clockworking your business using the system you are about to learn.

Let me clarify that I am not suggesting that you can *only* take a four-week vacation. For some people, four weeks may seem too short. Or, if you're thinking about having a baby, you may want to take three to six months off, or more, and you may not have a clue how you're going to pull that off while keeping your business alive. That's why we are going to *plan* to take a four-week vacation, so we can get your business running itself. Once that happens, you can take as much or as little time off as you want or need to. Imagine that—you may not have to put off major life decisions in order to keep your business running and growing!

When I tell people they need to schedule a four-week vacation, I get one of two reactions: laughter or tears. And sometimes I get that awkward for everyone, laughing-while-crying situation. But no matter what, I almost always hear some version of, "Are you kidding me?" And some say they don't need or want a vacation. (Whatever you need to tell yourself to get through the day.)

The thing is, even though it seems like the four-week vacation is all about you getting a vacation from your business, it isn't. It's about your business getting a vacation *from you*. The best way to get out of the way is to just get out. And let's face it—you are more likely to take the time away if you know it will benefit your business than if you think it is just for your own, I don't know, health and sanity.

Geno Auriemma is one of the greatest basketball coaches of all time. As the head coach of the University of Connecticut women's team, the Huskies, he led them to a record eleven NCAA Division 1 national championships. When he served as head coach for the United States women's national basketball team, they won two world championships and gold medals at the 2012 and 2016 Summer Olympics, undefeated in all four tournaments. The dude knows basketball and he knows how to build a winning organization.

Auriemma did a series about developing winning teams for

the online education series Masterclass. I took note of something he said about taking time off from coaching his team: "I could leave for a month and come back and the operation will actually be better than when I left because I won't come in and say, 'Hey, I want to change this and change that.' You have to give your key people autonomy to make decisions so they will feel ownership." A healthy organization never depends on one person's effort and availability. In fact, it is the opposite. Perennial success happens when the organization flows forward in the absence of any particular individual, including the boss.

A four-week vacation is a demonstration of trust in your team. You are not burdening them with your absence; you are giving them responsibility. You're not abandoning your company; you're helping it to become more resilient. Taking the four-week vacation shows you trust your team to handle it if something "bad" *does* happen, and it allows them to build resilience. Think of it like resistance training for your business. This is how we build muscles and strengthen our skeletal systems, and it will work for your company, too.

When I committed to taking my very first continuous month-long vacation, I started to plan eighteen months prior. I applied all I had learned about how to ensure my business would run like clockwork and ran multiple one-week tests away from the day-to-day work to prove that it was ready. And throughout those eighteen months, I thought about my business in a whole new way.

THE THREE PHASES OF CLOCKWORK

Gaining organizational efficiency so I could take my planned four-week vacation was a process that involved a lot of aha moments, plenty of trial and error, and more of my own big, fat ego trips than I'd like to admit. Some strategies worked like a charm, and some needed refinement. This is why I'm so grateful for my partnership with Adrienne Dorison. Together we founded Run Like Clockwork for business owners who want help clockworking their company. Since the publication of the first edition of this book, Adrienne and I continued to refine the system. If you read the previous book, you'll note some vital additions and changes to the sequence.

In the following chapters, we'll cover the shifts you'll need to take to make your business run itself. One phase may take longer than another, and you may find yourself having to go back and improve your implementation of the strategies from time to time. This system is not a get-fixed-quick scheme. The process of shifting to a business that runs itself is methodical and, at times, requires surgical precision. It may take some time, but if you commit to the process, you'll get there. To help you process all you'll learn in this book, I've identified three phases for clock-working your business. It's important to note that when you complete a phase, you will likely return to it again at some point. Your business is constantly evolving, and organizational efficiency is not a fixed state.

Here is an overview of the three phases to make your business run itself:

1. **Align**

   Align is the foundational phase on which organizational efficiency is built. What you gain in this phase you will never lose.

   To move your business forward toward your desired destination, everyone and everything must move in the same direction. If any part is misaligned, it will impede progress. And if your business has zero alignment—directional anarchy!—it will remain stuck indefinitely. In the Align phase of Clockwork, you will ensure that what the company does, why it does it, and who it does it for are in harmony.

First, you'll clarify the community you serve. Then, you'll determine your Big Promise to that group. With this new clarity, you'll determine your company's QBR or "Queen Bee Role," which is the heart of the Clockwork system.

2. **Integrate**

In the Integrate phase, you and your team start to see measurable results. This is when your company begins to run like clockwork.

Once your business is aligned, it must move forward with all parts in synchronization. In the Integrate phase, the goal is to refocus and reorganize every aspect of your company so your team can do the work in the fewest steps necessary, using the least required effort, to achieve the expected outcome.

First, you'll discover how you and your team will protect and serve the heart of your organization, the QBR. Then, you'll track your time and your team's time in a new way—breaking it down into the Four Ds (4Ds): Doing, Deciding, Delegating, and Designing. This is where you (and your team) will start to do more of the work that you (and they) love to do, the work that brings you (and them) joy and satisfaction. With these 4D insights, you'll learn how to offload and refocus your to-do list as you determine which tasks you can Trash, Transfer, Trim, or Treasure. To help you facilitate this part of the process, I'll show you how to capture systems easily and efficiently to ensure that anyone on your team can do almost any task.

3. Accelerate

In the Accelerate phase, you take organizational efficiency to a new level. Your team will become more empowered and resilient, you will completely remove yourself from the "doing," and your company will grow in impact and profitability.

In the Accelerate phase, you will put the best people and resources in place to improve integration. You will permanently help the organization avoid a single person being the "make or break" for the company's output. Your business will start to run itself.

First, you'll balance your team to ensure everyone is given the tasks and responsibilities that best suit them. Then, you'll learn a simple process to identify and fix the bottlenecks that interrupt organizational efficiency and slow your team down. Finally, you'll take your four-week

THE CLOCKWORK SYSTEM

PHASE	STEPS
I	**ALIGN** 1. Clarify who the company serves 2. Declare the Big Promise 3. Determine the QBR
II	**INTEGRATE** 1. Protect and serve the QBR 2. Optimize time utilization 3. Capture systems
III	**ACCELERATE** 1. Balance the team 2. Find and fix bottlenecks 3. Take the 4-week vacation

Figure 1

vacation. Or perhaps you'll start with a shorter intentional disruption as a quick test. Clockwork is about the continuous improvement of efficiency and effectiveness. To fix what isn't working, you will revisit and refine the work you did in the Align and Integrate phases.

For far too many of us, we celebrate twenty years of business ownership by realizing that we survived twenty years of a continuous near-death experience. But it doesn't have to be that way. You are not alone. There are millions of people just like you. And we can all make the transition, myself included. In fact, I'm still progressing further and further on my own Clockwork implementation, even as I write this. It's so easy to fall back into believing there's a magic productivity hack that will save the day. Whatever choices you made to get to *this* day, it's okay. They got you here. Now we will get you there.

As you go through this process, you will feel frustrated, or stuck, and want to give up. Don't freak out; those are just signs that you are getting comfortable with the uncomfortable new stuff I am teaching you. And don't you dare ever stop. Do you hear me? Never stop. As a result, you will achieve a business that runs on automatic. And *that* is what you are meant to do.

Time is everything. Every. Single. Thing. Time is the only thing in the universe (until someone invents a time machine) that is not renewable. Either you use it wisely, or you don't. Time will still tick, tick, tick away no matter how you spend it. I suspect even right now, you may have made a few nervous looks at the clock as time races by, hoping you can cram in this book (and your work) faster. Am I right? Even just a little bit? If you are experiencing that, I want you to know it's not your fault—it's Parkinson's Law.

And I want you to know that you are actually in a good position.

Better said, you are in a salvageable position. Your business likely has demand and you are delivering on it (although not efficiently). What we are going to do is make a few simple tweaks to have your business run like a well-oiled machine and, in the process, give you back that ever-precious time that seems to have vanished.

I want to be clear that this book is *not* about doing more with the time you have. It's about your business getting bigger and better results with the time *it* has, and about giving you the freedom to do what you wish with your time. It's about getting your life back while you grow the business of your dreams. That can happen. Actually, it *does* happen, all the time, for other businesses. Our job today is to do it for yours. But for this to work, you need to be all in on this with me. Are you ready, shareholder? Good. Let's get to work.

Scratch that. Let's get to *less* work.

 ## CLOCKWORK IN ACTION

Your primary focus is to design the flow of work through your company so that other people and other things can get the work done. Commit to putting your company's output first and your productivity second. How do you do this? Simple: you will find better answers when you ask better questions. Stop asking "*How* do I get more done?" and start asking, "*What* are the most important things to get done?" and "*Who* will get this work done?"

At the end of each following chapter, I'll share action steps you can accomplish quickly—usually in thirty minutes or less—and still experience big progress. For this first chapter, I only have one action step for you, but it is perhaps the most important. It will force an immediate adjustment in how you view your role in moving your business forward. The step? I want you to commit.

Send me an email at Mike@MikeMichalowicz.com with a subject line that reads: "I'm a shareholder!" That way, I can easily spot it among the other emails I get. Then, in the body of the email, please write something like:

"Starting today, I commit to designing my business to run itself." If you like, include what it means to you to be a shareholder from this point forward. Tell me how you will act for your business as a shareholder. Or tell me about the weird looks you will get from family and friends when you tell them you are a shareholder. But no matter what, promise me that forevermore you will only go by your new title, shareholder—because then you will act like one.

Why email me? Because, if you're like me, when you commit to someone else, your follow-through skyrockets. I will write you back—and hell yes, I use a process to be efficient, but every word is from me. I look forward to receiving your note. And that, my new accountability partner, is the perfect first step to owning a business that runs itself.

PHASE ONE

ALIGN

Imagine that you've created a new sport. It is a blend of water polo, football, and Texas Hold'em. You call it Texas Waterball. This sport is going to be big, and everyone loves the idea. You have recruited players and today is the first big match. All the major video networks are here to broadcast it. The world can't wait to watch. The one problem—the one *big* problem: none of the players know the rules or even the objective. How do you win? What's permitted? What's not? How does the team work together? Or is it everyone for themselves? Good luck bringing home the trophy.

If the other team has horrible players but they know the basic rules of the game, they will kick your ass six ways to Sunday. (Actually, the games are only played on Thursday evenings—it's a key Texas Waterball rule.) The other team may have inferior players with inferior tools and inferior skills. But if they are aligned on the rules of engagement, that overcomes a lot of weaknesses.

Lack of alignment is the most common operational problem among small companies, and it affects every aspect of business. When you serve any and all customers and any and all needs they have, it instantly becomes a free-for-all and you end up in constant reaction mode. And when there is no alignment around your company's promise to the customers you serve, no one really knows what to do beyond "just do your best." They don't see how things link together. They don't see how they contribute to the bigger whole. They may hear some pie-in-the-sky "corporate goal," but they don't see *their* goal. And the company fails to win.

Alignment is where everyone knows the goal, knows their relation to the goal, and is in it to win it. As the leader of the business, you are defining the game. It's time to play some Texas Waterball the right way—with everyone aligned. And showing up on Thursday night, of course.

CHAPTER TWO

CLARIFY WHO YOU SERVE

IDENTIFY YOUR BEST CUSTOMERS AND HOW TO GET MORE OF THEM

When I ask business owners who they serve, many respond by saying some variation of "everyone." For a business to run like clockwork, you must have a consistent delivery of your offering. You need a predictable process that yields a predictable output, and to do that you must reduce variability. Your predictability grows exponentially when you do fewer things for the narrowest set of expectations.

Have you ever noticed that fast-food restaurants have a limited number of menu choices? And that most of those choices are mash-ups of the same ingredients? The "Big Boy" Burger, the "Really Big Boy" Burger, and the "Insane-Oh Big Boy" Burger are all the same, except the meat is stacked once, twice, or an insane-oh three times.

What if you decided to focus on multiple types of clients? Would you be able to connect with all your customers in the same way? Would they respond to your choices in the same way? Would they have identical expectations of you? Would they all need the same type of education and support? Answer: that's a solid "no" across the board.

If you offer three products to five types of customers who each need their own variation of that product, you are delivering fifteen products. Better said, you are offering fifteen product variations, and for each one to be remarkable, you must get all fifteen right. That is fifteen areas of potential problems. And what if each product variation were made from ten parts? Now we have fifteen products times ten parts. That is 150 potential problems. Doing more things is the best way to grow a company? Don't get me started.

When my first company, Olmec, began to grow, our stability weakened. We provided tech support to businesses. As we got more varied clients, we needed more varied software to support them. We couldn't afford the necessary tools and infrastructure to meet their needs. As a result, my partner and I were unable to pay ourselves—again. Everything we did was a reaction to the needs of our varied customers. This caused us to make mistakes, which disappointed some of our clients. You know, the type of "disappointment" where they fire your company, don't pay the bills they owe you, and cap it off with a one-star review, everywhere.

A good external indicator of a company's stability is: Are they proactive (good) or reactive (not good)? To become a proactive company, begin by narrowing your type of clients. Let's say you have three products for one type of customer, where each customer has more or less identical needs. Now you only need to get three things perfectly right. It is far easier to get three things right than fifteen, and far easier to fix problems when they do arise.

Fewer things for fewer people result in fewer variations, which means you can get really, really good at what you do. And with fewer variations, you need fewer resources to get good results. Simply put, do less and you achieve more. (Yeah, I would highlight that one.)

To kick off the Clockwork process, you'll home in on that group within your customer base who are your best customers. I refer to them as "Top Clients." You may call them "dream customers" or "bestest friends" or, you know, "just like Mikes." Clockwork is more than just creating the engine of your company (getting the internal stuff right); it is also consistently adding the right fuel for your engine—your Top Clients.

THE CRUSH/CRINGE ANALYSIS

In *The Pumpkin Plan,* I outlined a process for identifying and cloning the best customers. I developed this at Olmec to get us out of reaction mode and to increase stability. The main point is, once you know who your Top Clients are, the next step is to clone them by attracting other clients or customers who have the same qualities.

The process begins with the Crush/Cringe Analysis.

1. First, evaluate your existing customer list. Sort them by revenue from most to least. This is important because the people who spend the most on your product or service, particularly if they repeat purchases, demonstrate through their behavior that they value you the most. Don't trust people's words; trust their wallets. In other words, people can say how much they love you until they are blue in the face, but it is the action of spending money with you, or *not* spending money with you, that points to their true feelings.

2. Next, evaluate the crush or cringe factor for each customer on the list. In other words, do you love them (crush), hate them (cringe), or feel somewhere in between (you know, a crunge)? You will automatically provide great service to the customers you love the most because it comes naturally to you. Conversely, you will find yourself avoiding or delaying work for the customers you hate, and the people in between will get hit-or-miss prioritization and service from you.

3. Document the community each customer is in (industry, vocation, consumer group, or transition point).

4. Finally, determine all the congregation points. These are all the places where they hang out together in an organized group. (More on that in the next section.)

CRUSH/CRINGE ANALYSIS

REVENUE	CUSTOMER	CRUSH/CRINGE	COMMUNITY	CONGREGATION POINTS

Figure 2

Sometimes the Crush/Cringe Analysis reveals that the cringe factor is more about the type of product or service a customer wants than the customer themselves. Hudson Lighting Ltd., manufacturers of outdoor lighting based in London, experienced exactly that. Most of their client base are contractors. Chris Hudson, the founder of the company, read *Clockwork* and just when he started categorizing clients, the phone rang.

"I had this moment where I thought, I don't want to answer the phone," Chris told me in an interview. "I could see who it was because I have all the contacts saved. And it hit me: Oh my God, this is a cringe customer."

He didn't answer the phone.

Chris finished his cringe list and then wondered, "What is it about these customers that makes me feel that way? What are they asking for that makes me cringe?"

Digging further into his list, Chris realized that the customers he wanted to avoid the most were smart home contractors.

"They build these amazing, beautiful, multimillion-pound homes," Chris explained. "And these homes have systems that automatically turn the lights on when you come home, that sort of thing. At first, it seemed like our lighting would fit in nicely there, that they were the ideal, high-end customer. The problem was, they wanted everything custom."

His cringe customers wanted variations on the existing products Hudson Lighting offered. "They always wanted something a little bit out there that took a lot of time to create. They'd say, 'Chris, instead of making this, can you make that?' Sometimes their requests weren't even lighting-related."

Chris had started taking on these cringe customers because he said "yes" to every request. He thought saying "yes" was how he would wow them. Plus, they were "easy upsells," and Chris desperately needed extra income. Since he started saying "no" to their cringe customers' requests, those customers have gone to other vendors for their requests. The custom work that drove his employees up the wall and made him want to avoid answering the phone disappeared. But what about those easy upsells and that extra income? Turns out those things are easy to say yes to but *really* hard to deliver on. Yeah, there was extra income, but it required disproportionately extra effort. The result? He lost money on the "easy extra" work for cringes. And almost lost his employees.

"Firing cringe clients has been fantastic," Chris said. "Now we're not doing all this silly stuff that tied us up for hours. Everyone was so relieved. And because we reduced some of our range of product to eliminate cringe customers, we've exceeded our goal of producing seventy-five lights per week; we are up to 110 lights a week now. Fewer variations meant increased output. And my team is happy. They are doing what they love without oddball distractions."

The Crush/Cringe Analysis will help you clarify who you want to clone and who you want to kiss goodbye. I have one disclaimer: there is no guarantee that any of your existing customers represent the ideal community for you to serve. I have mentored small-business shareholders on this process and a few of them did not have a *single* ideal client that they wanted to clone. In these rare circumstances, they created a cloneable client avatar by "stitching together" their favorite elements of their existing customers. That being said, the majority *did* have a client they wanted to clone, and if you have one, too, it represents a significant shortcut to a clockwork company.

CONSIDER CONGREGATION POINTS

Once you have your Top Client list, you can identify the market to which you want to focus your attention. Before you commit to a market, you must judge its viability based on its congregation points. This is step four, the final step in the Crush/Cringe Analysis.

Congregation points are where a like-minded community

converges on a recurring basis to connect, network, and/or share knowledge. If your market is active in many of them, that is proof that they are sharing with one another through established channels. Channels that you can access. Channels that you can market through. Channels where you can easily get a reputation for excellence. If you can't identify any congregation points, or if the points you do locate are few, scattered, and unestablished, you are in for a long slog. It is hard to be discovered when the community can't even find itself.

For example, my client Gary, who develops software for the food industry, said that his best client is a single mom running a bakery business who has achieved her first $1 million in revenue, is overwhelmed by the work volume, and is trying to raise a child by herself. And because she can't stand her own mom, she has no help.

Gary (whom I call "Big G") told me, "Give me a dozen of this client. My profit will skyrocket, and I only need to do one thing for them. I found my niche!"

I said, "Let me ask you something, Big G. What I just heard is that you are looking to get more clients who are 'single-mom entrepreneurs who hate their moms.' Right?"

"Exactly. That is exactly it."

I then asked Gary to tell me where their congregation points are. "Where do these people consistently gather to learn from and share with one another, Big G? Where does the SMH-TOMBC meet? You know, the Single Moms Hating Their Own Moms Business Club."

Answer: nowhere.

There are no meetups. No conferences. No podcasts. No websites. No single congregation point. Yes, two single-mom mom-haters could meet at some office holiday party and become besties. But happenstance is not a congregation point. A congregation point is a consistent space in which to learn and share, and it doesn't exist for this group. This means Gary is impeded—there's no group to access. He can and should ask his one Top Client where she hangs out with other like-minded people in similar circumstances because maybe there is some underground group. But there is little chance those groups actually exist, because Gary's psychographics are too narrow to locate an established community.

With this new knowledge, Gary took a fresh swipe at identifying a community. He asked himself what distinct characteristics about his favorite customer were also things that people formed communities around. She owned a successful bakery. That was one piece. She was overwhelmed with work. That was a second piece. She was a single-mom entrepreneur. That was another. She also hated her mom. That was yet another.

With the four pieces identified, Gary asked himself what elements spoke to his interests the most. Big G really enjoyed the bakery business aspect because he loved manufacturing and that is what this basically was. He also felt he could empathize and support the single-mom entrepreneur better than most vendors, since he was raised by a single-mom entrepreneur and was a single parent himself. The other characteristics were not areas where he had an interest or could contribute.

With the two characteristics identified, he ran the big test. Were there congregation points? With the power of the internet, the answer was easy to find. Gary searched "bakery associations." Simple, right? Sure enough, he found the American Bakers Association, the American Society of Baking, the Independent Bakers Association, and more. He found online forums. He found Facebook groups. This was an established community that congregated. This was an opportunity!

When he searched for "single-mom entrepreneur associations," he found nothing. When he searched for "single-mom entrepreneur groups," he found one meetup group with twelve members. There is no question that this was an important group of entrepreneurs, but it was not an easy opportunity for Big G. The congregation points were not established, so breaking into the community would be very hard.

Gary decided to go after bakeries. He spoke with his best client, who was already a member of one of the associations, to get some suggestions on how to get involved. With that, Gary was off to where his best prospects congregated. And like a good yeasty bread, his business started to rise.

Other people identify niches too broadly. They want to work with rich people or small businesses. Those are broad communities, and while they may have congregation points, the knowledge shared is general because their needs are all over the place. In other words, the few ideal prospects are mixed in these broad congregation points with a lot of non-prospects.

SAMPLE CRUSH/CRINGE ANALYSIS

REVENUE	CUSTOMER	CRUSH/CRINGE	COMMUNITY	CONGREGATION POINTS
$25,000	Example Co	Crush	Flooring Tile	The National Tile Association
$17,500	ABC Company	Cringe	Vineyard Owner	Winetime Podcast Winecon
$15,000	XYZ Inc	Crush	Long-Haul Trucking	Freight Carrier Association The Cargo Conference
$9,000	Alpha Co	Crush	Flooring Tile	The National Tile Association
$8,000	Omega Inc	Cringe	Office Cleaning	United Cleaners Association
$8,000	Another Co	Crush	Last Mile Trucking	The Cargo Association Truckers Meetup

Figure 3

You need to identify a homologous community that connects repeatedly at one or more congregation points to address their specific needs and wants. This is an area where you see the same prospects, vendors, and influencers appearing over and over. It doesn't need to be a physical meetup. It could be a social media group. It could be subscribers to a podcast or magazine. Ideally, there is a combination of ways for them to connect and learn. When you see this repetition of gathering and learning for a specific community, it means that, once you gain access to them, you can build a reputation as the leading vendor to serve their needs.

In addition to finding these gathering points, having clarity about your ideal customer allows you to market to them in an optimal way. You can—and should—craft your marketing to speak specifically to the customer you identified. And with less marketing variability, you have increased the efficiency of your marketing. You're welcome.

I need to make a critical point to you. It is your interest in the community and the fact that they have congregation points that is the most important thing. This is more important than how much you love your current customers. Having a great customer to clone is extremely helpful, but you can access a community even without a single client in that community. Further, a crush or cringe client may *not* be representative of their community. An instance of one is by no means representative of the whole.

The same is true for the customers you love. Realize that they represent a shortcut to the industry and possibly to other great clients. (Good people hang out with other good people.) Also realize that you may have bad customers within a great community, and that your jack-wad of a client is just not typical of that community and may not be the best way in.

After I wrote and published my first book, I discovered my ideal readers for that book, my true *who*: mom entrepreneurs who were entering or reentering the workforce after their children reached an age that gave them enough freedom to run their own businesses part time. Some friends suggested that my "niche" was all small-business owners, but I knew it was all about mom entrepreneurs as I was building my business. Did other people read my book? Absolutely. And I love them for it. (Shout-out to the dudes slogging their way through entrepreneur-land. I see ya, my brothers.) But had I focused on the broader community of all small-business owners right out of the gate, I wouldn't have been noticed. I lived the lesson Brian Smith, the founder of UGG, taught me: if you want big success, you need to focus on a small community and then empower that community to carry you to bigger markets. By definition, a niche is a very narrow group with very consistent needs. Be wary of targeting a broad community and telling yourself it is a niche, 'cause it ain't.

Choosing my community affected how I wrote my books and how I marketed and sold them. When I found out where the mom entrepreneurs congregated and showed up—at conferences and retreats hosted by other mom entrepreneurs who were achieving impressive business growth—that community carried me not only to other mom entrepreneurs, but also to other niche groups within the broader community of small-business owners. And the best part of that strategy was that I grew my audience, and my business, with minimal effort. See how that works?

FOR EMPLOYEES: CORA'S STORY

At the end of most chapters, you'll find a section for you, the employee. These sections include fictional stories about "Cora" that will help you understand your role in each phase of the Clockwork process. Her story begins here.

Cora Monroe served in the US army for ten years, achieving the rank of staff sergeant. During her tenure she led a squad of ten soldiers. She just got hired for her first civilian job since working at a pizza shop in high school. Her new employer, Job Turf Inc., specializes in sustainable, eco-friendly outdoor living spaces.

During the interviews at Job Turf, it was clear that Cora had the intangibles the company was looking for. They had hired veterans in the past, so they knew these individuals were trained to work as a team. They have self-confidence, can work under pressure, and are able to adapt to changing situations.

The fact that Cora was military gave her a leg up in getting the interview. But it did not guarantee a job. And now that she had the job, it did not guarantee she would excel. She had a lot to learn—especially about the Clockwork framework.

Her first day in the field, Cora received her five clean uniforms for easy rotation and four items that would prove essential for doing her job: a hard hat, a pair of gloves, a clipboard, and a client scorecard.

When she asked about the scorecard, her manager Gordon Sumner explained, "Every employee tracks the daily performance of the client and submits it to the project manager, which is me for most jobs, at the end of the project. The gold is out there in the field, where you actively measure the quality of our work and the quality of the client."

The performance of the client? Who does that? This company, that's who.

Her first day in the field, Cora noticed that while there were no issues with any of the clients, one particular client stepped out of their office to greet her and show her around the site. A customer who noticed she was a new hire *and* made sure she felt welcome? That deserved a note in the crush column.

By tracking their clients' responsiveness to questions, their participation in solving problems when they present themselves, their treatment of the company's employees, and their general positivity and enthusiasm, Job Turf can identify their Top Clients.

You may be interfacing with customers in a sales role or a support role, or maybe you simply hear the talk about customers among your fellow employees when the boss is away. No matter your role, you may have knowledge about clients that can help the company land better customers. And with better customers, everyone's job—including yours—is less stressful and more fun.

How can you help? Start documenting your observations. Keep a record of clients who are loved, and why. What are the crush factors? Which clients make it easier for you to do an effective job? Who seems grateful and expresses their thanks? On the flip side, who are your cringe clients and why do you feel that way? How do they affect you and/or your fellow employees? Why do you avoid them? What actions can be taken to strengthen the connection with those clients?

As a team member, you have your ear to the ground, and you may know more about certain clients than anyone else. So create your own crush list. Which customers do you love and which customers not so much, and why? What specifically do you like about the ones you love and what are the reasons the cringers make you cringe? With your crush clients, make a note of their attributes, behaviors, and congregation points. This can help your company get more clients just like them. How do they network with similar companies? What industry trade rags do they consume? What podcasts do they listen to? What makes them communicate well? How do they help you and your company navigate mistakes (because mistakes do happen)? What other notable aspects of them matter most? Write down all your observations about your crush customers and your strategies to help improve the behavior of cringe customers. Share your findings with the boss at your company to help bring in more great clients and improve the relationships with the ones you have.

CLOCKWORK IN ACTION

1. Do a Crush/Cringe Analysis to clarify who your Top Clients are.

2. Interview your Top Clients to discover what they value most about your company. That is what you stake your reputation on, so make sure you build rock-solid systems for that.

3. Find their congregation points. Ask your clients where they go to share with and learn from people in their industry. Research meetings they attend, conferences they visit, podcasts they listen to, social media and influencers they follow, and magazines and newsletters they subscribe to. These are all points of common interest for your potential Top Clients.

CHAPTER THREE

DECLARE YOUR BIG PROMISE

DISCOVER THE SINGLE PHRASE THAT DEFINES YOUR COMPANY'S REPUTATION FOR EXCELLENCE

We didn't go into places that promised big wins. We went into places we felt called to go into."

When Lisé Kuecker, owner of five Anytime Fitness franchises, shared her story with me over the phone, she made a point to tell me she had never lived in the same state as any of her franchises. Considering her husband was active-duty military at the time, that was some feat; they had moved states several times.

Growing up in New Orleans, where indulgent food is a major part of the culture, Lisé had seen obesity rates skyrocket. This influenced her interest in fitness, and soon, helping people lose weight and transform their health became her deep-seated passion. When she began opening gyms during her husband's deployments, she didn't look to the biggest cities or the areas with high-income residents. She didn't even look to the communities in her own area or within driving distance. She set up in the towns that needed her the most—small towns that, on paper, didn't seem to have the potential to support membership growth.

"When we bought a failing franchise in Minnesota, the bankers and other people thought we'd lost our minds," Lisé told me. "We bought it for $50,000, which was basically the cost of the equipment. The gym had been on the market for a year and a half and it was in bad shape—treading water the entire time. It was a miracle they had 350 members; that was in part due to the fact that the owners were local and well-loved."

Despite the fact that no one thought she could make a go of it, or should even try, Lisé was drawn to the dying franchise in small-town Minnesota. The obesity rates were quite high in the area, and she knew she could make a difference. She also knew that people who were living with obesity and struggling to lose weight were the people she wanted to serve. First, she cared about them and wanted them to succeed. Second, if she could help them, she knew she would have a better chance of retaining them as members than she would the average customer, who may not have the same challenges to overcome.

"I rolled up to the gym in the bitter cold of February, me from the Deep South in my rental car with four-wheel drive," Lisé said, laughing. "Right away we started renovation plans, and I started calling members."

Over the next month, Lisé called every single one of the 350 members herself. She sometimes stayed on the phone for an hour or more, talking to people, asking them their opinions about the gym and about the changes they'd like to see after it reopened. She listened to their stories, their health goals, and the intimate details about their lives that they wanted to share. After each phone call, she wrote down the most significant snippets about their life and their aspirations on a spreadsheet so she wouldn't forget.

Although she didn't realize it at the time, Lisé had already started the Clockwork process. As described in the last chapter, first she clarified who she wanted to serve: people with weight-related health challenges in communities with high obesity rates. Now, this is where many entrepreneurs would take that clarification and modify their offering to meet the needs of their customers—even if it took them off their original path. If Lisé had learned that a decent percentage of gym members wanted to train for bodybuilding competitions, conventional "wisdom" tells us that she should have created an offer for them. She knew better. She was on a mission to remove obesity from traditionally obese communities, and nothing would take her off course.

Traditional teachings tell us to first determine whom we are serving, and to modify our offering to meet their need. The popular word today is "pivot," but that term will change. It used to be "inflection point." Before that, it was "paradigm shift." And before that, it was "Soooo, what the hell should we do now?" The point is, you need to sell what the customer wants, otherwise you won't have anything to sell. On the surface, this theory seems to make sense, but it ignores the most important element of a successful business—you.

I have seen wonderful businesses pivot into failure and wonderful entrepreneurs pivot into disenchantment. I have seen many businesses pivot into something that the owner loathes. They keep shifting their offering to match what the customer wants until the customer starts buying. But in the process, they neglect to consider what *they*, the owners themselves, want. They ignore what their hearts call out to do. And while the business may win customers, it loses the heart of the owner and the soul of the business. The business experiences death by a thousand cuts.

Sure, an offering may make money, but at what cost?

Dreading work is no way to experience life, and it's not an efficient way to scale your business. This is why it is absolutely critical for you to determine what you want. What you intend to be known for. What your soul sings out to do. Don't pivot to your Top Clients' desires *unless* their desires align with yours. You want *them* happy and they need *you* happy. Don't pivot. Align.

By continuing to follow her mission, Lisé turned around her gym fast. In less than a year, her franchise ranked in the top 5 percent of all Anytime Fitness franchises. Do you want to know the real kicker? After spending the first month on-site, Lisé now works an average of five hours a week on her business. No, that's not a typo. Not fifty hours. *Five hours.* Five hours total for *all* five locations. How did she do it? It all started with her Big BANG (Big Beautiful Audacious Noble Goal), her company's greater purpose. That purpose brought alignment around the people she wanted to serve and how she wanted to serve them. The Big BANG made all the difference for Lisé and it will make all the difference for your company, too. It is the ultimate tool for aligning employees within a company and an energizing force that pulls your company forward.

WHAT IS YOUR BIG BANG?

Lisé wanted to help remove obesity from traditionally obese communities. That's her Big BANG. That's how she intends to change the world—and she's doing it. My Big BANG is to eradicate entrepreneurial poverty. I believe business owners can save the world by innovating solutions to big problems and providing good jobs. To do that, they need strong, healthy small businesses, which is why I'm on a mission to help them achieve that. (And that means you, too.) That's how I intend to change the world.

What's your Big BANG? As the poet Mary Oliver said, "What is it you plan to do with your one wild and precious life?"[3]

Now, if you don't have a Big BANG aimed at impacting the masses, such as ending obesity or eradicating entrepreneurial poverty, that's okay. Actually, it is more than okay. Your driving purpose must be meaningful to *you*. It is enough to have an impact on *your* world, not necessarily *the* world.

When my friend Malik told me about his Big BANG, he said it was to put food on the table for his two daughters. His wife had passed away and his focus wasn't on changing the whole world or even a small part of it. His mission was to change his *children's* world, to provide the stability they needed. If your Big BANG is along those lines, that's massive. Absolutely, humongously massive. You are changing *their* world, and that is changing *the* world.

What do you want for your world, however big or small?

When I consider new members for my team, I talk about what our company's Big BANG means, how I hope it impacts our world, and why it is important to me. They may or may not find it important. Some can relate; others can't. Those who can't, even if they are great employees, won't have a compelling mission pulling them forward. They may do well but they are not motivated to stay at the company or do extraordinary things because the great aspiration does not speak to them.

Your purpose needs to outweigh your effort. That is what keeps you going when you don't want to carry on. When I wrote my first book, I assumed I'd sell thousands of copies in the first week, but I only sold a few. That was a massive wake-up call, a "how are you *really* going to make money?" moment. But then my wife reminded me of a specific note from a reader who mentioned that the book "had saved them." Chalk one up to the Big BANG being served, and it was the emotional juice I needed to keep going. Even when you aren't seeing the monetary results, the emotional wins can serve as the fuel to stay the course.

When you have a purpose beyond the transactions, speak

about it often and in different ways, inside and outside the company. Tell stories about its impact. Share company folklore of what your company has done to deliver on it. Highlight and publicly reward employees who help keep your purpose alive. The greater mission is the reason you are doing what you are doing, and it is the wind in your sails.

WHAT IS YOUR COMPANY'S BIG PROMISE?

If you aren't sure of your Big BANG, that's okay. You don't have to pause this important work until you find it; you can keep thinking about it as you continue to Clockwork your business. What you cannot save for later is this next part—declaring your company's Big Promise.

At the heart of the Clockwork process is that thing—that thing you most want your company to be known for, that thing on which you stake your firm's reputation, that thing your clients value most. I call that thing your Big Promise. When you align every aspect of your business with that Big Promise, it provides the level of clarity and certainty you need to design your business to run itself and get your employees on board.

I asked you to consider your Big BANG first because sometimes entrepreneurs confuse the two. Your Big Beautiful Audacious Noble Goal is a driving force for you, and it is your corporation's purpose. It is not your thing, though. Your thing, your Big Promise, is what you ultimately deliver to your clients and customers. To further clarify, it's not a specific product or service. It's what you intend your company to be famous for, that thing your Top Clients value most.

For Lisé's Anytime Fitness franchise, the Big Promise was strong, personal connection. She knew that one of the biggest challenges in her industry was customer retention. People would sign up for the gym and then quit within a few months. She knew she could inspire member loyalty and commitment to their fitness goals if they felt truly supported by the gym and its staff. (Do you see how this also helps her fulfill her Big BANG?) Recall that Lisé's first step when taking over the gym was to call the existing members to learn more about them. From that point forward, her policies, her business practices, and her team were all focused on maintaining that connection—and establishing it from the start with new members.

Losing weight is more than a physical change; it also requires a mental shift. When customers felt they were being heard by Lisé's team, they were able to share more about their challenges and fears. This, in turn, empowered them to change the beliefs and alter the behaviors that contributed to their obesity. The equipment at her gym was not different from the equipment at other gyms. The exercise classes were the same types of classes you could get at other gyms. What customers couldn't get at other gyms was a feeling of deep connection with Lisé's team. She would not give up on them, so they did not give up on themselves—and they did not give up on her gym.

> The Big BANG = The driving purpose for what you do.
>
> The Big Promise = The number-one thing that your customers value you for.

As I shared already, my Big BANG is to eradicate entrepreneurial poverty. My Big Promise to my customers is to simplify entrepreneurship, and I do that through my offers of products (books, videos, swag) and services (education, training, consulting, speaking).

Notice how my Big Promise is tied to my Big BANG. Don't get tripped up on that. Declaring a Big Promise works even if you don't know exactly what your Big BANG is yet. You may go to work every day with an intention to wow your customers. That drive is from your Big Promise. That is how you build your reputation with others. But you may not have defined your life's purpose yet, and that is cool.

The Big BANG is your company's reason for existing and it is how you build cohesiveness across operations. I don't want you to get buried trying to figure out your company's purpose, since it may not come naturally. Shoot, there are entire books dedicated to discovering your company's purpose, such as Simon Sinek's *Start with Why*. You have permission to skip the Big BANG for now, even for a while, but you cannot skip the Big Promise. Your company's reputation depends on it.

To further distinguish them, here's a handy-dandy chart with examples:

BIG BANG / BIG PROMISE EXAMPLES

COMPANY	BIG BANG The driving purpose for the organization	BIG PROMISE What your Top Clients value most
Lisé Kuecker (Franchise of Anytime Fitness)	Remove obesity from traditionally obese communities	Deep, personal connections
Mike Michalowicz (Small-Business Author)	Eradicate entrepreneurial poverty	Simplify entrepreneurship
Google	Information universally accessible and useful	The best daily use online tools
Disneyland	Inspire imaginative possibilities for the child within all of us	The happiest place on earth
World Wildlife Fund	Save the planet	Maximize the benefit of member contributions

Figure 4

In the last chapter, I mentioned the struggles I experienced at Olmec when we took on any and all clients. Once we identified our Top Clients and stopped dividing our attention, we became more efficient, for sure. The business really started to click, though, when we discovered our Big Promise.

We knew that, among IT companies in our industry, other companies had greater tech abilities. Some had better geographic coverage. So what was it about Olmec that worked for our Top Clients?

We started with the client at the very top of our list: Larry O'Friel, the CFO of a hedge fund. His company was unique among our client roster in that they paid us well and they paid us early.

I asked Larry, "Why do you keep buying from us? What are we doing right?"

"You respond fast," he replied.

When you ask your customer, "What are we doing right?" they won't tell you what you are doing right. They will tell you how they are measuring your performance. And since that is how they are observing you, the thing you are doing right is actually the thing that you need to do better—*if* it aligns with how you want to serve your customers.

Ask all your Top Clients what you do *right* and their answers will tell you the one thing that determines your reputation above all else. It's a Jedi mind trick that works every time. Default thinking is that we need to improve where we struggle. Not so. Exploit and enhance your reputation. That becomes your world-dominating force—your Big Promise.

After Larry revealed that it was our speed that mattered, I went through several stages of grief. I was better in so many ways, not *just* speed. I first went through denial (you know, the Egyptian river of disbelief). Then I went over the mountain of anger and through the valley of depression. Finally, I landed in an ocean of acceptance. I thought about my own vendors. If I had a problem and needed to order computers, for example, there was one thing I most cared about: Did the computers function correctly? I didn't put special significance on much else. Your clients don't care about all you do, either. They care about what *they* care about.

As I continued to interview our Top Clients, I heard similar responses. They may have used different words than Larry did, but it seemed our ability to respond quickly was the primary reason most of our favorite clients chose us and stayed with us.

Although we didn't call it that at the time, our Big Promise became lightning-fast response to tech problems. With this new declaration, we refocused every aspect of our company to ensure we delivered on our promise and came up with inventive ideas that not only changed our business but changed our industry.

Declaring your Big Promise is the key to designing your business to run itself. Without this clarity, you will continue to be in reactive mode, chained to your business. Worse, you will continue to stunt growth. Take the time to nail your Big Promise and a whole world of possibilities will open up for you, your team, and your company.

To recap, today my Big BANG is to eradicate entrepreneurial poverty. That is why I am driven to write books. My Big Promise as an author is to simplify entrepreneurship. And the promise of this book is to deliver on that by giving you your time back through an easy-as-pie process. When you have an uncomplicated path to being worry-free about the operation of your business, I am delivering on my Big Promise. When your business is running without you, your experience with entrepreneurial time poverty—where your business sucks up every waking moment of your life—has been further addressed. And maybe you will even join the movement by empowering employees to work with more efficiency and gain more time for living. And maybe the word will spread to other entrepreneurs. And with that, my Big BANG will march forward.

FOR EMPLOYEES: CORA'S STORY

Job Turf is famous for their environmental responsibility. In fact, the owner, Calvin Broadus, is a recognized horticulturist and environmentalist who actively works with the local government on environmental law. He believes a home can have a beautiful outdoor space and help foster the natural habitat.

Cora's first day at Job Turf was different than she'd imagined. Calvin and Gordon both greeted her when she arrived. After getting her new gear and that unique client scorecard system from Gordon, she expected the rest of the day would include filling out paperwork and watching training videos. It did not.

Instead, she met the GTers (Green Teamers), her fellow employees. They asked her questions about her life. They shared stories about why they had come on board with Job Turf. The recurring theme was clear: most people were there because they wanted to improve the environment. The outdoor electrical and plumbing work they did adhered to the highest environmental standards. Every project was a way to make the environment better. A new firepit, for example, was designed to be aesthetically appealing, to reduce pollution, and to include insulated alcoves and cutouts where wildlife could set up new homes. By the end of the first day, Job Turf had won Cora's heart.

Cora understood that while she didn't know 99 percent of the stuff she would do at her job, she knew the 1 percent that was the most critical: the company's purpose (its Big BANG) of harmonious integration of people and nature. And she knew their Big Promise: outdoor living spaces in harmony with nature. Then she did what every employee should do. She said, "Tell me more."

No matter your job description and responsibilities, clarity about your company's Big BANG, the why behind the work you do, serves as your true north. When you are clear about your company's Big Promise, it helps you understand how you serve the company and clients.

How can you help? As an employee, you have your own interpretation of what your company's Big BANG and Big Promise means to you. When presented with opportunities, share the company mission in your own words. And when you see something out of alignment, say something. You don't have to be a hall-pass monitor, but do report any major diversion from the company's driving purpose and promise so it can be fixed before it becomes a big issue.

 ## CLOCKWORK IN ACTION

1. Consider the impact you want to have on the world and declare your Big Beautiful Audacious Noble Goal (Big BANG). Often, life-defining moments, traumas, or childhood dreams are catalysts for a personal purpose that your company can serve. The financial trauma I experienced by grossly mismanaging money and seeing my nine-year-old daughter compelled to save our family from financial ruin by volunteering her piggy-bank savings was the spark for my Big BANG. Your reason for doing what you do may come from a dark place or a bright one. Consider what you are serving not just to

your clients, but to yourself, every time you deliver your offering—and you may find your Big BANG there.

2. Interview your Top Clients to help you home in on your Big Promise, the thing you do best and want to be known for. Is there a common thread in what makes you special to them? Additionally, you can decide independent of client feedback what you want your reputation to be. Simply ask yourself what you want your company to be famous for—that can be your Big Promise.

CHAPTER FOUR

DETERMINE YOUR COMPANY'S QUEEN BEE ROLE (QBR)

PINPOINT THE CRITICAL FUNCTION WITHIN YOUR ORGANIZATION THAT DETERMINES ITS ULTIMATE SUCCESS

f you see something, say something."

The US Department of Homeland Security has a very important Big Promise: to prevent terrorist attacks. And they have determined that the best way to prevent terrorist attacks is to identify and disclose suspicious activity. We don't see most of their work, but we do see the posters that blanket our public transportation facilities: "If you see something, say something." With this message they are recruiting everyone, including you and me, to help them deliver on their promise.

And that call to action has paid off. A study conducted out of San José State University found that since the popularization of the phrase in 1970, detection rates have improved by 14 percent in economically advanced countries. And as the phrase was promoted more often and more publicly, the rates of prevented terrorist attacks increased.[4]

Just as Homeland Security depends on all of us to help it

deliver on its promise, you depend on your team to help deliver on your company's Big Promise. The final determination you'll need to make in the Align phase is to identify the core function that delivers on your biggest commitment. When everyone on your team is aware of it and has a clear path to be of service to it, even if it is as small as calling a phone number to report a package that seems out of place, your ability to deliver on that commitment improves.

WHAT IS THE QBR?

Years ago, I started looking for solutions for running a more efficient business with a simple question: What is the most efficient organization in the world? That is what we all aspire to have—an efficient organization that generates money on automatic, which, in turn, gives us the freedom to do what we want, when we want. My Google result? Squat-o-la.

Then, one fateful day during a long drive, I flipped through radio stations and came across the most random report about bees. An NPR field reporter was out there with a beekeeper, reporting on how these insects do the amazing work they do. And, in typical NPR fashion, they shared some of the live action, including a sting that the reporter took when he got a tad too close to the hive.

As I listened, what impressed me most about bee colonies was their ability to scale extremely fast and nearly effortlessly. You may have seen it for yourself. A bee buzzes around outside your window one day, and what seems like the next day, you spot a massive hive there. How do bees do it?

Each bee in the colony knows it needs to do just two things, in the same order every time. First, each bee must ensure that the production of eggs is protected—nothing is more important than this role, which is served by the queen bee. Then, and only then, do the bees go do their Primary Job, their most crucial job in terms of their regular activity. As a result, their buzziness (I swear I will only do that once) grows quickly and easily.

Here's how bee colonies operate:

1. The most important function in a beehive is the production of eggs. Most bees have short life spans of four to eight weeks, depending on the species. So new bees are needed constantly. Therefore, the queen bee serves the most critical function in the hive: making eggs. The task of laying eggs is the Queen Bee Role—the QBR. If the QBR is humming along, enough eggs are created to keep the colony thriving. If the QBR is not served, the entire hive is in immediate jeopardy.

2. Every bee knows that the most critical function for the colony to thrive is egg production, so that activity is protected and served. In a bee colony, only the queen bee can produce eggs, so she is groomed, fed, and sheltered. She is not distracted by anything other than doing her job.

3. Don't confuse being the queen bee with being the most important part of a colony; it is the *role* she serves that is most important. Healthy eggs need to be made quickly and continuously. One specific queen or another is not critical; the QBR is what is critical. So if the queen bee dies or is failing to produce eggs, the colony will immediately get to work spawning another queen bee so the QBR can get going again.

4. Whenever the bees are satisfied that the QBR is being fully served, they go off to do their Primary Job. This could be collecting pollen and nectar (food), caring for the eggs and larvae, maintaining the hive temperature, or defending the hive—from being exploited by NPR.

After learning how beehives scale so efficiently, I had the epiphany of a lifetime. I realized that identifying and serving the QBR would radically improve any entrepreneur's business, and an entrepreneur's quality of life. What activity in your company is equivalent to egg production? What is *your* QBR? Let's find it right now.

HOW DO YOU FIND YOUR QBR?

If your package absolutely, positively must arrive tomorrow, which delivery company will you use? FedEx, of course. Why? Because that's what they stake their reputation on. It's their Big Promise. Since the QBR is the activity that most ensures that the promise is met, what is FedEx's QBR? Customer service? No, because that is more about answering questions and handling problems than it is about getting packages delivered on time. Their business center locations, where you can print, make copies, ship packages, buy office supplies, and generally pretend it's your office-away-from-the-office? Nah. Aside from the shipping counter, there's not much in the actual building that will help them deliver on their Big Promise. All these aspects of the company are significant, but they don't fit the requirement for the QBR. And there can only ever be *one* QBR. So what is the most critical activity? For FedEx, it's logistics—the management of package movement. When logistics are humming, their Big Promise is delivered consistently, day in and day out.

But imagine that FedEx decided to shift their focus to customer service and let logistics take a backseat. Now everyone in the company rallies around this new QBR. What do you think the headline would be in the newspaper just a few days later? FEDEX CAN'T FIND A SINGLE @#$&! PACKAGE, BUT THEY ARE BEING REALLY NICE

ABOUT IT. Sounds like the beginning of a sad tale about a ridiculously successful industry dominator that goes out of business.

If, on the other hand, FedEx decided to crank up their logistics (QBR) even more than they already do and kill their customer service, what do you think the headline would read? NO ONE ANSWERS PHONES AT FEDEX BUT EVERY PACKAGE DELIVERED ON TIME. They may get some bad press, maybe a few funny-annoying memes, but ultimately, they won't go out of business. Know why? Because the QBR continued unscathed. They kept delivering on their Big Promise.

When Jessi Honard and Marie Parks of North Star Messaging + Strategy started their copywriting company in 2018, it was the "Jessi and Marie Show." They did all the work themselves and had no hope of sharing the load with other writers, much less taking a vacation from their business. When they started the Run Like Clockwork program, they identified their Big Promise: we get you.

"We had a client once tell us that outsourcing copywriting was like outsourcing the heart and soul of her business," Jessi told me in an interview for this book. "One of the things Marie and I realized even before we started the Clockwork process was, we tend to work with business owners who have been in business for a little while. And they would come to us with the same consistent frustration that they had tried to outsource it, and even if that person was a good writer who understood their business, the copy still didn't sound like them. Our clients were saying, you got us, you made me sound more like me than me."

With their Big Promise clear, they settled on their QBR, the main activity that would ensure they continued to deliver on that promise: capturing the voice of their clients.

With the "capture clients' voices" QBR in place, it set North Star apart from their competitors. It also set in motion the shifts that led to dramatic business growth, and to organizational efficiency. Identifying the QBR helped Jessi and Marie realize they had to train other writers on their team to serve the QBR, which led to the eventual end of the "Jessi and Marie Show" and gave them the space to do more of the work they love.

Now it's your turn. I love it when you sit down to do your homework and realize you already did most of it in class. Well, guess what: if you completed the action steps in Chapters Two and Three, you already did most of your QBR homework. The final piece in the Align puzzle is an easy one to fit. To find your company's QBR, simply determine the one activity that most ensures you deliver on your Big Promise.

The QBR is the activity at the heart of your company—it must always be beating for your company to stay alive. It's the thing that the whole team must get behind; it can't break or stop, or the regard customers have for your organization will tank. The QBR is the activity that makes your vision a reality and brings your company's reputation to prominence. Everything else is secondary to the QBR, and some tasks and activities won't contribute to the Big Promise at all. You can likely abandon those things to bring more focus and efficiency to the things that do have an impact on the Big Promise. And, unlike a beehive, your QBR does not need to be served by one individual. Ideally it will have multiple people and/or multiple systems serving it for redundancy protection and efficiency gains.

THE IMPACT OF THE QBR

In the last chapter, I shared how at one of my previous companies, Olmec, we interviewed our Top Clients and, based on what they valued most about our service, we came up with this:

Big Promise: lightning-fast response to tech problems.

And the activity that ensured we would consistently deliver on that promise:

QBR: minimize the time of "hands to keyboard."

Notice how our QBR had nothing to do with providing excellent overall service. Our focus had to change so that we got working on significant tech problems the fastest. This was the mid-'90s, mind you. *It's a Wonderful Life* actor Jimmy Stewart was still alive and the PalmPilot was the "smartphone" of choice. If the PalmPilot was before your time, know this: it was neither smart nor a phone. At the time, remote dial-in access wasn't adequate technology for most troubleshooting, and the "cloud" didn't exist in an applicable form yet, so it meant getting technicians to jobsites as quickly as possible so they had their hands on the physical keyboard. And this meant finding ways to streamline dispatch. I started carrying three beepers (hot tech at the time) on my belt to manage the dispatch of myself and other techs to client sites. Sexy, right? Perfect with my '90s balloon-fit jeans.

We also changed the structure of our company. Prior to determining our QBR, I serviced my thirty clients; Barry, my business partner, serviced his thirty clients; other techs serviced their clients; and so on. This setup seemed to make sense at first because we figured clients wanted to work with "their guy" and not have multiple techs fixing their computers. We didn't know that our QBR was speed, so our organizational structure was based on pure speculation. We tried to never cross the streams, à la *Ghostbusters*, so if one of Barry's clients needed service and he was across town at a different site, they would have to wait until he could get to them.

With our declared QBR, we made a change to support better efficiency in that area. We trained each tech in the critical technical needs of every client. Now each tech still served as the point-of-contact for their respective clients, but any available tech could service any client if critical technology malfunctioned. So if Barry couldn't get to a jobsite he could dispatch a tech right away and, if needed, help the tech troubleshoot over the phone.

We looked at every aspect of our work through the lens of serving the QBR to deliver on our Big Promise, and this led us to a creative solution we may not have come up with otherwise. For the hands-to-keyboard QBR to work, we also had to be able to take the user off the computer we were repairing. Sometimes a machine would stop functioning in one capacity (e.g., they couldn't access a stock exchange's real-time feed) but continue to work in another (e.g., they could still do trades). In these cases, the user wanted (needed) to keep working while our technician stood there, unable to resolve the problem. This triggered an idea that was unheard of at the time. We bought extra computers for our top clients, preconfigured them to run the software they used, and stored them at our facility.

In the past, the first step was to wait for the user to get off the computer. Now the first step was to get the user moved to the replacement machine. The client would be up and running in minutes instead of hours while we fixed their malfunctioning computer. By continually optimizing our QBR, we wowed customers. Word got out about how fast we were in getting the job done and how different (in a great way) that was from the industry norm.

As we addressed our Top Clients' problems faster, they started to focus on growth with new technology, and they gave that business to us. More sales came in without us having to get more clients. And we kept serving and enhancing our QBR by adding a lead tech who stayed at the office to do phone support for our dispatched techs. The lead tech built and maintained a knowledge base of problems and fixes, giving us warp speed to fixing problems upon arrival and allowing that tech to get to the next client faster. Which meant hands to keyboard even faster.

We also stopped installing a specific antivirus package that seemed to confuse our remote access with a virus attack and would lock us out. The software slowed down our access, so out it went. We found a better way to secure our clients' technology and ultimately eliminated a time-consuming step, which helped us serve the QBR.

Before we declared our Big Promise and discovered our QBR, I was worried every day about how I'd feed my family. Honestly, it wasn't worry—it was sheer terror. That's why I worked exhaustively, sometimes from five a.m. one day to five a.m. the next day. I know that's a twenty-four-hour shift. You've been there, too, I know it. That workload is not sustainable, but I didn't know of any other solution besides working more and working harder to dig us out of our hole. As it turned out, the answer was working less. When we were finally able to shift to a normal, forty-hour week, I was able to direct my attention to expanding the company.

Do you see how focusing on the QBR is essential for your company's efficiency and its reputation? I hope your mind is buzzing right now and that your heart is filled with hope for all the awesomeness that is about to come your way once you declare *your* QBR.

THE QBR IS NOT . . .

I need to repeat a few words of caution. Most entrepreneurs automatically assume that they are the QBR, but this is key: the QBR is *never* a person, or a machine, for that matter. It is always an activity. So while you may be the one fulfilling the QBR right now, and perhaps are even the only person serving the QBR, that doesn't mean it always has to be you. In fact, it *shouldn't* always be you.

If you are the owner of a small business with five or fewer employees, the QBR is likely being served by you. If you are a solopreneur, it almost certainly is being served by you. And if you have a larger organization, it is often (but not always) served by your most skilled people.

As a reminder, the Big Promise for a beehive is that the colony will thrive. And the QBR, which is handled by the queen bee, is the production of healthy eggs. More healthy eggs means more healthy baby bees, which means the colony will grow. Simple. Simple, yet I want to reiterate a point I made earlier to clear up any potential confusion. The queen bee serves the most important role, the QBR, but is not the most important bee. She can be "disposed of," as they say here in New Jersey, if she fails to produce healthy eggs, and can be replaced by another queen bee. And she certainly is not the brain of the colony; the swarm is. The queen bee is the ovaries.

The same is true for your business. The people serving the QBR are not the most important; they are serving the most important role. They are replaceable, duplicatable, and interchangeable. The QBR is not. The QBR is the most important function, and the people (or person) serving it are simply doing the most important job. But by no means are these people (or that person) the brains of the organization; they are simply serving as the ovaries.

Here's a business example. Jesse Cole is the owner of the Savannah Bananas baseball team, arguably one of the most remarkable teams in all of baseball—majors, minors, or college. And not because they are a great team with great players. In fact, the players are all-star college kids who rotate every season. The team is constantly changing, and many of the fans don't know the name of a single player on the team. Why? Because extraordinary baseball is not the Bananas' Big Promise.

As Jesse puts it, "Baseball is the break between the entertainment." The show must always be fresh. I mean, imagine watching your kid's soccer game twenty weekends in a row; that would get draining. Wait a second, you already survived that. I mean, their first game is fun. But when it starts repeating, it becomes somewhere between boring and frustrating. Just kick the ball. Stop picking dandelions in the field. Just kick, kid. Just kick the damn ball! (As you sip wine camouflaged in your coffee thermos. By the way, everyone knows you are doing it. And they are impressed!)

Jesse knows baseball is even worse. Everyone is just standing around waiting for someone to hit a ball, and in this case your kid isn't even out there. So Jesse set the Big Promise to "fun family entertainment." One family trip for a game is fresh, but anything and everything gets stale if you see it again on the next family outing. As a result, Jesse is constantly cooking up new ideas for crazy stunts his team can perform and fun games the fans can play in between innings. So the number-one activity that ensures the Big Promise of fun family entertainment is the continuous creation of fresh ideas. And that, mi amigo, is the QBR.

Your company, my company, and every company on this planet has a reputation. What you need to realize is that you can build your reputation deliberately or be assigned a reputation by your customers. And if you don't master the one thing, your reputation will be that you are marginal at everything. The words customers typically assign to marginal reputations are things like "yeah, they're good-ish," or "meh," or "they're okay, but . . ." or "they kinda suck, but I'll deal with it for now." But when you first decide what you want to be known for (your Big Promise), you can then determine what is the most important, uncompromisable, never-ever-screw-up activity in your business that delivers on that Big Promise. And that is your QBR.

Jesse invited me to throw out the opening pitch at a game in front of five thousand Bananas fans. What an honor! Except it wasn't a baseball I threw out; it was a roll of toilet paper (in honor of my book *The Toilet Paper Entrepreneur*) and the crowd went wild. It was fresh, fun, silly entertainment. Big Promise delivered. For the Savannah Bananas, the QBR is served not by Jesse alone, but by everyone who entertains the crowd. And for that one game, for that one opening pitch of toilet paper, the QBR—for a few seconds—was served by me.

A couple of years ago, I met my friend Clyde and his wife, Bettina,* for dinner in Frankfurt, Germany. Clyde and I have been friends for years, but this was my first chance to get to know Bettina. Over dinner, I discovered that she was one of fewer than fifteen hundred physicians in the United States who are licensed and board-certified to practice pediatrics in an intensive care unit. To get to that point, she'd completed eleven years of school and training.

For most of us entrepreneurs, eleven years of higher education seems like forever and a day, but equate it with the early years of running your business. Or if you're an employee who happens to be reading this book, equate it with the time you put in getting an education, training, and learning your industry from an

---

* To protect their privacy, Clyde and Bettina are *not* their real names. Sadly, their story is all too real. Should you be curious about how I came up with their names, it was simple. I asked them what names they would never have wanted their parents to give them when they were born. The answer was Clyde and Bettina. So there you have it, meet Clyde and Bettina.

entry-level position. Just as Bettina invested time and money into her career, you've invested time and money into your business.

Like us, Bettina was passionate about her work. Extremely so. She loved working with the most critical pediatric patients in the city she lived and worked in, and she loved teaching attending physicians. She even loved the research she was expected to do in her free time. The only problem was that she knew she wouldn't be able to sustain it for much longer. She already had multiple years in the industry as a doctor, and with the relentless volume and variety of demands put on her, she figured she would be lucky if she made it ten years. Cumulatively.

Imagine this: You have five twelve-hour shifts, followed by a thirty-hour shift. In addition to patient care, you have training and mentoring related to your professorship. Then add two to three hours of patient and administrative documentation. Then pile on top of that billing and dealing with insurance company disputes. After your shifts, you have more admin work related to teaching interns. Then, when you miraculously have the energy to pull an unpaid all-nighter, you have to write research papers so that you can get promoted, if you're lucky—a few years from now. You're so exhausted you need to invent a new word for exhaustion, one that probably rhymes with "please help me."

"I love my job, but I just don't think I'll be able to keep this level of intensity and maintain mental and physical health," Bettina told me. "I had to come to grips with the fact that I won't be a full-time practicing physician my entire life. And I'm not the only one. Ten years seems to be the burnout rate for physicians at the hospital where I work."

It blew my mind that Bettina, who was an elite physician with specialized training, training that patients desperately need, had to come to terms with the fact that unless something changed dramatically, she couldn't stay in her position for much longer. It blew her mind, too. She was just entering her prime, yet she was in such drain pain that she was about to tap out.

"You plan for the eleven years of additional schooling, but no one tells you how the workload will affect you. It was a big shock, knowing how much time and money I've spent on my training. I just can't keep up this level of intensity and stay healthy and sane, and I have to be okay with that decision."

Bettina is being forced to change her life plan, and the hospital is losing one of its best doctors because it has set up a never-ending workflow—aside from patient care—that cannot be sustained. Would giving Bettina a productivity hack help to reduce her stress? No, because the hospital has already given her dozens of them, and then quickly finds a dozen new ways to fill up her "free time" with more work, like processing insurance-claim disputes. Imagine that: you're having lifesaving heart surgery and your surgeon takes a break in the middle of the operation so that he can argue with an insurance agent about why he used ten stitches during the last operation instead of the insurance-mandated three.

You know the saying "Don't busy the quarterback with passing out the Gatorade?" This is because the QBR is so important. The quarterback has a job to do. He has got to move that ball down the field, not dole out drinks to rehydrate his teammates. Similarly, Bettina shouldn't be bothered with tasks that interfere with serving the QBR. It's so obvious that it is hiding in plain sight. Bettina needs to save lives first, last, and all the time in between, yet she is often stuck passing out Gatorade. It's more than just a shame; it's a sin.

And it's a sin if you don't cherish the QBR, either. In the next chapter, I'll tell you how to make sure you and your team empower *your* quarterback—whoever is serving the QBR—to get that ball down the field and all the way into the end zone, with a "hokie" touchdown dance and all.

FOR EMPLOYEES: CORA'S STORY

Job Turf's Big Promise is "outdoor living spaces in harmony with nature." And the QBR is the activity that ensures it: ongoing testing. Installing a backyard pool, patio, and pergola in the traditional method can really mess up the habitat for little creatures and disrupt the environment for vegetation. So the crew takes extensive training on sustainable practices. Every day, they check in to make sure their work is environmentally sound. At the end of any project, they bring in an outside party from a national park or environmental group to review the project and rate the quality of their work.

Attention at this level is unheard of in this industry, and it is the reason why Job Turf is heralded by clients.

Cora will be doing a lot of hands-on work installing pipes and other materials. But she is also responsible for protecting the QBR, along with everyone else at Job Turf. The saying at Job Turf is "See something. Say something. Immediately." Even though Cora isn't working the big machinery yet, or overseeing the work, she has the power to stop the entire project if the QBR is compromised. They call this "Code Red," and it is triggered by a page sent through their smartphones.

How can you help? Make sure you know the QBR. If you don't know, ask. Working with clarity of the big picture makes it easier to understand why you do what you do. How do you serve it? Do you serve it directly or in a support role? Once you understand the QBR, keep an eye out for areas where it may be compromised or could use improvement. What is your plan to keep an eye on it? What is your "see something, say something" strategy? If the QBR is struggling or stalled, what can you do to get it running and moving again? What is your backup plan for when you need to help with the QBR and your other work is on hold?

CLOCKWORK IN ACTION

I have only one action step for you: determine your QBR.

Yes, that's it. Once you do this, you will start to find your way out of the weeds. The QBR is the linchpin to a business designed to run itself.

Here's an exercise to help you find your QBR:

1. Once you have determined your Big Promise, ask yourself how you will make it happen. Consider all the activities that serve the company. Which one is most directly connected to delivering on the Big Promise? This is not necessarily easy to pick out of thin air. They may all seem to be the most important activity. But by definition, only one activity can be the most important.

2. You can use the sticky-note exercise to employ deductive logic to find the QBR among all the others. To do this, write each activity on a sticky note. For example, if your Big Promise is extraordinary support, you may have answering phone calls, responding to chat messages, answering emails, and talking with customers as the important activities required to deliver on that promise. Note each one on a sticky note. In the example, you'd have four, but there is no magic number.

3. Looking at your sticky notes, take away the two that are least connected to your Big Promise. Repeat this process until you are down to your final two or three. With the remaining sticky notes, pick the one that is most important to deliver on your Big Promise. That is your QBR. For me, important activities that support my Big Promise of "simplifying entrepreneurship" include speaking, podcast interviews, writing books, video training, and some coaching. But when I start to peel things away, out of all of them, writing books is the one activity that best supports my Big Promise. So writing books is my company's QBR. My business's health, like the health of a bee colony, depends on the production of healthy eggs (books). The other tasks matter, for sure. But nothing matters so much that I can ignore the quality of my books in order to handle it.

4. Still struggling to nail down your QBR and think it could be a few things? Here is a simple tiebreaker: Call your Top Clients and ask them, "Of these things we do, what is most impactful to you?" For example, if you are not sure if your QBR is sales proposals or creating content or collections, call a handful of your best clients and ask them. Where they see the value in your company is where you are making your reputation. I can't speak for them, but in this example, I assume your clients will get the most value out of the content you create for them. Therefore, content creation is the QBR. The sales and collections are important, but they are secondary to content creation.

PHASE TWO

INTEGRATE

The first articles about Amazon featured this guy who had decided to move to Bellevue, Washington, and open an online bookstore. I can still see the picture of Jeff Bezos cranking away at his computer in his home garage, which doubled as a makeshift shipping center. He was the perfect example of an entrepreneur grinding it out to make a dream happen. In those early days of what would quickly become the biggest book retailer in the world, Bezos stocked certain titles, kept up with inventory, processed orders, updated the company's website, and handled customer complaints.

Bezos also had a vision—a big vision. I assume it was world domination because he's pretty much there. Or maybe it was to do something completely out of this world, which he also achieved with his (seriously phallic) rocket ship. Now imagine if he tried to make his vision happen, to make his Big BANG happen, by continuing to ship all the books from his garage himself. Where would Amazon be today?

To realize his vision, Bezos gave up the grunt work and let his team handle the day-to-day operations. Sadly, many business owners never make this vital shift. They may do some big thinking about their business, they may have a big dream for their business, but they don't get out of the way so it can become reality. They don't change, and therefore their company doesn't change. They don't run the company; they run around *inside* the company.

In the second Clockwork phase, you will begin to integrate the clarity you gained in the Align phase into the day-to-day operations of your business. Now that you know your Top Clients, the Big Promise you offer them, and the QBR that ensures you deliver on that promise, you can begin the process of stepping out of your hustle-and-grind entrepreneur role and into the capacity that will help you guide your company to greatness: shareholder.

CHAPTER FIVE

PROTECT AND SERVE THE QBR

UTILIZE THE METHOD THAT GETS YOUR ENTIRE TEAM
WORKING TOGETHER IN THE OPTIMAL WAY

Mrs. Wilkes' Dining Room in Savannah arguably has the best family-style Southern cooking in Georgia, perhaps the world. It's a great place to visit before you head off to a Savannah Bananas evening game. In 1943, Mrs. Sema Wilkes took over a boardinghouse in historic downtown Savannah with the goal of making the area's best Southern meals. Mrs. Wilkes' Dining Room feels like two dozen of the world's-best-grandmother cooks whipped up their favorite dishes for a family dinner, but instead of plopping it down on the dining room table, they scootered it over to the fabled Savannah restaurant. The food is that good.

If pressed to answer, I'd bet the owners would say their Big Promise is "a dining experience just like eating at Grandma's house." The activity—their QBR—that *most* delivers on that promise is cooking quality food, hands down. The servers exude Southern hospitality. The restaurant is basic but spotless. The ambience is very much family-oriented; you'd better be ready to meet strangers because you will surely be sitting with them at the large tables that seat ten people. And when you are finished, you will be carrying your plates to the kitchen to be cleaned. Great food, good service, and fun times. All those things are necessary to keep you in the restaurant business, but you stand out on your Big Promise (in this case, "like eating at Grandma's"). If the food wasn't exquisite, the restaurant would be more of a gimmicky place. If the food disappointed, the Big Promise would be left unfulfilled.

Your QBR must be run optimally to make the Big Promise happen. The "to" being the link. When you determine your Big Promise and your QBR, run a quick "to" test to make sure they are linked. For me? I "write books" *to* "simplify entrepreneurship." Mrs. Wilkes' "prepares the best food" *to* "make it taste like Grandma's." You do your QBR *to* deliver on your Big Promise.

The entire Mrs. Wilkes' Dining Room team rallies around the QBR, and the result speaks for itself. The typical waiting time to get in the restaurant is one and a half to two hours. People start to line up hours before the place opens, not just on holidays or during vacation weeks, but every day.

The goal of the team, just like yours needs to be, is to protect and serve the QBR. Every employee plays a role in either directly serving or protecting the QBR. The chef and team in the kitchen are directly serving the QBR by gathering the finest and freshest local ingredients and cooking them just right. Serving the QBR is their Primary Job. The rest of the team protects the QBR. For example, the serving team's Primary Job is to ensure each customer has a lovely, frictionless dining experience. That said, they also protect the QBR (making the most delicious food) by ensuring that it is served at optimal temperatures. The food is on the table *before* you get seated and the dishes are rotated quickly to keep it warm and fresh. If a table's food delivery is slow, another team member will jump in. Everyone knows what they are known for. And their job is to make sure the food is top-shelf.

Sema Wilkes passed away in 2001. Her granddaughter runs the

restaurant now and she maintains strong relationships with the local farmers, ensuring the restaurant has top ingredients. The granddaughter knows that their business's success hinges on serving the QBR, not on Sema herself. And while Sema is sorely missed by all who loved and knew her, the QBR continues unabated. If the kitchen needs a hand with prep work, one of the serving team will immediately take on the role. The entire team helps with preparation and gives feedback if there is any problem. Is the chicken slightly dry? If a dish is even just a little off from grandma-level perfection, the team rushes that input back to the kitchen. It almost never happens, but it could, and the team knows that the food quality, the QBR, is everything. It's everything because it makes their Big Promise a reality.

Protect and serve the QBR as though your life depends on it because it makes your Big Promise a reality and your business becomes a "must go there" for customers, just like Mrs. Wilkes' Dining Room is for foodies.

That's it. That's the main goal. That's the one thing that will make your business rocket to organizational efficiency.

In this chapter, you'll begin to Integrate the work you did in the Align phase into your day-to-day operations. You'll learn how to determine each team member's Primary Job and how to differentiate between serving the QBR and serving one's Primary Job. This clarity is crucial as you begin to assess how everyone on your team spends their time.

THE QBR VS THE PRIMARY JOB

Now you know that your team's main goal is to protect and serve the QBR. Always. If the QBR is good, then and only then can they focus on their Primary Jobs.

Your employees may occasionally get confused by the difference between the QBR and their Primary Jobs. Heck, you may get confused from time to time. The distinction is important because although everyone protects the QBR, that is not necessarily the primary function of each employee's job. Let's break it down for clarification.

You already know that QBR stands for the Queen Bee Role. The main objective (Big Promise) of a bee colony is survival, and the one activity that most supports that is the production of eggs. You can only have one activity that is *most* important, and that's your QBR. One big point of confusion I hear readers share is that they hear "Queen Bee" and think, "Hey, I'm the Queen Bee in this joint, therefore if it's the most important activity, I need to be the one to do it." Now I'm not saying you were thinking this, nope. But just in case *someone you know* had these thoughts, let me tell you straight up that this is a) false, and b) all about your ego—I mean, *their* ego. Been there, done that, have all the T-shirts from every time I let my ego take over, so accept it, let it go, and move on.

The QBR can be directly served by one person, sure, but that means your company would be dependent on one person. I think you might just know what that feels like, and what happens when everything hinges on one person. I sure hope that person doesn't get sick! Or need, say, a long lunch break. Even bees in a hive don't rely on one queen. She has a lofty title but she has to crank out a ton of eggs. Some of the drones are designated "queenslayers" (good band name!) and will rise up and kill the queen if she doesn't produce enough eggs. Brutal, right? *If the QBR is not fully served, they kill the queen.* Likewise, if the offspring of the queen are lazy, hungry, or sterile—boom! The queen dies. So it is about the *role*, not about the queen herself.

Sometimes a team thinks only one person can be the queen.

That is where my analogy is weak, I'll admit. The QBR sounds like one person's job, but multiple people can directly serve the QBR. In fact, it doesn't have to be just a few people. It could be an entire department, or robots, or systems. Again, the QBR is not a person; it is an activity.

A simple example of this is American football, or any other team sport, for that matter. Let's assume the Big Promise is a championship season. Note that some teams, such as the Savannah Bananas and the Harlem Globetrotters, have a different Big Promise: family fun and entertainment. For this example, though, let's go with the promise of a championship season. The QBR is the activity that will accumulate more points than the opponent. In this case, to get the ball into the end zone or between the field goalposts.

Here are the individuals on a football team who directly serve the QBR:

- The center, the first person who touches the ball and (almost always) transfers it to the quarterback.
- The quarterback, who then transfers it to another player or runs with it toward the end zone.
- Possibly another player who catches or is given the ball, then runs with it toward the end zone.
- The kicker, who tries to kick the ball between the field goalposts.
- And, occasionally, the defensive player who finishes a play with the ball in their respective end zone (through an interception, fumble, or safety).

The other players' jobs on the team are to act as decoys, to block, or to interfere with the other team's attempts to prevent the forward progress of the ball. Who will directly serve the QBR is determined in advance when deciding which play will be attempted in an effort to move the ball forward.

When players are not directly serving the QBR, they are doing their Primary Job, the most crucial job any individual has in terms of their "regular" activity. Before he is hiked the ball, the quarterback is serving his Primary Job of communicating changing plans to the team. When serving the QBR, the center takes the ball from the ground and hands the ball to the quarterback, and then reverts to his Primary Job of blocking. The receiver's Primary Job is to run a specific, preplanned pattern intended either to confuse the other team's defense or to get them to an open space where they can catch the ball. When they catch the ball, they are now serving the QBR.

Because they serve the QBR, the quarterback is the most important player on the field—but only when they have the ball. When the receiver gets the ball, *they* are now the most important player on the field.

Football über-fans have reminded me that even the crowd itself plays a support role with the QBR. The home fans can get pretty raucous before, during, and after a play commences in an effort to interfere with the communication of the opposing team, therefore supporting the QBR of their team. This is one of the rare circumstances where having too many drinks can be an asset. The other being when your mother-in-law tells you she is extending her visit at your home for another day.

Again, the QBR is never an individual. It is always the most important activity within an organization. All employees must be aware of it. Some will serve it directly at all times. Some will serve it part time. Some will only serve it occasionally. When they do, they are the most important people on the team, and everyone must "block" for them so they can serve the QBR.

The only thing that supersedes the Primary Job is when the

team member is called upon to directly serve the company's QBR. The Primary Job of a lineman is to block opponents so the player carrying the ball can get to the end zone. In football, if a player running with the ball fumbles it, the lineman is expected to jump on the ball, no matter what. The QBR is to get points, and the only way they can do that is if they maintain possession of the ball. You may have seen the pure chaos when a football is fumbled and a pile of bodies ensues as everyone scrambles to get the ball. They are all immediately reverting to serving the QBR.

To help clarify this further, I made a chart for you. Don't you love charts? Recall that the Big Promise is your number-one commitment to your clients. The QBR is the number-one activity that

QBR / BIG PROMISE EXAMPLES

COMPANY	QBR SERVED BY	QBR	BIG PROMISE
Football team offense	Player(s) moving the ball forward	Actions that get points to…	Win enough games for the championship
Football team defense	Player(s) preventing forward progress of the ball	Actions that stop or prevent the other team's progress and regain possession of the ball to…	Win enough games for the championship
Me (author guy Mike)	Person(s) writing the book	Write books to…	Simplify entrepreneurship
FedEx	System managing package flow	Manage logistics to…	Deliver packages on time
Zappos	Customer service department	Provide customer service to…	Give the feeling of happiness
Amazon	The website	Seamless online ecommerce to…	Provide the most convenient shopping experience
A deli	The purchaser(s) of ingredients	Serve the most complementary ingredients to…	Make the tastiest sandwich
A different deli	The maintainer(s) of ingredients	Serve the freshest ingredients to…	Make the freshest sandwich
Yet another deli	The assemblers of sandwiches	Assemble sandwiches in the most efficient manner to…	Provide the fastest service

Figure 5

delivers on that Big Promise. The Primary Job for any individual is the most important function they serve within the scope of their job.

The QBR is the heart of your organization. Some people (and/or resources) will have the Primary Job of directly supporting the QBR. Others will have a Primary Job that is a supporting role to the QBR and other company functions.

You need to know both the QBR for your company and the Primary Jobs of your team. And everyone needs to know how to step in to serve the QBR when it is compromised. This happens to FedEx every holiday season. Demand for shipping skyrockets and the QBR is challenged since the regular drivers can't keep up with the pace. So the managers, whose Primary Job is to manage, get out from behind their desks and get into the trucks to help deliver. They help serve logistics (the QBR) directly when it is compromised.

Four years into clockworking his business, Trevor Rood had grown Foghorn Designs from $300,000 to more than $1 million in annual revenue. He had stepped out of serving the QBR directly and had handed off nearly all the hats he'd worn trying to do all the things. Gone were his twelve-hour workdays and seven-day workweeks. Then COVID-19 arrived, and his branding company was hit hard.

"In February of 2020, we had a $60,000 month," Trevor told me. "Then in March, it was $27,000. By April, our revenue was down to $3,200."

His clients had shut down and they weren't ordering signage, screen-printed products, or embroidered items for branding purposes. There was no reason to do that—the whole world had hit the pause button. Thanks to the changes he'd made in his business by applying the principles he'd learned in *Profit First*, he weathered the storm. By the end of the summer, they brought in $50,000 a month. The problem was, he no longer had the same team. This meant Trevor had to put a few hats back on—he had to focus on serving the QBR himself and take on work that, before the pandemic, had been his employees' Primary Jobs.

The good news was, he had removed himself from these jobs before and he knew he could do it again. He was sure of this because he had already designed his business to run itself. Once clockworked, always clockworked. Or, at least, always clockworkable.

"It's a struggle to find good people right now, but I'm optimistic. I have the systems in place. I know my metrics," he explained. "When COVID hit, I was about two months away from taking my first four-week vacation. I had to cancel it. But we've built to that point before, and we can do it again."

Trevor's new goal: to see all sixty-three national parks with his family. He's going to need a lot of time away from his business to pull that off. And he'll get it. He knows that for sure.

In this chapter, you've learned how to help your employees identify their Primary Jobs and differentiate between serving it and serving the QBR. This is a crucial first step in the Integrate phase because it provides them with the clarity and context they need to make critical decisions about how and where they focus their attention.

When you Clockwork your business, it gives you the confidence to weather almost any storm. You may have to jump back into a job for a period of time, but eventually, you'll be able to pull out again and do the work you love to do and the shareholder work your company needs you to do.

FOR EMPLOYEES: CORA'S STORY

After two months at Job Turf, Cora has come to understand and appreciate her Primary Job: the installation of inhabitable landscapes. This is not to say it is her only job. She has a lot of responsibilities. She has started manning some of the machinery and now operates a skid steer (imagine a mini-bulldozer) the company uses to move materials around. And she is directly involved in the installation of piping and foundation work. Cora must attend to all these jobs, but her Primary Job is ensuring that the landscape installations are inhabitable. She always has her eye on that work. And if at any time she sees that it is being compromised, she takes care of it. And in circumstances where she can't fix it herself, she brings the issue to a site manager's attention immediately.

Cora and her fellow team members focus on their Primary Jobs while always keeping an eye on the QBR. If the environment is being negatively impacted (meaning the Big Promise of "outdoor living spaces in harmony with nature" is in jeopardy), she is expected to report it immediately and initiate new testing. If something affecting the Queen Bee Role requires immediate attention or testing, then she, like everyone else, is expected to stop the project on the spot. If the QBR is down (no testing), it needs the available and capable resources bringing it back up. Stat.

By definition, only one thing can be the "most important" thing that you do. That is your Primary Job. This is not to say that other things won't be important. In fact, a lot of the things you do *are* important. The Primary Job is the *most* important thing in the domain of work you do, above all else. If the shiitake mushrooms hit the fan, stay focused on your main work—as long as the QBR isn't compromised. If the QBR is in jeopardy and there is no way to serve it without your direct intervention, and you have the capability to serve it, you may do that. And if the QBR is down and the people who can bring it up to speed efficiently are working on it and don't need your help, continue with your work responsibilities.

How can you help? Work with your manager to clearly define your Primary Job. Again, this is not your only job, but this is the most important thing you do within the domain of your job. Also, know the QBR of the company so that you can protect and, if needed, serve it. Maybe—hopefully never, but maybe—you will be called upon to serve.

 ## CLOCKWORK IN ACTION

The next step in the Integrate phase is to help your team determine how they serve the QBR and, if they don't serve it directly, identify their Primary Job.

Here's a variation on the sticky note from the last chapter, to help you and your team find their Primary Job:

1. Ask each team member to jot down the top six tasks they do on any given day, and then write each one on a sticky note. For example, for a receptionist, that might include answering the phones, responding to voicemails, greeting customers, processing mail and deliveries, scheduling appointments, and accepting payments.
2. Looking at the sticky notes, ask each team member to determine if they serve the QBR directly or are in a protection role, expected to jump in where needed.
   a. Since you have already identified the QBR for your company, it is easy to see which team members' tasks

directly serve the QBR. If no tasks match up, then their QBR-related role is to protect it when called upon.

3. Then, to identify their Primary Job, ask each team member to take away the three tasks they do that have the least importance to the company. Then, using the same parameters, take away one more sticky note, and then one more. The remaining task is their Primary Job (as they have identified it), the work that cannot be compromised—except when protecting the QBR.

   a. Company leadership must ensure that the Primary Job identified by the employee is in alignment with what is expected. Sometimes, individuals identify a Primary Job that is not accurate. In that case, leadership needs to explain what they see as the Primary Job and determine why the team member thought otherwise.

4. Finally, if a Primary Job has already been identified for a position within the business, leadership can simply explain what it is. But the exercise is still a helpful tool for a team member to go through so they can understand how the different elements of their job work together.

CHAPTER SIX

TRACK EVERYONE'S TIME

BRING TO LIGHT INEFFICIENCIES, UNNECESSARY WORK, AND THE OPPORTUNITIES TO DO MORE WITH LESS

Entrepreneurs are natural DIYers. We do everything as we build our businesses from the ground up because we *must* do everything. We can't afford to hire others, and at this stage, we still have the time to do everything. We aren't usually that good at most of it (even though we convince ourselves that we are), but we get the stuff done well enough. While it makes sense that we have to take on many different roles when we first get our businesses off the ground, it's not healthy and it's not sustainable. Finally, we make that first hire, and even with the added financial pressure,* we feel some relief because we couldn't keep up the insane pace of doing everything. But the sprint-like pace does

---

* The financial dilemma of hiring people is very difficult for small-business owners. When you hire an employee, you might have to cut your own compensation, which is already sparse. So we delay hiring until we can afford the employee, but we never get there. We are stuck between a rock and a hard place. Work even harder, which you can't. Or hire someone, which you can't afford. There is a solution, though, which I detail in *Profit First*. I also made a video explaining exactly how to address this situation successfully. It is available at clockwork.life.

not, in fact, go away. Even when we hire people to help us (employees or subcontractors), we often still end up "Doing" a ton of work—scratch that, *more* work—because we are the linchpins.

Designing a business that runs itself is doable. In fact, it is very doable. To pull it off, you have to shift away from *Doing* and focus more and more of your time on *Designing* the flow of your business. In this chapter, you will gain a better understanding of how you and your team utilize your time. With this knowledge, you will have the data you need to fully Integrate the understanding you gained in the Align phase.

THE 4Ds OF RUNNING A CLOCKWORK BUSINESS

Every company engages in four elements of work. These are the Four Ds (4Ds)—Doing, Deciding, Delegating, and Designing. Although you were engaged in all four of these types of activities to varying degrees during the course of your business's evolution, and while your business will always have a mix of all four Ds, our goal is to get you, the business owner, Doing less and Designing more—which is the job of a shareholder.

Shifting from Doing to Designing is not a "Monday morning makeover" kind of shift. It's not a switch you flip; it's a throttle. You build toward this. You become more and more of a designer over time, and there is no finish line.

1. **Doing:** These are the activities of productivity, the necessary work required to serve clients and maintain operations. You know it well and you do it well (enough). When you're a solopreneur, doing everything yourself is a necessity. This is where almost every startup starts, and

where most of them get stuck permanently. Of the nearly thirty-two million small businesses in the United States, nearly twenty-six million don't have a single employee.[5] In other words, the owner is doing everything.

2. **Deciding:** This is the process of making choices and assigning tasks to other people. Whether they are full- or part-time employees, or freelancers, or contractors, they are really only task rabbits. This is because you are doing the work of making decisions. They try to do the one task you gave them and then come back to you to ask questions, get your approval, have you solve problems, and help them come up with ideas. If there is any unexpected hiccup with the task at hand, the person seeks your decision. When they finish a task, they either sit idle or ask you, "What should I do now?"

    Most entrepreneurs confuse Deciding with Delegating. If you assign a task to someone else but need to answer questions to get the task done, you are not Delegating—you are Deciding for them. Business owners who have two or three employees often get stuck spending most of their time on this activity. Your employees do the work, but the business owner's "job" becomes answering a constant and distracting stream of questions from them. It eventually gets so bad that you may even throw your hands up in frustration and make the decision to "go back to how it was before" in an attempt to return to the "easier times" when you did all the work yourself. Before long, you get overwhelmed with the Doing and then hire again and return to the frustrations of the Deciding stage. You flip-flop back and forth for the life of the business between doing the work and deciding for the few employees, over and over again.

3. **Delegating:** In this activity, you assign an outcome to an employee *and* empower them to make decisions about executing the tasks to make that outcome a reality. The person is fully accountable for the achievement of that outcome. They are on their own. As you spend more of your time Delegating, you will feel some relief from your workload, but only if you delegate in the right way. Initially, you *must* reward your employees' ownership of an outcome—*not* the efficiency in achieving it—because the goal is to shift the responsibility for decision-making from you to them. If they are punished for poor decisions,* or slipups, you will only be training them to come back to you for decisions. You, too, have made poor decisions in the past; that's how you grew. They will make poor decisions, and that is how they will grow. The Delegating stage can be extremely difficult for entrepreneurs because we can do everything perfectly (in our mind) and get frustrated when they don't (in our mind). You must get past this perfection mindset if you ever want your business to successfully run itself.

4. **Designing:** This is the activity where you work on the ever-evolving vision for your company and strategize the flow of the business to support that vision. When your team handles the other three Ds, the business runs itself. When you are in Designing mode, you will not only be free from the daily grind, but you will likely experience the most joy in your work. Your job is elevated to managing the

---

* A poor decision can be in the eye of the beholder. I have judged decisions by others as bad because they did not make a decision consistent with mine. But that doesn't mean it was a bad decision. The goal is to achieve the outcome, and the decisions to get there may vary. Put the most emphasis on the outcome and the efficiency in achieving it.

company by numbers and fixing the flow of business to ensure that everything aligns with your vision. When you are devoted to Designing and are no longer needed to do the work, you are now overseeing the work (to the degree you want to) and doing only the work you want to. But don't confuse deep thinking, the work required for Designing, with easy work. This is the work that makes a company (and its owner) healthy, wealthy, and wise. This is the good life, my brothers, my sisters, and my nonbinaries.

FOUR TYPES OF WORK

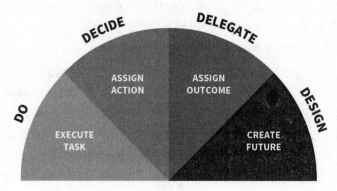

Figure 6

DOING IS GETTING YOU NOWHERE

I still struggle with the urge to "just do everything myself."* In my nearly thirty years as an entrepreneur, "doing everything" was something I expected of myself. I was a "serious" entrepreneur. I

---

* The urge to do everything myself has diminished significantly since I started taking my annual four-week vacation. This is the keystone to a business that will run itself. You will discover how to do it in Chapter Eleven. And you *must* schedule it before you finish reading this book.

did "whatever it took" to grow my business. And because I (somewhat) succeeded, I attributed much of that success to my "tireless" work ethic. Even when I had a team of nearly thirty employees, I still burned the midnight oil, doing much of the work and overseeing the rest of it because "no one can ever do the stuff only I can do" and "no one cares as much as I do." I just wished that my employees would "step up" and "act like an owner." But they didn't. They just bothered me with an endless stream of questions. Notice all the quotation marks in this paragraph? That's because most of my perceptions were, like I said, hype—total BS.

Again, as a business leader, your time is best spent *Designing* the work, not *Doing* the work. What do I mean by "Designing the work"? Let's use another football analogy. (Go Hokies!) It's the story of the team owner, the coach, and the players.

The players are empowered to make split-second decisions on the field of play, the coach creates the game plan and calls the plays, and the team owner designs the team. The owner lays out the vision for the franchise, picks the coach(es) to manage the team, and then watches from afar as the team puts the game plan into action. For the outsider, it may be a bit confusing. It just looks like a rich old guy eating mini-wieners in the glassed-in suite. But there is much more going on than you can see. The owner optimizes every element of the franchise: the team, the sponsor deals, the seat sales and the upsells, the marketing, the budget, etc. The owner is the shareholder.

As a designer, you think several steps ahead. You are strategic. You measure opportunities and risk. Is every move you make the right one? Of course not. But you measure the outcomes of your moves and make adjustments accordingly on your subsequent moves. And to be your company's designer you must get off the field and up in the suite. You must make big, calculated decisions at a deliberate pace. And you must ensure that the organization fulfills those plans. Just avoid those mini-wieners. Nothing good ever comes from those things.

Every entrepreneur starts out as a doer because doing things is what we're good at. The problem arises when you get stuck in that phase, and all the Doing keeps you from your bigger vision of building a business. You're already familiar with Design work. It's what you loved when you first started—creating a vision for your company and considering the big, bold, strategic moves you could make. So this is also work that you have the firsthand knowledge of to do effectively—directing the flow of the business.

When you spend most of your work time in Design mode, your company achieves absolute efficiency and scalability potential. As the designer, you are giving your company your best—your genius, the genius that started it all. You are also removed from the day-to-day operations so that your business can run without you, which means it can also *grow* without you. Your purpose is to design the flow of your business, point it in the direction of growth, and then make strategic decisions to fix, change, and/or improve things when the flow is not right.

Even when we appreciate the value of Design work, most folks still devote too many hours to Doing. This doesn't just apply to the solopreneur who hasn't delegated anything yet, but also to leaders of teams of five, or fifty, or five hundred. Owners, managers, and C-suite teams can get trapped in the Doing just as much as any solopreneur.

A 2009 study by the Max Planck Institute for Biological Cybernetics in Tübingen, Germany, determined that people trying to find their way through a forest or a desert devoid of landmarks (and without the sun as a beacon) tended to walk in circles. People walked in circles as tight as sixty-six feet while thinking they were walking perfectly straight. That is like putting a blindfold on and trying to walk across a football field the short way, one sideline to the other, and never making it across.

Researchers concluded that in the absence of clear markers of distance and direction, we make a continuous stream of micro adjustments to what we think is straight, but those adjustments are biased toward one side more than the other. Our constantly changing sense of what is straight keeps us walking in a loop. We circle and circle, ultimately perishing, when we could have easily gotten out of the woods (and weeds) by just walking straight.

You can overcome this tendency if you have a distinct landmark to move toward, and if you are lucky enough to be equipped with a compass or GPS. The distinct and distant landmark allows us to constantly recalibrate our direction and stay straight. Even when an obstacle presents itself, we can avoid it, move around it, or run from it, then spot our landmark again and use it to correct our course.

A business that doesn't devote time to determining where it wants to go, seeking ways to get there, and identifying the landmarks that will offer the most direct route is destined to spin in circles for eternity. The struggle to escape the Survival Trap is constant. The business owner and team toil away, month after month, year after year, hoping to move forward, but without a clear sense of direction, they are surprised and frustrated when they keep circling back to the same spot.

The worst part about walking in circles? We don't believe we are doing it, even when we see proof. In the study by the German researchers, one group of participants was dropped in the middle of a German forest and another group in the Sahara Desert. With GPS tracking devices attached to them, they were given simple instructions: walk straight for a few hours. When the sun or moon was visible, people stayed on a somewhat direct course.

But on a cloudy day or a night with no moonlight, people reverted to their looping patterns immediately. Worse yet, the terrain caused even more complications with direction, creating a channeling effect. People can't walk straight without a landmark, and when complications present themselves, they often send people in a whole new direction yet again.

Trying to build a business by just Doing and without Designing is like walking through a dense forest while blindfolded. It is inevitable that you will walk in circles and be thrown off course if you come across a substantial obstacle. Navigating the terrain of growing an organization requires a designer who looks beyond the constant stream of challenges and opportunities immediately in front of them and instead charts a path toward the company's long-term vision. And that designer is you. Yes, even if you've lost touch with the vision you once had, even if you feel like you haven't seen your creativity in the last decade, and even if you wonder if you truly have what it takes to navigate your corporate ship to new, prosperous shores—you are the best person for the Design job. You can do it, Captain.

THE DELEGATION COMPLICATION

When you first want to scale your business, the Deciding phase comes quickly. The process is easy—hire people and tell them what to do. Getting them to do the work without your input? Not so easy. And we bring this problem on ourselves. Every time my team had a question and came back to me for a decision, it made sense. They were new employees and they needed to learn the right way to do things—my way. So I gave them the answers they needed and sent them on their way to do the work. Plus, every time they had a question that only I could answer, it pumped my ego and fulfilled my need to feel important. I'm just being real with you here. And you need to be real with yourself, too: knowing what others don't is an ego boost.

I thought the need to answer everyone's questions would be short-lived. They were learning the tools of the trade, and I expected the questions to slow down. But oddly enough, they increased. The problem that I didn't realize until it was too late was that I was teaching them to always get the answers from me.

Leaders often unintentionally encourage the "I'll decide, you do" behavior in new employees. It starts with the "better than sliced bread" moment. You bring on virtual help, a consultant, or a part- or full-timer. On the first day, the only person more excited and anxious than that employee is you. Within days you're thinking, "This new hire, she is taking so much work off my hands. Why didn't I do this sooner? She is better than sliced bread."

The newbie has tons of questions, but that is to be expected. In fact, that is what you want: a learner. But a few weeks later, this person still has tons of questions. She's asking questions she should know the answer to by now. What is going on? Then, in a few more weeks or months, that new "bread" has become a total distraction. The questions never stop. You are pulled from your own work constantly to serve her. That is when you realize this bread is that icky, gluten-free kind. You know, about as flexible as concrete, with the rich flavor of cardboard. And then that buried thought reappears: "It's just easier to do all the work myself."

When you give your employees all the answers, you exhaust yourself with all that dynamic thinking and decision-making. You also block their learning. I suspect that when you first learned to drive a car, you only figured it out for real by driving the car. Yeah, you went through that six-hour, in-classroom driver's-ed course where you were told that the gas pedal is on the right and the brake is on the left. But even with those instructions, when it actually came to driving the car, chances are you over-accelerated or hit the brake way too hard. I bet that as you learned to steer a car, you went a little too tight and crushed a cone or two . . . dozen.

The learning—the true learning—is in the doing. You must experience it for it to become ingrained in you. Our employees must experience the decision-making for it to become ingrained in *them*. When you hire someone to do the work, you are making the hire so you can reduce your work. But, ironically, if you allow yourself to make all the decisions for them, your work increases and their growth stops in its tracks. If you want your team to drive their work forward, stop steering for them. (See what I did there?)

Having to oversee my team didn't reduce my hours. I actually worked more because they constantly pulled me away from the work I should have been doing. Then, when I got back to my work, I would have to sync up again—which, as you know all too well, takes time. The distraction of being the decider made *me* super inefficient. Employees would put their work on hold as they waited their turn to ask me a question. They literally *stopped* taking action until I gave them direction. My work stopped and so did theirs! Trying to do my job and supervise my team was like trying to type a letter *and* handwrite instructions at the same time. Try it. You can't do it.*

This experience led me to believe that I had to get more work off my plate, so I would hire another person. And another. And another. Until I was making decisions for an entire team and trying to do my work at night, on weekends, at the crack o' dawn.

---

* If you want to try to prove me wrong, please send me a video of you typing and writing at the same time. I would love to see it.

As a result, the company became more inefficient because all those people were waiting for me to make decisions. Instead of capturing and utilizing the most powerful resource I had—their brains—we were all dependent on mine. As an added bonus, all those salaries drained my bank accounts.

I decided to get back to what worked—me and me alone. I fired everyone to get back to getting *my* stuff done. I thought that would be easier. I had romanticized notions of being the lone-wolf entrepreneur who "gets shit done." I was delusional; it was as if I forgot what it was like to do every job. The cycle started all over again. Flipping between Doing and Deciding is more common than you think. That's why most businesses don't ever get past a handful of team members.

Answering their questions made my work wait, and doing my work made my employees wait for my answers. According to Daniel S. Vacanti, author of *Actionable Agile Metrics for Predictability: An Introduction*, more than 85 percent of a project's life span is spent in a queue, waiting for something or someone. While waiting time is inefficient, it's also exhausting. If we can reduce waiting time, we can improve growth—and gain sanity.

Many businesses with just a few employees get stuck playing the waiting game and in the back-and-forth between the Doing and Deciding activities. Business owners start with "I need to do it all" and move to "I need to hire people to do it." Then, when they discover that their workload hasn't lightened up and they are more stressed and strapped for cash than ever, they end up thinking, "Everyone is incompetent, and I will fire them all and just do it myself," which eventually leads them back to "Oh God, I can't keep doing this, I need to hire people desperately," and back around to "Is everyone on this planet clueless?"

No, the people around you are not clueless. Far from it. They just need *you* to stop Doing and Deciding and start Delegating not just the deeds, but the decisions. For real. If you are an employee reading this, I suspect you are nodding your head right now in enthusiastic agreement. And if you are a business owner, I suspect you are shaking your head in disbelief. That's the disconnect we need to resolve, and it starts with the shareholder releasing some of the decision-making, permanently.

What could you accomplish if your team was not focused on completing tasks, but on delivering outcomes for your company? That's a game-changer, right? Let's start by getting your buy-in on the delegating concept. Ask yourself: Would my life be easier if my team members were empowered to make decisions, and I felt confident that they would routinely make decisions that would sustain and grow my business? Would my life be easier if my employees acted like owners?

The only answer is, "Damn straight, Mike! My life would be an endless string of awesomeness!"

When *your* desired outcome is also *their* desired outcome, you are better able to let go and let your team *do their jobs*. And it will be okay. It will be more than okay. You're going to be a delegating machine. You'll be the Oprah Winfrey of delegators: "You get a project! And you get a project! And *you* get a project!"

If you're going to save your Saturdays and your soul *and* scale your business, being acutely aware of what phase of the 4Ds you are in is essential. Will you ever stop Doing entirely? Maybe not—but you will do a fraction of the work that you do now, and you will transition to doing only the work you love.

Deciding every little thing—you can kick that phase to the curb. You won't stop Deciding entirely; you will just move from making minor decisions to making only the most critical decisions as the people to whom you delegate become more comfortable making decisions on their own. As for Delegating, because your business will evolve and change, you'll have to dedicate some time to it. You will delegate until you hire a delegator, whose Primary Job is to continually empower the team to make on-the-field decisions and protect you while you do the Design work. Reminder: this is not a switch from one phase to another; it is a throttle. The goal is for you to spend *most* of your work time controlling the flow of work and designing your company's future. If you want to make your business run like clockwork, you must concentrate the majority of your effort on being a designer.

THE 4Ds—TARGET PERCENTAGES

Setting a goal of losing one hundred pounds is not a good idea if you only weigh one fifty. If you want to improve your body or your business, or anything else for that matter, you need to know what you intend to accomplish and where you are today. Clarity comes from knowing your ideal target *and* where you are starting. That is what we are going to do for your business in this step. We will determine how much time you and your team spend in each of the Four Ds (4Ds)—Doing, Deciding, Delegating, and Designing—and then optimize it.

The 4Ds are being executed within your business and every other organization on this planet. This is true if your business is a company of one, one hundred thousand, or any number in between. And this is true for every single person in your company. From an intern to an executive board member, from the nice folks in C-suite to the sweet folks with feet on the street, everyone is working on the 4Ds.

Each person in your organization is doing their own blend of the 4Ds, although you may not (yet) be deliberately directing it. Some people may be Doing work constantly. Another person may be Deciding what other people should be executing while Doing the work of ten people, and with the few seconds left trying to Design a forward-looking strategy. Sound familiar?

Collectively, the 4D work of each person combines to form a 4D Mix for your business. If the business is just you, the solopreneur, your own 4D Mix *is* the company's 4D Mix. If the company has multiple employees and other team members, the aggregation of each contributor's 4Ds is the *company's* 4D Mix.

OPTIMAL 4D MIX

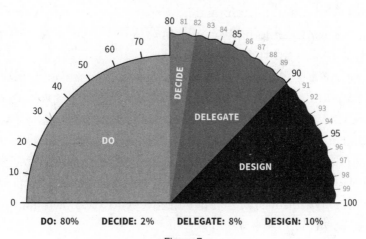

DO: 80%   DECIDE: 2%   DELEGATE: 8%   DESIGN: 10%

Figure 7
Note: To make this chart easier to read,
this graph is not drawn with balanced increments.

The ideal mix for most companies is 80 percent Doing, 2 percent Deciding, 8 percent Delegating, and 10 percent Designing. Why does a business need to dedicate so much time to Doing? Because businesses need to do things that customers want and that create value in the marketplace; that's how businesses make a profit. The other 20 percent of that ideal 4D Mix is spread over managing and guiding the business. For you to design your company to run itself, you need to master the mix. Simply put, you need to know what your company's 4D Mix is as compared to the optimal 4D Mix, and then use the Clockwork system to continuously optimize your business.

Critically Important and Helpful Shortcut: Analyzing for the optimal mix can be arduous and time-consuming. Since business is dynamic, it is very difficult (perhaps impossible) to nail down that mix. So the one thing you should focus on above all else is the big piece, and that is the 80 percent of Doing time. Is your company spending most of its time serving clients (that is, the 80 percent Doing), but not all of it? If you are at 95 percent Doing, you can tell instantly that there is not enough Designing or other work going on because there is only 5 percent of company time left for the other three Ds. If the Doing is at 60 percent, that also tells you that you're in trouble, since your business isn't spending enough time getting things done. So if you simply track the Doing and target 80 percent, the other three Ds will often come into alignment. Focus on spending as much of the remaining 20 percent as possible on Designing, and the Delegating and Deciding will often just fall into place, as long as you commit to empowering your employees to take ownership of their work.

THE TIME ANALYSIS

Hang on—I'm about to throw a whole bunch of numbers at you. Like Dorothy in *The Wizard of Oz*, you may not want to walk through the woods to get to the Emerald City. For her, it was scary. For you, it may seem tedious or overwhelming. Percentages, percentages, percentages, oh my! I realize you might not be a business geek like me, who gets turned on by allocation exercises and analysis. But stick it out for me, would ya? You need this information to get where you're going. (Which, incidentally, I hope is the great land of Oz, not the dust bowl of Depression-era Kansas. Why *did* Dorothy want to go back, anyway?)

You will now track your typical workweek (five days, er, seven days) and use it to see your way forward. If you want to shortcut the number-crunching, go to clockwork.life to get our free Time Analysis system. It does all the math for you.

1. As you go through the day, write down the date and the activity you are working on, along with the time you started it. Then get to work on that activity. The moment you shift to a different activity, any activity—including a distracting question from a colleague, going down a social media rabbit hole, or putting out yet another fire— quickly jot down the finish time for the current task (even if it is not finished; it is just finished for the moment). Then write down the new activity (e.g., answering your colleague's question) and when you start it. Then, once that activity is complete, fill out the time you finish it. Then do the same for the next task. Repeat for the entire day. Include all activities, even "downtime" activities, like the social media rabbit holes.

TIME ANALYSIS WORKSHEET

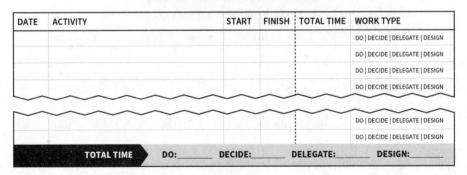

DATE	ACTIVITY	START	FINISH	TOTAL TIME	WORK TYPE
					DO | DECIDE | DELEGATE | DESIGN
					DO | DECIDE | DELEGATE | DESIGN
					DO | DECIDE | DELEGATE | DESIGN
					DO | DECIDE | DELEGATE | DESIGN
					DO | DECIDE | DELEGATE | DESIGN
					DO | DECIDE | DELEGATE | DESIGN
TOTAL TIME	DO:_____	DECIDE:_____	DELEGATE:_____	DESIGN:_____	

Figure 8

2. When the day's work is done, make sure all the date fields are completed. Add up the total time for the day, and then prepare a new sheet for the next day.

3. Repeat this exercise for one week. Do it for two weeks if you want to play at the varsity level. Warning! You don't want to collect data on an atypical week. You'll get far better analytics if you do this exercise during a typical period of time.

4. Now that you know the optimal 4D Mix, let's figure out where you fall within it. Ultimately, you will need to evaluate how your entire team utilizes their time, but since you are the person reading this book and possibly serving the QBR, we will analyze your mix first. And if you are a one-person business, then you are the team.

5. Next to each documented task, review the activity and categorize it as Doing, Deciding, Delegating, or Designing.

6. If you aren't sure how to categorize an activity, pick the lowest level of those in consideration. For example, if an activity could be either Designing or Delegating, choose Delegating.

7. Add up the time devoted to each category and divide it by the time recorded on your sheets to get your 4D Mix percentages. For example, if you worked eighty hours in a week, and the Do total was seventy-three, the Deciding time was five, the Delegating time was zero, and the Designing was two, the percentages would be:

   a. Doing: 91.25 percent (73 hours divided by 80 hours)

   b. Deciding: 6.25 percent (5 hours divided by 80 hours)

    c. Delegating: 0.0 percent (0 hours divided by 80 hours)

    d. Designing: 2.5 percent (2 hours divided by 80 hours)

8. This analysis reveals how much time an individual—you—is putting into each of the 4D categories. Complete this analysis for each team member and you will have a clear picture of how they utilize their time. Add up everyone's analysis numbers to understand how your entire company utilizes its time.

While each work type is necessary, many businesses are unbalanced. We will look at the entire business in a moment, but for now, let's start by just looking at where you stand. What do you notice? What are your realizations?

Many solopreneurs fall into the trap of having upwards of 95 percent of their time allocated to Doing. They are living in a

4D MIX

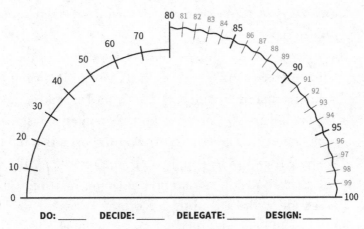

DO: _____ DECIDE: _____ DELEGATE: _____ DESIGN: _____

Figure 9

Note: To make this chart easier to complete,
this graph is not drawn with balanced increments.

time-for-money trap where the only way to grow is by Doing more, but they can't because there is no time.

I've also seen solopreneurs trap themselves in a Design-heavy 4D Mix. Putting 40 percent of your time into Designing (which is way more than the optimal 10 percent) might indicate that you are a dreamer, but it surely means that you aren't spending enough time Doing the work to turn those dreams into reality.

The optimal 4D Mix, of course, works for multi-employee companies, too. For example, if you have two employees (you being one of them), the average of both your individual 4D Mixes constitutes your company mix. So if your 4D Mix is 50 percent Doing, 0 percent Deciding, 0 percent Delegating, and 50 percent Designing, and the other employee's is 80 percent Doing, 20 percent Deciding, 0 percent Delegating, and 0 percent Designing, it is the average of each category that gets you your business mix.

(Note: I realize that you may work seventy hours a week and your employee forty hours a week, and therefore more emphasis should be put on your percentages. But that level of detail does not do much to impact the results, so let's not get that nitty-gritty. Plus, our goal is to reduce your time way down from seventy hours. Remember?)

In this example, the company's mix is 65 percent Doing (the average of 50 percent and 80 percent), 10 percent Deciding (average of 0 percent and 20 percent), 0 percent Delegating (average of 0 percent and 0 percent), and 25 percent Designing (average of 50 percent and 0 percent). So this business is 65/10/0/25. Compare that with the optimal 4D Mix of 80/2/8/10, and we can see that we need to ramp up the Doing (getting things done) and reduce the Deciding for others (perhaps we outsourced to virtual help, and they need way too much direction). There is no Delegation going on, and we want about 8 percent of the time spent on empowering others to drive outcomes. Twenty-five percent of the time between these two people is spent on the Designing (vision and future thinking) of the business, which is too much (it should be around 10 percent).

If you have a large company with dozens, hundreds, or thousands of employees, you can still do this exercise for everyone. But do it in groups, by department and responsibilities. For example, say you have two hundred employees, and your accounting department has ten people. Have each person in the accounting department do a 4D Mix analysis. Then average out across the department. Now you will have the 4D Mix for your accounting department. Do the same for the other departments, then create a chart for each department. Add up the departments' 4D Mixes to see what your company's 4D Mix is.

When I interviewed Amanda Bond over videoconferencing for this book, she was drinking coconut water—out of a coconut in a bar in Playa del Carmen, Mexico. Surrounded by other digital nomad entrepreneurs who were probably also videoconferencing, she looked like she had just stepped off the beach to take my call.

Amanda's company helps its clients create automated cash flow using social media ads. Before implementing Clockwork,* she did most of the work herself. Then she created online courses to teach people how to do the work themselves, and sold those courses using the method she teaches. Super meta! So she clockworked her business model while she clockworked her business.

When Amanda completed the Time Analysis, she discovered she'd been spending *too much* time designing—a whopping 25 percent. Before she started this process, she had been running her business "slapdash," and she eventually burned out. The design time was her "fantasy time," and it was also a much-needed

---

* She also completed the Run Like Clockwork program. Details are available at runlikeclockwork.com.

break. But after nine months of overdesigning, she didn't have one new program to show for it.

"It was as if I was 'playing' business," she told me. "I spent all my time thinking and coming up with ideas, but no one was executing on those ideas."

Amanda had to go back to Doing more so she could produce results, and eventually work her way to the optimal 4D Mix. Sometimes we overcorrect, but this is the beauty of Time Analysis. We can see where we need to make shifts and get back on track.

YES, YOU CAN MAKE ANY BUSINESS RUN JUST LIKE CLOCKWORK

If you're a creative entrepreneur, or an entrepreneur with a special skill set on which your business depends, how do you shift from Doing to Designing? I get this question often, mostly from doctors, lawyers, performers, and other highly skilled folks. It's important to remember that Doing, Deciding, and even Delegating maintain your business. Designing *elevates* your business. And even if you are in an industry as specialized and independent as, say, painting, you can be the designer of the business. Don't believe me? I'll let Peter explain.

Seventeenth-century German artist Sir Peter Lely was certainly not the first artist to systematize his art, but he was arguably the first to make his company run like a well-oiled cuckoo clock. (That's a shoutout to all *one* of my Black Forest woodcarver readers, I mean, reader.) Lely painted in the Baroque style that was popular at the time. After he moved to London, he quickly became the most sought-after portrait artist, and then the "Principal Painter" for the royal family. He was best known for a series of ten portraits of ladies of the court—the "Windsor Beauties"—that hung in Windsor Castle.

His art in high demand, Lely opened a workshop and trained other painters to help him complete his paintings. This fella didn't just have a few assistants; he had a massive operation that allowed him to do what he was known for, what he did best: paint faces, leaving the rest of the portrait to his assistants. When customers wanted some of that "Windsor Beauty" magic, it was all about the face. But if Lely painted every portrait in its entirety, including the subject's attire and surroundings, he would be spending the majority of his time working outside his zone of genius, i.e., capturing faces. If he stayed in the Doing, Designing, and Delegating phases exclusively, the only way he could scale was to work harder and longer.

So jumping right into the Designing phase (while never fully abandoning the other phases), Lely sketched a variety of poses and numbered them. He often used the same dress design and the same props. After he finished a subject's face, his lead artist would assign someone on the team of artists to use a template for the numbered pose required and paint the rest of the painting. Lely was the godfather of paint by numbers.

Business boomed because he delivered on the one thing his clients wanted most: Lely's interpretations of their faces. The rest—the setting, the color of the dress, the props used—didn't matter much. And because he was able to focus his Doing solely on painting faces and Delegate the rest, he was able to turn out thousands of paintings over his lifetime while his contemporaries were lucky to turn out a hundred.

The next time you dare to say, "My business can't be streamlined" or "I need to do all the work," take a pause. You are lying to yourself. Your business can run on its own. If an old-school painter could do it hundreds of years ago, surely you can do it today.

For the longest time, I struggled with the idea that, in my business, others could do the core work or, from my lips to God's ears, *all* the work. My enemy was my ego. I believed I was the smartest person in the room—at least when it came to my business. But it all changed when my friend Mike Agugliaro told me about a simple change that he and his partner made.

Mike and his business partner, Rob Zadotti, grew a plumbing business from the days of the two of them racing around in a beat-up truck to a $30 million home-service business. How did Mike make the shift from Doing to Designing a world-class business (which was acquired in the summer of 2017 for, as Rob put it, "a sick amount of cash on the barrelhead")? They did it by changing the question they asked. They no longer asked, "How do I get the plumbing work done?" Instead, they asked, "*Who* will get the plumbing work done?" That simple change of question started to bring the answers that made them business designers. For you to become your business's designer, you can no longer ask "how" but "who." That one question—"*Who* will get the work done?"—will open your eyes to a business that will cruise right to the Design phase.

I can't tell you how many times entrepreneurs say to me, "My business is too unique. It can't be systematized." Sorry to break it to those people, but they're not that special. Yes, they have a few things that are special to them, but 90 percent of their business is the same as everyone else's. So is mine. So is yours.

Few businesses in the world are that unique. And when they truly are unique (and are successful at it), everyone else copies them. Say goodbye to the uniqueness. Now don't get your undies in a bunch. Your mom was right, you are special and different and all that. I'm just saying the business fundamentals stay constant for all businesses. Since you're reading this book, I'm going to assume that you are at least willing to put your ego aside and attempt to run your business using the Clockwork system.

The best part is, streamlining your business doesn't take a ridiculous amount of work to build a bunch of new systems. In fact, it is ridiculously *easy* when you realize that *you already have all the systems.* The goal is to simply extract them from where they are already documented—in your head. You'll learn how to do that in Chapter Eight. And when you do that, you will be free to do what you do best. Whatever work you do, it can be broken down into steps and delegated to someone else.

And if you don't want to give up too much of the Doing because that's what you love? Then by all means, do what you love. Your business should make you happy. The point is, you *can* delegate more than you realize. Even if your business is a work of art.

PLAN YOUR DOWNTIME (THE FIFTH D)

The team at Run Like Clockwork has been serving business owners in the implementation of Clockwork. The president of our organization, Adrienne Dorison, realized I neglected to include a fifth D in the prior version of this book: Downtime. A study reported in *Scientific American* shows that we are more productive when we have mental breaks.[6] We just can't run at an optimized productivity level for eight straight hours. Or, more likely in your case, an entire *eighteen-hour* workday. Our brains drain. And when our brains are tired, we are easily distracted or we look for distractions. Smoke breaks have been replaced with social media, which is easy to justify because having a presence on these platforms often feels "mandatory." But can you really count the time you spend answering a "What kind of cheese are you?" quiz as productive? When we're really overwhelmed, we end up down internet rabbit holes. Or maybe we blow off steam in other non-productive ways.

By building Downtime into your workday, you can use it intentionally. And when you use that time intentionally, you'll reap the full benefits. Planned breaks from work are proven to be more efficient than time wasted on unplanned distractions. This also removes any guilt you may feel when your social media doom-scrolling reveals that you are simply a Muenster (cheese). That ain't healthy, my friend. Planned Downtime is.

START WITH 1 PERCENT

Making changes in your activity allocation is hard. If you are constantly Doing, making cuts there to increase Designing time may seem impossible, so let's start small. Set aside just 1 percent of your work time for Designing. If you are Doing forty hours a week, that's twenty-four minutes a week, rounded up to a half hour. If you do all the work you need to do in forty hours, surely you could do it in thirty-nine and a half hours. Now you have one half hour for Design time.

If working sixty hours a week is closer to your reality, that can be rounded to just one hour of Design time. You don't even have to block off an entire hour (or whatever your 1 percent equivalent is) for Design work. You can break up the time into what you find more manageable, as long as the manageable blocks are actually productive Design time. Chopping up sixty consecutive minutes of Design time into a few seconds here and a few seconds there is not concentrated work effort and therefore won't be beneficial.

One way to allocate your Design time intentionally is to insert something in your calendar that disrupts your Doing time. For example, I get my lunch from a deli that is a fifteen-minute walk from the office. I call in my peanut butter and jelly sammy order and then head out on foot to pick it up. My phone goes in my back pocket and my Design work goes to the front of my mind. As I walk to and from the deli, I consider a business challenge for which I need to apply strategy. This results in deliberate Design time and some healthy physical activity. Then I top it off by getting some deli jelly in my belly. Noice!

With even 1 percent Design time, you can focus on optimizing your 4D Mix and other strategies to help you streamline your business. You know what else you'll be able to do? You'll finally be able to pick up that folder of "someday" ideas that you keep in the drawer and figure out if you still want to pursue them. The articles about industry trends that you've been meaning to read, the training videos you've paid for but haven't yet watched, the Big Promise you haven't documented yet (yeah, I see you)—you can use your 1 percent time to finally get around to doing that important stuff. Even with just thirty minutes a week, you'll have time to do one of the most important analyses of your business: ask what is working and find ways to do more of it, and ask what is not working and find ways to do less of that.

Once you get in the habit of setting aside the time, you'll become more comfortable taking the time—and making good use of that time. You'll start to see changes in your attitude toward your business, and changes *in* your business, as you begin to implement some of the ideas and strategies you came up with during Design time. And once you get used to taking Design time as a matter of course, you'll want more of it.

Katie Keller Wood is the executive director of CMStep, a training and certification program for teachers who want to be certified in the Montessori method. Developed by Maria Montessori, an Italian physician and educator, the method fosters independent learning and child empowerment. I learned about this approach from Katie when I interviewed her for this book. She and her team were in the early stages of the Run Like Clockwork program, and she wanted to share an observation with me.

"Clockwork is like Montessori for your business," she said. "The Montessori teacher plans and designs the learning environment and tweaks it when it's not working. The goal is student empowerment to unlock their potential. We want them to be free to make choices and we give them appropriate limits so they don't go off the rails."

In working toward the optimal 4D Mix, you create a work environment that fosters independence and empowers your team. Your job is to set the guardrails to keep people on track, but let your team members run their races. Imagine what you could achieve with an independent, empowered staff that gets it done.

Katie told me, "The greatest sign for a teacher is to realize the children are working as if the teacher does not exist." That's the greatest sign for a business owner, too.

FOR EMPLOYEES: CORA'S STORY

At Job Turf, time tracking is used to look for efficiency opportunities. Calvin, the owner, has a saying: "Just because you are doing something doesn't mean it is something you should be doing, dogg."

After six months learning the ins and outs of the job, Cora was asked by her manager, Gordon, to keep track of her time for five days. She received a simple handheld recorder to attach to her belt. She set an alarm for every half hour on her phone. When she heard the beep, she would speak into the recorder, saying the time and what she had been doing for the last half hour. At the end of each day, Gordon and Cora would listen to the recording, make observational notes, and mark each task as a Do, Decide, Delegate, Design, or Downtime activity. During her review, she expected to find that most of her time was spent Doing, but was surprised to see how often she stopped what she was doing to ask Gordon a question. Most times, he simply confirmed that she was on track. Tracking her time helped her realize that she knows the answers to a lot of things, and that she should trust her instincts rather than go to Gordon for confirmation. This frees up some of her time—and Gordon's as well.

How can you help? The time required to finish a task is often much more than we think it will be. The objective of time tracking is to get a true understanding of how much time you need for different parts of your work. The analysis helps you determine your own 4D Mix and adjust accordingly. And in the next chapter, it will help you offload some of the tasks altogether.

Time tracking is *not* about comparison. The goal is not to see if you do things faster or slower than others. This is not a race. All people perform tasks at different speeds. Michael Phelps would kick my ass in the pool. I could be doing the crawl stroke and he could be doggy paddling, and he would still swim circles around me. Writing a business book, on the other hand, might take Phelps a bit longer than it would take me. While Time Analysis is not for seeing who is faster or slower, it does identify where your natural talents lie. For me? It's probably better to put me behind a keyboard than in the pool.

Track your use of time at work over the next week. If you want to get a more accurate picture, track a longer period. Do everything you can to track a "typical" week. You can record your time on a piece of paper or download a worksheet from clock-work.life.

The goal is for you to track time, not for you to feel as though you are being tracked. You don't need to fill in idle time or break time, unless you are intentionally tracking the Fifth D (Down-time). Our goal here is to simply see how long it takes you to do specific tasks. Then, review your Time Analysis with your manager and discuss how you can optimize your work.

Please remember this: time tracking is challenging. Not so much in the effort required to do it, but in the level of transparency it will give you. It can be scary and force you to come to terms with how effective (or not) you are. But with knowledge comes power. Don't deny yourself this power. On the other side is a better company and a better you.

 ## CLOCKWORK IN ACTION

1. It's time for you to get some Design time. In *Profit First*, I implored readers to commit to setting aside a minimum of 1 percent of their revenue for profit. Even if they didn't follow any of the other steps in the book, I knew that the action of taking 1 percent profit would accomplish two things: they would discover how easy it was to set aside that money, and they would learn to live without it. For this action step, I'd like you to set aside 1 percent of your work time to focus on Designing your business. Just 1 percent. No matter how big your to-do list or how demanding your customers and team, your business can survive you taking a tiny amount of time each week to do the work that will help your business move forward.

If you are an overdesigner (someone who relentlessly plans and learns at the expense of doing work) and are not so much an overachiever, we need to enforce a faster shift. In this case, cut your Design time in half and allocate it to Doing time.

2. Block out this new allocation of Design time every week for the next eighteen months on your calendar. As you move along, you will be throttling up (or, in rare cases, down) the amount of Design time, but for now, you and I just need to ensure that 1 percent is protected for a long time.

3. Just as you need to take your profit first in your business, you need to allocate this 1 percent of time *first* in your week. Don't wait for the end of the week to do the Design work. Instead, allocate the time right at the beginning. If you work on the vision at the start of the week, the rest of the week will naturally support that vision, therefore getting you to it faster. Run the Time Analysis on yourself for the next five business days, then determine your 4D Mix.

CHAPTER SEVEN

TRASH, TRANSFER, TRIM, OR TREASURE

ELEVATE YOUR ENTIRE TEAM TO BRING MORE RESULTS—AND FALL IN LOVE WITH THEIR WORK IN THE PROCESS

The longer we do something, the longer we will continue to do it, even if it doesn't serve us. Welcome to the sunk cost effect. An investor buys stock that they expect to go up in value. When instead that stock goes down, rather than sell it, they invest *more* into it, expecting it to go up higher. When it fails again, they double down.

When you've spent years creating a process, you are more likely to stick with it than to abandon it, simply because of the sunk costs. Even if that process hurts your business, you'll probably keep doing it. That stops today.

Now that you've completed the Time Analysis, you can both work toward a more optimal 4D Mix and Integrate delivery on the Big Promise and service to the QBR through the Trash, Transfer, Trim, Treasure process. It's as simple as looking at the list of everything you do and, if it's not in service to the QBR or your Primary Job, Trash, Transfer, Trim, or Treasure it. The goal isn't to make your job easier at the expense of someone else on the team. The goal is to reduce the cost in time and money and to improve results.

WHAT DO I TRASH, TRANSFER, TRIM, OR TREASURE?

If you haven't figured this out by now, the person or people serving your QBR are probably spending too much time doing everything *but* serving the QBR. Likewise, your team is also spending too much time doing other things when they could be protecting the QBR and serving their own Primary Jobs. And they are possibly, despite good intentions, detracting from the QBR and their Primary Jobs.

With this simple exercise, you and your team will be able to clearly see how focused you are on serving or protecting the QBR and doing your Primary Job, and how distracted you are by other tasks. Then you will know which tasks the person(s) serving the QBR needs to offload to someone else, which tasks need to be automated, and which tasks need to be dumped.

To begin, go back to the Time Analysis sheet you created for everyone on your team. Then highlight the work done during that period that was directly serving the QBR. Next, highlight the work done on the Primary Job, if that person's role is not in service of the QBR. Tally up the highlighted time and compare it to the total work time. You can get the percentage by dividing the highlighted time by the total work time.

To get the hang of it, do this analysis on yourself first. Then do it for each person who is or should be serving the QBR (you may likely be one of them). Then do it for the rest of your team, where the highlighted work is their Primary Job. This is not only easy, it's eye-opening.

When we completed this step in my company, we noticed two big opportunities to improve organizational efficiency—one to Transfer and one to Trash. The Transfer insight had to do with handling my schedule. My assistant, Erin Chazotte, gets a ton done. She's a *producer.* Sometimes when a person is highly productive, you don't notice that part of their job could be improved. After doing the Time Analysis I explained in the previous chapter, Erin and I noticed that more than 68 percent of her workday went to handling my packed schedule of appearances, podcasts, presentations, and travel. A lot of these hours were spent going back and forth with people to find times that would work for both parties. We realized she could transfer some of that work—not to a person, but to scheduling software. The Time Analysis revealed my blindness to the issue. Because Erin is such a powerhouse employee, I would have never known there were inefficiencies in her day-to-day work. Using the Trash, Transfer, Trim method, we freed up her time so she could focus on bigger things and provide more value to the company.

The Trash insight hurt, let me tell you. Looking at my own Time Analysis, I realized that I spent a lot of time recording my own podcast. Interviews and summaries took a big chunk of time. Even more time-intensive were the editing and promotional work my team did to support the podcast. Because it technically helped me simplify entrepreneurship, my Big Promise, it was of service. But it was in a secondary role to and taking time away from my QBR of writing books. To add insult to injury, the show didn't have many listeners. I bet you didn't even know I had a podcast. So even though it hurt my ego, I had to let the show go.

As you utilize this approach, what do you do if you encounter tasks that are transferable, but there isn't anyone to transfer them *to?* That is often a signal to make a hire.

As you transfer work away from the QBR and away from the Primary Job, you will see that less-skilled tasks are the first ones to be transferred. This typically means you can employ less expensive people, part-timers, freelancers, vendors, or contractors for that work. The goal is to have a few expensive, skilled team members at your business, focused almost exclusively on doing the most skilled work, and transferring all the other necessary, but easy, repeating tasks down the skill chain. That's a streamlined business. And that is exactly what the Trash, Transfer, or Trim method supports. Now, let's get busy doing it in your business.

1. Trash. Evaluate a task and determine whether you can Trash it. Does it support a necessary objective of the business? Does it add measurable value to your clients or to your team? You see, not everything is necessary in a business. In fact, many tasks that may have been necessary at one time are no longer needed, but they hang around because "that is what we've always done." Trash the things that are not necessary. And if you are unsure, just stop it for a period of time to see if there are consequences. No consequence = not needed. Trash it.

2. Transfer. Next, seek to transfer work to other people or systems that will free you and your expert people to take on bigger, more challenging tasks. Transfer work down to the most inexpensive resources and empower the new owner(s) of the task to achieve the intended outcome more efficiently.

3. Trim. For the stuff you must keep, evaluate how it can be trimmed. Can an existing task be done faster or more easily? Can the cost of materials and time associated with this task be reduced? If a task can't be Trashed or Transferred, it can still often be trimmed. Seek ways to reduce the time and cost of completing a task while achieving the necessary results.

4. Treasure. I've added a fourth T in this edition of *Clock-work:* treasure. These are the few select tasks or responsibilities you *should* keep on your plate because they are important to you, because you love them. This is the work that fuels you, that makes you excited to go into the office. We don't want to trade joy for organizational efficiency.

DON'T CLONE YOURSELF

The refrain of the small-business owner is, "I need to find someone like me." Alas, you won't. You are irreplaceable. So is everyone else, for that matter. Each of us is a unique makeup of many parts: experiences, genetics, our education, what we do every day. All those things make up the human experience and our individuality. You can't find someone else like you. At least not just like you. Plus, if you did, wouldn't they be running their own company? You are, after all.

So the objective is not to find another you. It is to find little bits and parts of you. I call it fractionalizing.

Let's say you are really good at sales and pretty darn good at doing the work, too. Let's also assume you can do the accounting, the billing, and the collections. Let's say you suck at the ongoing communication with clients and prospects. Not because you don't have the talent, but because you struggle to find the time. Sound about right?

All those elements of work make up your capacity. When you operate a small business, or the smallest of small businesses (where it's just you), you don't try to (and can't) find your clone. You try to find your pieces. And then put them together.

Stop looking at your work as the entirety of the tasks that you do. Instead, look at your work as a stack of individual tasks that you happen to choose to do. With that understanding, you can selectively Trash, Transfer, and Trim the tasks. You can find individuals to do one task, or another, or a few. But they don't have to do it all.

You also need to get away from the all-too-common belief that you need a full-time person, or a worker who is fully dedicated to your company. A task can be given to an existing employee or a new one. It can be for someone who works part time or full time. It can be given to a contractor or a vendor. It can be virtual help or offshore help. It could be your mom. It could be my mom. (At age eighty-seven, she "kiddingly" offered to help Ernie, my landscaper, with his customer calls and scheduling. He was too busy to interview her.)

The point is this: You don't need (or even want) to immediately take everything off of your plate. But you sure as shit need to take one thing off your plate. Start with the small stuff that you don't like. Get one thing moved over and out. You will build confidence in your ability to stop doing. Then transfer another thing, and then the next. Trash the things that no one needs to do. Do it in parts. Fractionalize yourself, then Trash, Transfer, and Trim accordingly.

WHEN YOU'RE THE ONE WHO SERVES THE QBR

What if it really seems as though you're the only one who serves the QBR? How can you pull back from the business? How can you Trash, Transfer, or Trim? The objective is simple—get others serving the QBR.

Sometimes you'll have to let go of your role serving the QBR. At Vitality Med Spa and Plastic Surgery Center, the integration of the most cutting-edge procedures (their QBR) to keep patients looking and feeling young, fit, and healthy (their Big Promise) was handled by the boss. Maybe it's obvious; maybe it's not. The clientele commit to major procedures such as weight-loss therapy, plastic surgery, Botox applications, and discreet matters such as, you know, discreet matters. There is a lot of complexity to some of these, so the perfection of the operations is a necessity. The founder of Vitality Med Spa, Monique Hicks, did all the work to develop new cutting-edge processes herself. She could no longer scale the business this way, and she was exhausted. So she empowered her team to protect and serve the QBR in many ways, including one unique "trick." More on that in a minute.

I first met Monique in the fall of 2017 and was blown away by what she had accomplished. She had grown Vitality Med Spa to a $3-million-plus operation while raising a daughter as a single parent. She recounted how for the first three years of business, she exclusively served the role of the QBR. She was researching procedures and working hand in hand with clients to make everything perfect for them. She swooped in like a superhero when problems arose. She did everything to protect and serve the QBR, by herself.

Monique explained, "Then one day, it became very clear the business was dependent exclusively on me. The energy and effort I brought to the business was what customers were getting out of it. I realized the business was only as strong as I was on any particular day. It was exhausting and not scalable. That's when I taught my team about how I was serving our QBR, which I had been calling my 'zone of genius,' and how I needed them to protect and serve me in that role."

The teaching part was easy. Monique had one-on-one meetings with each employee, explaining how to customize experiences for customers, learn about their individual needs, and specify the optimal procedures. She used a daily huddle to highlight how people were making both big and small improvements, and empowered employees to learn from one another. She had employees share best practices.

Monique also showed respect for the employees' domains. In the past, when she had swooped in to fix things, employees had sometimes interpreted it as interference. With clarity on how to protect and serve the QBR, Monique stopped swooping in and employees felt more confident in the service they were providing. Morale increased. Things got better—for the most part.

There was just one problem: Monique was still the only one doing the QBR work. Her employees weren't coming to her with ways to further improve the company and their services, even though they were the ones doing the work.

Remember that unique trick I alluded to earlier? It was a special hire Monique made. The QBR is the essence of the business, and it is the responsibility of all the employees to protect and serve it in some capacity. Even when—especially when—the boss is failing to protect and serve the QBR.

Monique is human, like all of us, and is prone to mistakes. And she is the first to admit that she isn't always sure about how to improve or change the company's services. She realized that, even at times when she wasn't identifying the newest procedures to implement, employees noticed that clients said things like, "I'm surprised you don't do the new fat freezing method," but they did not mention it to Monique. The employees had a hard time speaking up to her because they were too timid or couldn't believe a company existed where the QBR was more important than even the boss's opinion.

Monique saw the blockage in the communication lines and took a unique measure. She hired a "strong-voiced" individual who wasn't intimidated by Monique in any way. The new hire was put in charge of day-to-day operations, including collecting "frontline feedback" from the team and sitting with Monique to discuss it, uncomfortable as some of it was. The company leaped forward in the rollout of cutting-edge service and continues to grow accordingly.

"The QBR is an all-in commitment, Mike," Monique shared with me. "The team needs to know it and act upon it. And if either is not happening, it is the owner's fault. Their inability or fear of being honest with me about our lack of application of research was not their problem, it was mine. So I set out to fix it immediately."

You have the right to do what you want in your company. That is a dangerous truth, but it is still the truth. It is dangerous because, as we've discussed, most entrepreneurs continue to do everything in the business, believing that their freedom to do anything they want is a mandate to do everything that is needed. Refrains like "the buck stops with me" or "if you want it done right, you need to do it yourself" are tired and not applicable. The "buck," also known as a problem, needs to be solved by the system. Doing it right must be built into the system.

If you go to a McDonald's and your burger comes out undercooked, the owner is not the person listening to your complaint and giving you a free Happy Meal to make you, well, happy. The owner isn't even there. The buck stops with the store manager. And that undercooked hamburger? How many of those have you ever had? None, because the system ensures that it doesn't happen. An undercooked burger happens so infrequently that when a raw burger comes off the line, it makes headline news.

Back in 2021, the *Daily Mail* reported that a customer in Brisbane, Australia, was "horrified" by his "completely raw" Quarter Pounder. The customer's burger was replaced, and he also got a free apple pie. The owner did not have to swoop in. The team and a gooey slice of pie handled it.

You may want to work in your business. You may want to do the stuff you love. Me? I love writing and speaking. So I do. My business does not need me to speak since we have created systems for speaking. For example, there are hundreds of people who are trained and authorized to speak on Profit First. I am blessed to be invited for big main-stage events, which are my favorite to do, and there are countless other events that our certified Profit First Professionals present at, even (often) at the same time that I am doing a main event. You can have a business running itself and still choose to work in the business. You can do what brings you joy.

Writing makes me happy, so I will continue to write my own books. I also have other authors furthering my ideas by writing industry-specific derivatives of my books. I am on a mission to eradicate entrepreneurial poverty, and I need all the help I can get. For example, you can read *Profit First for Minority Business Enterprises* by Susanne Mariga, *Profit First for Contractors* by Shawn Van Dyke, *Profit First for Lawn Care and Landscape Businesses* by Christeen Era, and more. There are Profit First books for dentists, microgyms, real estate investors, real estate agents, therapists, ecommerce businesses, salon owners, restaurants, and more.

You are welcome to work in your business. But only when you are not needed. That is the catch. We need to free the business from dependency on the owner, or any individual, for that matter. As a business owner (shareholder), you may vote for yourself to still do the work that gives you joy, as long as you are not necessary for the company's health and efficiency.

FOR EMPLOYEES: CORA'S STORY

Cora appreciates that everyone at Job Turf cares about her work enjoyment, not just her outcomes. During her weekly one-on-ones with her manager, Gordon, he always asks her, "Is there anything we need to change to make the job better for you?" Part of that discussion includes identifying any tasks or responsibilities that could be Trashed, Trimmed, or Transferred to help the company deliver on the Big Promise.

A few months into her job, Cora noticed a transfer opportunity—not to pass on, but to take on. Gordon was the only certified crane operator in the business. It is a job that requires excellent manual dexterity, exacting depth perception, and masterful hand-eye coordination. Even though crane work was rarely needed, when it was, everyone had to wait until Gordon arrived.

Cora really enjoys the skid steer work she does, but now that she has mastered it, the work has become monotonous. Opportunity, please meet preparation. In Cora's former life, she was a highly skilled tank operator. Like a crane, a tank has a big spinning turret and requires excellent manual dexterity, exacting depth perception, and masterful hand-eye coordination. The only difference is, with a tank you blow things up, and with a crane you build things up.

A quick meeting with Gordon and the deed was done: he assigned Cora to be the company's second crane operator. After completing the necessary training and certifications, she too is now building things up with that massive twisting and turning machine. And Gordon has transferred a big portion of his work, which enables him to manage sites without disruption. All done by a great employee who saw a great opportunity to transfer work to herself.

How can you help? Doing more stuff does not mean you are doing more. The goal is not to be busy for busy's sake. The goal is to maximize your work on the things that really matter. Be vigilant in protecting your time. If you get pulled in multiple directions, say something. Ask for help.

Looking at your Time Analysis, note which tasks do not

benefit the company and which tasks may distract you from doing work that matters. Determine if you need to Trash, Transfer, or Trim some of your responsibilities. And make note of the work you treasure as well. If you could bring more efficiency to the business by taking a job that one of your colleagues does, propose the transfer. Your boss wants you to love your job, so seek ways to better serve the company as you better serve your Primary Job.

 # CLOCKWORK IN ACTION

1. Now it is time to clear the plates for the people serving the QBR. Take the easiest and most distracting thing off their plates. Even if it's just one thing, the impact can be huge.

2. Consider how your team is working currently. Do you have your most skilled people doing unskilled work? If so, that approach is costing you. Use the Trash, Transfer, and Trim method to move work to the appropriate people. Usually, you will find that most of a company's work is highly repeatable and requires little skill. An army of interns or part-timers, and subsequently fewer highly skilled (usually expensive) people may get more work done faster, better, and cheaper.

3. Once you've taken steps to ensure that the QBR is being protected and served, it's time to make a choice. Do you want to be the heart of the business and do the QBR work yourself, or do you want to be the soul of the organization and have others serve the QBR? If you choose the latter, you need to take another simple step. How? We'll get into that in the next chapter.

CHAPTER EIGHT

CAPTURE SYSTEMS

CREATE PROCESSES FOR ANY PART OF YOUR BUSINESS AND ARCHIVE YOUR COMPANY'S KNOWLEDGE FOREVER

The loud, squealy voice echoed though the office. "Create systems? I don't even have time to get the work done, and now I have to create this detailed step-by-step document? We don't need no stinking systems! I just do the stuff. My people just do the stuff. We are the system. Jeeeez." That outburst was mine. Just a moment of weakness as I struggled to transfer some recurring tasks to my intern. Admittedly, my voice gets a little Peter Brady pitchy when I am frustrated. If you don't get the reference, Michael, Carol, and Alice the housekeeper will all be disappointed.*

Creating systems takes a lot of time! Doesn't it? At least I thought it did, and you may feel the same way, too. The idea of creating systems so that whoever is serving the QBR (or doing a Primary Job) can offload other tasks is overwhelming. It is extraordinarily time-consuming. And it is often a waste of time

---

* Google *The Brady Bunch*. And make sure you watch their "Time to Change" music video, where Peter Brady demonstrates his pitchy voice.

because by the time the system is fully documented, it is no longer relevant. First, we must think about the outcome we need to achieve, then figure out a step-by-step sequence to get there, and then document it. Soon—no, strike that—much, much later, as in many moons later, we have a shelf full of three-ring binders representing our systems: best practices, workflow guidelines, chains of command, and more. Blood, sweat, tears, late nights with coffee, and early mornings with tequila went into those binders, and does anyone ever really use them? I mean, does anyone ever really use them for something other than kindling? I think not.

I used to believe this laborious process, as painful as it is, was necessary. I had done it dozens of times in the past, never with any success, mind you. But nothing else worked, either, so after I tried and failed to roll out yet another system, I would attempt to eradicate my frustration by doing the process "just one more time." And my frustration grew. Like a boil. A gross, monster-sized boil only seen in sci-fi movies (or on an especially unfortunate teenager).

I remember doing this for used-book shipments. I had discovered a great marketing and money-making opportunity in used books. To get closer to my optimal 4D Mix, I decided to streamline the entire process so I could get if off my Doing list. I easily spent four hours creating a step-by-step standard operating procedure (SOP). The final document was a fifteen-step recipe with each step written simply and clearly, complemented by pictures and diagrams. When the masterpiece was done, I gave it to my intern and she got to work. Problems ensued.

First, the document was not perfect. As she went step by step, there were variables I had forgotten and steps I had inadvertently skipped, which threw her off. Within minutes, she was back in my office with questions, which put me right back in the Deciding phase. She had the hands to do stuff, but I was the sole decision-maker for all the arms. You know the Indian goddess Kali? She has many arms but only one head to control them all.

I updated the SOP to fix what I had missed, and soon found that I had missed more. Then there were anomalies. What if the order was expedited shipping? What if the order came in on a weekend? What if, God forbid, the customer ordered two books? Do we ship them separately or together?

Before, I just used my judgment to do whatever made sense in the moment, but now I was committed to turning this into a document that could handle anything. The SOP expanded to address anomalies. I spent more time developing it. More going back and forth. And then all hell broke loose: the US Postal Service updated its website. Every picture and step that was documented in the SOP about the shipping process needed to be redone. And in the midst of all that, Amazon changed *its* back-end system, too. *Ugh.* The hours and hours, and days and days it took to document one simple procedure was all out the window. I couldn't even make one SOP foolproof, let alone the hundreds that I would need to create for my business. It just wasn't worth it. The thought of doing this for my entire company had me thinking that renewing my driver's license at the DMV—just for the hell of it—would be a more appealing option.

I remember a meeting with Kaushik, the editor for the first edition of this book, at the old Penguin offices. We were meeting in his office when my eyes wandered and landed on a very large book on a shelf behind him. It must have had more than 1,000 yellowed pages and it was covered in thick dust. It looked like something from an Indiana Jones movie. Or maybe it was the Bible—like, the first one Gutenberg printed.

"What's that?" I asked, gesturing toward the book.

Kaushik glanced over his shoulder. "Oh, that's our standard operating procedures manual."

"Do you use it?"

"I've never looked at it. It was left there by the last person who used this office. I don't think they ever opened it, either," he replied. "Anyway, you learn on the job, here."

That's what happens at a lot of companies. You spend all this time creating SOPs, but no one refers to them. It becomes an artifact, like Penguin's dusty manual—which, ironically, the team refers to as "the Bible."

We humans are like rivers. We will seek the path of least resistance to get where we are going. And when you see your employees ignoring your SOPs, that is a sure sign that the SOPs aren't working. The goal of every organization should be to seek constant efficiency and improvement. Waste of materials, waste of money, and waste of time are the bane of every business and must be addressed constantly. Traditional SOPs don't serve that goal anymore.

Of the thousands of entrepreneurial companies I have communicated with, a minuscule few have active documented systems. They also don't have SOPs, at least not in the traditional sense. And when I visit an entrepreneur's office and ask to see their operating manual, there is usually nothing but a mix of documents and emails that are buried away on some virtual cloud drive that no one can find.

What most companies do is on-the-job training. In technical terms: "We are just going to wing this puppy." Whatever they tell you to do, do. And when someone else tells you to do something else, do that. And if those directions conflict with each other, just do the best you can to serve both, and make sure you teach the next person that.

This process may sound familiar. After all, it is woven into the fabric of humanity all the way back to prehistoric communications. Since they didn't have much of a written language, people drew pictures on cave walls and told stories to one another around the campfire about things like how to make a campfire.

One person would tell the clan, "Ugh. Strike rocks. Big rocks make big spark. Me got biggest rocks, if you know what I mean. Ha. Ugh. Ha. Ha. Ugh." Stories would go from one person to another, and like the telephone game you played as a child, the original message would turn into something else. "Strike rocks" would morph into "spike fox," and those goons would go off to poke animals with sticks, and when they got back, no one would know how to start a damn fire.

To make sure the QBR is humming along, and that your company is operating with the optimal 4D Mix, you'll need to systematize both the QBR and everything around it. The whole goal of an SOP is to have a consistent process to produce a consistent outcome. But SOPs are really hard to make, since you don't have the systems yet. And they are super hard to maintain, since things change constantly. There has to be a better way—and there is.

YOU ALREADY HAVE SYSTEMS

First, let me clear up the most common misconception about systems right off the bat. You may be thinking, "I don't have any systems," or something like, "I need to create systems from scratch." Wrong. So wrong! In fact, you have every single system for your business already. Every single stinking thing. All your systems are in your head and/or the heads of your employees. All those tasks that you need to delegate are already being done by you. You already follow a process in your head. You don't need to create anything new. Nor do you need to painstakingly extract them from your head onto paper. The goal is not to create systems. The goal is to *capture* systems—and do it easily. This is how you transfer the knowledge of tasks and get your business to run like clockwork. The best part is that anyone can do captures, and it is ridiculously easy. First, let's get the method that *doesn't* work out of the way, shall we?

Perhaps the most inefficient way of extracting stuff from your mind is to write it down sequentially so that someone else can understand it. You force yourself to slow down and overthink things. Going step by step from what you currently do to paper (or word processor or a flow chart or anything written out) is painstakingly slow and fraught with missed steps. In short, don't do this. It doesn't work.

Now let's talk about the simple method that does work.

The far better way to create a system for a process is to capture the process as you do it. The magic here is that you actually get the work done while creating the system for others to follow.

The idea of capturing systems is that you take your best-established processes and transfer them in the simplest and easiest possible way to your team so that they can do it properly going forward. Simply put, do whatever you currently do that works best, and record it as you do it.

Captures are not just about freeing up your time; they ensure that anyone at your company can handle the job if needed. The key is to have each person capture their own system, thereby teaching it to someone else. The last thing you want is for one of your employees to leave without passing on their knowledge—the little tweaks and shortcuts they used to get their job done efficiently that no one else knows about, and the pitfalls and variables that have to be addressed. All that should be passed on through Captures.

When a process is captured by an employee and another employee is given the work, or at least trained on it so they can back up the role, the person who learned the process must also teach the system via a recording. You read that right: the person who is now responsible for the process does a Capture. This is a way to both retain their knowledge and reinforce the best practice they were just taught. If you can teach it, you must know how to do it. Teaching is the ultimate form of learning. And when they capture the process properly, they retain knowledge and prove their ability to do the task.

SYSTEMS FOR STARTUPS

If your business is brand-spanking new, you can easily argue that you have no systems. I mean, you don't have anything, even in your head, to tell others to follow. What do you do then? Two things.

Remember that the transition from Doing to Designing is like a throttle, not a switch. You want to do the work for a period of time so you can learn and relate. Then you can capture what you learn to Transfer it. Or you could take a shortcut and become a curator of other people's systems.

One search on YouTube will deliver dozens, if not hundreds, of systems for almost anything you need. Most of the work has been done for you. It may not be how you want it or the way you would do it, but the systems are there, rated and reviewed by others. Want to have an invoicing process your team can follow? Search for "how to invoice customers." In the deck-building business? Search for "how to build a deck." Need your team to dig holes, pour concrete, and hammer in joists? Search for "how to dig a hole for a deck post," "how to pour concrete for deck footings," and "how to install deck joists."

The systems have already been created. Your job is to capture what is in your head, or to use what other people have already captured from their heads. Then you go about designing the process for your team to use the knowledge that is all captured, recorded, and ready to be rolled out.

When it comes to picking what to systematize first, the priority is to always protect and serve the QBR. Capture it if you can, even if you can't transfer it (yet). But, and this is a big, important but, you need to build your systems-capturing muscle first. The first thing to do is to get used to capturing systems with something easy.

For example, do you notice that you respond to the same questions over and over? Create a system for it. Capture the process of how you respond and make an easy-to-use, copy-and-paste template for the response, then assign that task to an assistant or other colleague. I realize there is sophisticated software that can do this, and perhaps better approaches. The goal is simply to learn how to get stuff off your plate fast and assign it to someone else to further develop and improve it. Capture, assign (Transfer), then have them do another Capture of how they are doing the work, and have them find ways to do it more efficiently (Trim).

Pick things that are "easy" but that you shouldn't do and/or don't like to do. Capture and Transfer. Then start capturing things that are taking away from your focus on the QBR.

HOW TO CAPTURE SYSTEMS

Once you have identified what you need to systematize first, you determine which primary process you are following. Are you 1) doing something physical (moving something, talking with someone), or 2) interacting with something (working on the PC, pushing keys on the cash register)? Of course, it can be a combo of both.

Let's start with work done on a computer, since that is so common. Let's say I invoice clients (which I have done), and my QBR is writing books (which it is). I use computer-screen-recording software to record my process. (I don't want to make a software recommendation here, as it is constantly changing, but I do have a list at clockwork.life.)

As I perform the task, I just record the screen and narrate what I am doing. I then store the video in a directory labeled for that task. Sometimes, I also have the video transcribed, which is easy to do. Now the person who is doing it has a training video *and* accompanying written instructions, which they can use to replicate the process over and over again. Easy to find in the directory and easy to do since it is recorded, step by step. Plus, the video and written instructions work for different learning styles.

Will the video capture address every anomaly? Not likely. But because it is much more of a show-and-tell, it conveys a lot more than you can with a written script. I know of a gymnastics studio owner who films students doing backflips so she can record how she coaches and teach her method to others. And I know a CNC machinery guy who records how he troubleshoots machinery so others can do the same. Record what you do as you do it and give a running play-by-play voice-over of the steps you're taking.

This is more than just a captured process. You also did the work while creating the training material. So there is no time lost in building the system. Boom. Bam. Slam.

For other activities where you are only talking (a type of physical action), all you need is a voice recorder. You probably already have one in your pocket: your smartphone. And for the moving stuff, you just need a video recorder, which you already likely have, too. That same smartphone.

Capture the activity, store the recording in a system that is accessible to your team, and then delegate it to another team member. Just get it off your plate. Protect the QBR at all costs!

> A note about storing Captures: Use an index system, such as a spreadsheet, to make your videos easy to find. Standardize naming conventions so any newbie can locate the video they need. If it takes someone more than sixty seconds to find it, something is wrong with your storage system, and now it's a distraction. So get the help of your team. If something is hard to find, task them with creating ideas to make it easier.

In the beginning, employees may come back with basic questions that you forgot to include in the captured content you made. Maybe you made a video on how to ship stuff using the computer but didn't include the log-in. This is where you give them the answer, and then request that *they* make the next, new and improved, video. That is right. They start working on improving the system right away, and by recording, they become the teacher. And we all know the best student is always the teacher.

Doing this has had a massive impact on my business. I noticed that administrative tasks were clearly time-consuming and doing things like shipping books (which I did myself for years) and invoicing took me far from my QBR. I wrote the original SOP for shipping books, which quickly became irrelevant and was ignored. I would then have to teach the person myself, which was time-consuming and never retained. So I would teach it again. Then when a new intern replaced the old one, all the knowledge went out the door and I had to do it all over again.

I then went to the Capture process I outlined above, and it was like magic. I just used a screen- and video-recording software package to capture the process of taking an order and getting it ready to ship. I took out my handy-dandy iPhone and filmed myself packing an order and explaining details on how to pack. Those recordings were all it took. I haven't shipped a book since. The team does it.

When the next person starts the process, they review the video. Amazon changes its shipping process pretty regularly, so when the process needs to be updated, whoever is currently doing the process records a new video. They are the responsible party for this task, so they are also invited to make improvements to the system. And since the person making the new video (teaching) is the best student, they both reinforce the process in their own mind and have a training video ready for the next person.

We did the same for invoicing and paying bills. Video done. Recording done. The work gets done to the standard. And invoices go out.

Once the systems are Delegated, determine how the output will be measured and monitored. For example, I want to know that invoices are going out and money is coming in. The metric is simple: What new projects have come in, and what do the accounts receivable look like? After a five-minute review, I know whether the system is humming along or if there is an issue that needs to be resolved. I'm not trying to seem too manic about efficiency, but I do want to drive the point home: I have the report taped to the left side of my computer monitor once a week. When I come back to the office from a speaking tour, I see the report instantly (without even needing to turn my computer on). If I have been away for three weeks, then there are three new reports. Simple. Fast.

The key is to always have one person responsible for the outcome. Make that point abundantly clear. That way, you know who to talk to when there are problems in need of solutions. On the wall in my home office, I have a quote from George Washington in which he addresses the importance of singular accountability: "My observation is that whenever one person is found adequate to the discharge of a duty, it is worse executed by two persons, and scarcely done at all if three or more are employed therein." If a founding father of the free world felt this was of critical importance, you and I should feel the same.

As you move into the Designing phase, always look to simplify processes to get the same (or better) results than in the past, with less effort.

While on a speaking tour in Australia, I had dinner with Craig Minter at the Potting Shed in Sydney. Craig is an efficiency consultant who goes into businesses and looks for obvious opportunities for the business owner to create organizational efficiency. After chatting over a beer about everything from tinnitus to long-distance running to optimal footwear, Craig explained how he works.

"You often can make the biggest strides in streamlining a business through effective delegation. That's why the first thing I look for is where the owner may not be delegating decisions. Then, I determine the decisions they must make for their business to run like clockwork, and where those decisions are distractions," Craig explained.

According to Craig, the owner is usually doing something with the QBR (though he doesn't use this term) or other important tasks, and then they get distracted with decisions that take them off their game. If decisions are being pushed up the organization, distractions are happening and time piles (idle or waiting time) appear. And if time piles appear, some significantly long, Craig looks to change the process so that decisions happen faster and with less distraction. He usually can.

Craig went on to tell me what he calls his "traffic light" story, about Debbie Stokes and her curtain manufacturing company R&D Curtains. "Debbie was spending two hours a day making decisions. Every time a job was done, the leader of the work crew would come knock on Debbie's door and ask what they should do next. She would stop what she was doing, go to the floor, and evaluate the work. It only took her a few minutes to figure out what the next job was, but then another fifteen minutes or so to get back to the project she had been working on before the interruption. Then the next knock would come."

Debbie hired Craig, who implemented a system where they put a red, yellow, or green tag on each job order. Now, with this traffic light system, Debbie's crew knows which job to work on next and they don't knock on her door to ask her for guidance. She spends about ten minutes a day sorting all the jobs for the next day, adding red, yellow, or green tags. Red signifies something that is urgent and needs to be done next, green is a project that still has adequate time before it is due, and yellow is in between. The team knows the simple rule: make decisions throughout the production day that keep projects in the green. Debbie can now spend more time making big-picture decisions and strategizing the next steps for her company.

While you may not be able to reasonably capture every task and delegate it, with a simple solution like Craig's traffic light system, you can find ways to Trim down the work for the individual serving the QBR and Transfer the rest out to the team.

YES, YOU CAN CAPTURE THAT THING YOU DO

I've got news for you. That thing you do, that thing you think no one else can do, or do as well as you, it can be captured. I know you want to think you have a special magic touch that can't be replicated, but it probably can. Even tasks that seem to be about raw artistry can be captured. It was true for Peter Lely's painting and it's true for modern artists, too.

Remember the copywriters Jessi Honard and Marie Parks of North Star? I shared their story in Chapter Four. They determined that they are known for capturing their clients' voices, their QBR. But when they ran into a capacity issue and couldn't handle all the work, how could they be sure that other writers would be able to do that voodoo that they do so well? Wasn't it just their "thing," something they intuitively knew how to do? What if other writers didn't have the same ability? How could they teach something like that?

Marie told me, "The Clockwork framework you created for us helped us make the mindset shift and realize, 'Hey, we're not that special.' It's not just intuition. There is a process happening here. We just haven't taken the time to figure out what it is."

Once they started to examine their process, Jessi and Marie realized that, even though their clients were different, they asked the same questions of their clients each time, looking for similar information. They used a road map to come up with a code for how each client communicated.

"It's about what someone *doesn't* say, as much as what they *do* say," Marie explained. "It was specific stories they shared. Even punctuation. Do they use a lot of em dashes? Do they like emojis? Where do they stand on Oxford commas?"

"It took time," Jessi chimed in. "And even now, we're still making tiny tweaks and refinements. But we were able to come up with a way to train the team, a repeatable, systematized process that could be used for any of our clients."

In essence, they captured their system for capturing brand voice. And it worked. The work produced by their team needed fewer revisions, and they were able to pretty much nail the voice from day one, which helped them protect their QBR. Customer satisfaction improved and clients were more willing to stick with North Star over the long haul.

Of course, Jessi and Marie don't hire just anyone to do this work; they hire other writers. So their Captures work for other writers, but not for, say, the bookkeeper—unless they are one of those secret novelists with a manuscript in their desk drawer.

It's one thing to hand off a menial task to someone else, but to hand off something you take pride in being great at, something you're known for, that's a whole other ball game. When I asked how Jessi and Marie handled it the first time, they said it was "absolutely terrifying." So they mitigated the risk a bit. They ensured that the first time another writer used their voice-capturing system, it was with a client who wouldn't be likely to get upset if the work wasn't just so. That gave them a little bit of insurance.

It wasn't long before their internal discussion board went quiet and they no longer fielded questions from the writers. The clients were happy and their QBR was safe and sound. Eventually, they created a writer-mentor role and moved two of their writers into the position to take their place. Now Marie and Jessi are no longer the "holders of all the writing knowledge," which frees them up to focus on growth and other passion projects they've left behind—the novels in the drawer.

You and I are not special, either. You can capture that thing you do. It may take some time, but it can be done. It can always be done.

But wait, Mikey boy. Are you saying that someone else could paint the Mona Lisa? Maybe. Maybe not. What I am saying for sure is that the process of painting the Mona Lisa could be captured. And then the process of someone else doing the same is far easier. They need the right talent and experience, but the pathway has been outlined. There is a reason legendary land-scape artist and PBS icon Bob Ross says to paint the clouds first. (Notice how Bob's teaching process also involved video? Dude was ahead of his time.) If viewers don't follow the right sequence, they'll have muck. Maybe they're not the next Bob Ross. But they'll be a better painter than they were before.

RIVERS FOLLOW THE EASIEST PATH

As you give your workers tasks, especially the responsibility for making decisions, some may still keep coming back to you for your input—even if you have captured the systems you want them to follow. From their perspective, it makes sense, because what if they make the "wrong" decision? They are concerned about being reprimanded by the boss (you), or worse, fired. They surely don't want to lose your trust. But if you make the decisions for them, they can do no wrong. If you give them an answer and it works, they are rewarded for following your instructions. If you give them an answer and it doesn't work, it's not their fault. Either outcome, as long as *you* make the decision, is safe for them. And bonus—they don't have to think! They just have to do. (And you already know that "doing" is your preference, so why wouldn't it be theirs, too?)

The natural tendency of people is to defer decisions. We do it at work and at home. Ever been asked the most challenging question of all time after a long day of work? You know the one: "What do you want for dinner?" I dunno. Whatever you want. It's easy for your team to do the same. They dunno. They want whatever you want.

If you are meeting resistance from employees you've empowered to make decisions, whatever you do, don't make their decisions for them! You must let them do the research, determine the course of action, and then commit to it. After all, we are trying to get you out of the business, and you can't do that if you keep making the decisions.

Your employees may resist this by coming to you for assistance in decision-making, but you should always push the decision-making back to them. If they ask for direction, respond with: "What do you think we should do?" If the resistance to making a decision continues with the popular "I don't know, that's why I am coming to you" answer, respond with: "We hired you because you are smart and driven. We hired you to find answers. Please come back to me with your best answer and the decision you would make, and we will discuss." When they do come back, get ready to smile, nod, and give your okay.

Even when they offer up ideas that you disagree with, bite your tongue and support them. Then, after the decisions and actions have been carried out, for anything with significant outcomes— either positive or negative—do a debrief and have the employee share what they have learned and what they will do differently the next time. Always do the debrief *after* they make and execute a decision.

The only time to intervene is if you see them making a decision that will have dire consequences. If you spot severe danger, make your team aware immediately. Now you are mentoring them, not deciding for them. And remember, there is a big difference between the right decision and your decision. We all process in our own way. So when observing an employee's decision, rather than comparing it to the decision you might have made, ask yourself if it is a decision that serves the company.

In a must-see interview, billionaire Sara Blakely, the founder of Spanx, explained the foundational belief that spawned her success: failure should be embraced.[7] Blakely explained, "My dad growing up encouraged me and my brother to fail. It's really allowed me to be much freer in trying things and spreading my wings in life." The only way to make progress is by moving through challenges, mistakes, and errors, and learning along the way. This requires making your own decisions. Ultimately, as Blakely explained, the only true failure is idleness, where you don't make any decisions. Stop training your employees to be idle by deciding for them. Have them move your business forward by empowering them to make decisions.

How do you empower someone to make decisions? Brace yourself—you must reward mistakes. When something doesn't go right and you punish the person (lecture, point out what went wrong, chop their pay, roll your eyes, anything), you instill the fear of making the wrong decision, and therefore it is safest for them to just come back to you for decisions (keeping you in the Deciding phase). But if you say, "Hey, the outcome was not what we expected, but I am proud of you for making a decision to move us forward. I want you to keep at it. Tell me, what can I do to serve you?" you will not only start to see your business run without always needing you, but you will have improved your relationship with a member of your team.

Toyota's world-famous lean manufacturing process is based on the same core belief. The decision-making must be pushed "down" to the people making them. When a line worker has a problem, they can stop the entire line (you read that right), and the managers hurry over to provide support for that person. The line worker gives out the commands and directions, and the managers provide the support to get the line up and running again. That is giving decision-making power to the right people—the people closest to the problem.

FOR EMPLOYEES: CORA'S STORY

Job Turf was constantly looking for new equipment. New to them, that is: they loved to buy used stuff. But they wanted new equipment that was 1) more efficient and effective, and 2) better for the environment. Cora loved learning about the new tools. When they bought a new machine to transplant trees, she was assigned the task of mastering the tool and creating a system to operate it.

The newest purchase was a specialized spade that connected to their existing skid steer. Cora went to practice at their lot, moving a dead tree from one spot to another, and another, and another. She spent a few hours learning how to use the spade, and once she felt she was ready to do it in the field, she filmed a demonstration of the process with the dead tree. She had two cameras going, one filming the skid steer with the spade and the other showing the control panel. She filmed the process while explaining the steps. She then uploaded the video files and stored them on Job Turf's cloud for anyone to view.

Over the following weeks, as Cora used the new spade, she found more efficient ways to use the equipment. Big underground boulders interfered with removing or replanting trees, so she developed a simple method to test the area first using a rod and a sledgehammer. She also made a few tweaks to how they used the equipment itself. Then, she filmed the process again and replaced the old training video with the new version in the cloud.

The day came when someone else on the team had to use the tree spade. Cora was traveling for a vacation in Lanai, Hawaii, where she got engaged to her longtime sweetheart, and her return flight was cancelled due to storms. No problem. Gordon watched the "capture" of the tree spade process and did the work. Though it took him a bit longer than if Cora had done it, he got the job done properly.

How can you help? Create a video teaching one of the processes you do for your job. Start with something small and easy. Then ask a fellow team member to do the process you just captured. Note the results—do they meet your standards? If not, improve the captures until they do. Once someone else can successfully complete the task, you have made yourself even more valuable to the organization. You can do important things, you can capture those important things, and you can transfer those important things, which allows you to take on even more important things.

Consider different ways to capture the process so others can learn it easily. For example, aside from video capture, you could create a checklist or a flow chart.

The more processes you record, the more you elevate yourself, especially when you capture your Primary Job. The employee who makes themselves irreplaceable may think they've secured their job, but they are compromising the company's stability (if they don't do the work, no one can) and preventing themselves from growing beyond the job. Capturing systems is a way to provide the knowledge you accumulate to the company. It also enables you to grow into new work and opportunities.

When your Primary Job can be done by others, you have backup and you can take breaks. You may even be able to take a four-week vacation. (Ask your boss. Tell them I said so.)

CLOCKWORK IN ACTION

1. Capture a system. Yes, you have hundreds of systems that you will ultimately capture, but you won't capture any of

them if you don't get started. Take the first step now—something small and easy, and something that you can take off your plate permanently. Capture that first system and see how it works for you. And then have the person to whom you assign the system make the next version of the recording.

2. Store your first captured system in a directory. This should be the same directory that everyone on your team uses. You can use whichever cloud storage software works for your company and/or your own server.

PHASE 3

ACCELERATE

Your business is about to blow up—in a good way. Your team will be empowered. Your company will start to find and fix its own problems. So where does that leave you?

While in the process of writing this expanded and revised edition of *Clockwork*, I took a break to attend a quarterly meeting for my writing and speaking business, planned by our president, Kelsey Ayres. If you read the first edition of this book, you might remember that she was my assistant at that time. Kelsey started out as a part-time, $10-an-hour employee, and now she oversees the execution of our vision as the president of the company.

At the quarterly meeting, we conceptualized new products that further served and could expand our established community, including merchandise and a children's book inspired by *Profit First*. (That became *My Money Bunnies: Fun Money Management for*

Kids.) We brainstormed new strategies in a way that I had not experienced before. The meeting concluded with an announcement that we had had our most profitable quarter ever. This was remarkable, because my speaking gigs, a significant revenue source, had all but dried up due to the COVID-19 pandemic. All of this was possible because we clockworked the company and kept improving our systems. Then the meeting really ended, with celebratory wine and appetizers—only the good stuff, of course, because that is how you recognize achievement.

Integrating the clarity about your company's Top Clients, Big BANG, Big Promise, and QBR that you gained in the Align phase will enable you to start achieving organizational efficiency. The next step is to take your systems to the next level.

In the Accelerate phase, you'll balance your team according to their strengths, remove bottlenecks, and incorporate vacations *from* your company and *for* your company. You will become relevant to your business in a new, more important way. You will no longer be the heart of your business. You will be the soul.

CHAPTER NINE

BALANCE THE TEAM

GET THE RIGHT PEOPLE, IN THE RIGHT ROLES, DOING THE RIGHT THINGS, IN THE RIGHT PORTIONS, RIGHT

From the moment you make your first hire, part time or full time, or bring on your first virtual assistant or contractor, your company now has multiple gears that need to mesh harmoniously. If you build a balanced company (one that is 80 percent Doing and 20 percent Deciding/Delegating/Designing) from the get-go, you will have a stronger foundation and it will be easier and smoother accelerating growth from that point. This is a Designing skill that will carry you far.

As Verne Harnish says in *Mastering the Rockefeller Habits*, we need to get "the right people, doing the right things, right." This is true. Very true. But I would like to add one more element. The right people need to be doing the right things in the right amount. My modified version of that maxim reads like this: "Have the right people, doing the right things, in the right portions, right."

Here's how that sentence breaks down:

1. "Have the right people . . .": This means that you know the super strengths of your team, aka their zones of genius. Not what they do most, currently, but what they are best at doing and get the most joy from. When a person is great at something and loves doing it, they will excel. Unfortunately, most business owners and leaders don't know the strengths of their team. Determine your people's strengths (and evaluate the strengths of people before you bring them on) and use this knowledge to put them in a position where they will excel.

2. ". . . doing the right things . . .": Identify what your business needs and what it doesn't. Trash what it doesn't need so that no one is distracted by those tasks. Transfer the work to the right people. Trim the work that can be done more efficiently. Treasure the work that needs to stay with them. When you do that, you are aligning the right people with the right things.

3. ". . . in the right portions . . .": People and businesses both need balance. All the Doing in the world will fall short if there is no clear direction. And all the direction in the world is useless if no one is taking action on the strategy. Even if they are great at something, your team needs balance, and they need their own appropriate level of variety. Target an overall balance of 80 percent Doing, 2 percent Deciding, 8 percent Delegating, and 10 percent Designing time for your company.

4. ". . . right.": This is about education. Provide your people with the relevant captured system. Have a clearly defined goal and a process to follow. Educate them on their Primary Jobs, what the QBR is, and the need to serve and protect it.

THE RIGHT PEOPLE

After I delivered my first main-stage keynote on Clockwork to four hundred people at a conference in San Jose, California, I stayed in the room for another forty-five minutes answering questions and listening to entrepreneurs' stories about what they were doing to streamline their businesses. As the audience funneled out of the room, I noticed one gentleman waiting patiently for me. If you are a speaker, you will know this is usually the weirdo, and you should avoid eye contact at all costs. But this guy I recognized. It was Darren Virassammy, cofounder of 34 Strong.

Darren is *the* expert on balancing teams and bringing about extraordinary engagement from every employee. His company has taken the StrengthsFinder system, which measures an individual's talents (among other things), and developed a powerful process to move the right people into the right roles at a business.

Darren and I started chatting and decided to continue our conversation over dinner, where he proceeded to school me on balance. I realized then that, even though the QBR strategy worked and resonated with audiences, a company would still have to balance its team in order to achieve organizational efficiency.

"The mistake organizations make, both big and small, is that they see all people as basically the same. If you can talk well at an interview, you are hired. If you can kiss ass well once you're hired, you get a promotion. The work, of course, matters, but the measurement is simply whether you can do an adequate job in the time allotted," Darren said. "What's missing is the realization that every person has an extraordinary talent. The person who turns red-faced in an interview and can barely spit the words out may be the best analytical mind in the world. The person who talks about the importance of serving others may not be a good salesperson who is motivated by numbers but may be a powerful customer service person who is motivated by impact."

He continued, "You need to know what people are inherently strong at, and then match them to the role in your business where they are applying that strength as much as possible. In other words, if you measure a fish by how well it can climb a tree and a monkey by how long it can breathe underwater, you have set up both for failure. But if you measure the fish by its ability to breathe underwater and the monkey by its ability to climb a tree, you will find they excel."

For your people, match their strength to the role. How do you find their super strength? You ask them. Well, it is a little bit more involved than that. For example, if you are interviewing someone to write content for your website and you ask them what their strength is, if they have even a modicum of desire to land the job, they will likely say, "I'm really good at writing copy."

So the question is not what they are good at; the question is what do they naturally love to do. For example, "What are your three favorite things you have ever done at work?" "If you were able to have any job on the planet, doing anything you want, what would you do?" "Ten years from now, what is the perfect job you see yourself doing?" "If you had all the money in the world, and simply wanted to work for the joy of working, what would you do?" Seek out their interests. Seek out their hobbies. Seek out what gives them joy. Because if it gives them joy, it is usually their strength.

That's the shortcut. For my own business, I use a far more thorough approach. I did 34 Strong's team evaluation and took their direction in moving the right people into the right roles (which we'll discuss in a minute). As new hires are considered, we interview with the questions above and have Darren test them out for us.

As we said goodbye, Darren reached out to shake my hand. I, not being the master of human cues, didn't even notice, leading to the most awkward hug of all time. His outstretched arm was now pinned between our abdomens, and I clung to him for an inappropriate length of time. We both cleared our throats, but nothing would overcome the pinnacle of awkwardly long, pinned-arm man-hugs. And alas, the weirdo hanging around after my speaking event wasn't Darren; it was me.

One final strength detector, and perhaps the most effective detector of all, is observation. Watch your colleagues at work. What do they naturally excel at doing? What do they want to do more of? What do they want to learn more about? Those are all likely indicators of their strengths.

Now that you are working toward a target 4D Mix, have identified your QBR, and are mobilizing your team to protect and serve the QBR, you'll notice that your team may need to shift to accommodate these changes. This is where you will sometimes get push-back from your team. People may worry about their job security, or they may have a difficult time letting go of their old roles because doing "less" makes them look like less of a team player, although the exact opposite is true. Or you may find yourself locked in your own awkwardly long hug. As you go through this process, keep in mind that transitions can be difficult for some people. In this chapter, I'll share how to ensure that you have the right people, doing the right things, in the right portions, and also address some potential issues that may come up in the process.

WHEN SHOULD I HIRE?

I get this question almost daily. Before I can answer, the person asking already has their own answer. They'll say, "I can't afford to hire someone now," or "No one will have the skills I need without a huge price tag," or "Everyone else sucks." The entrepreneur's conclusion is almost always the same: "I guess I just need to grind it out longer by myself." They decide that they need to delay the hire, and in doing so, stay stuck longer and longer in the Survival Trap. A good rule of thumb is, if you feel you could use help but need to grind it out longer, take that as a desperate subconscious plea to yourself that you need help now, and should make that hire.

First, let's address your mindset about doing the work yourself. Let me ask you a question. Would you rather make $50 an hour or $5 an hour? Of course you want that 50 bucks. What if I asked you if you would rather make $50 an hour doing all the work yourself or $5 an hour doing no work at all? This is where the Survival Trap reveals itself. Fifty dollars an hour is still better on an hourly return than $5 an hour, but how much you ultimately earn is determined by your effort and your ability to sustain those efforts. The $5 an hour (after expenses) comes in regardless of whether you are working or not.

When you figure out that you can keep multiplying $5 an hour into infinity, you might change your thinking. Let's say that with one good hire you can make $5 an hour without working, and with two hires you can make $10 an hour. With ten hires you can now make $50 an hour without lifting a finger. You're sick, you make money. You go to your daughter's school play, you make money. You go on vacation, you make more money. That is the goal of a Clockwork company—that the company runs itself without any dependency on you, all while serving you, the shareholder, with the money it creates.

Now that you see that you *can* make money even (or especially) if you don't do the work yourself, when should you hire? Hiring can't happen too soon. But it *can* happen too fast. Those are two different things. If you hire too fast, you are hiring without proper consideration. That is a mistake. But you can't hire too soon. Meaning, any size business will benefit from the right hire, hired under the right parameters, sooner rather than later.

For example, say you are in a routine of doing the work yourself, and that it is relatively consistent, but you are not making nearly enough money for yourself and you're burned out. It's time to hire. Don't be distracted by the immediate feeling of "I don't have money." Think long term: "I need a way to make more money without working more." This is a time to hire, under the right parameters. Meaning, maybe you aren't ready to hire someone full time with benefits. Maybe you want someone to work five hours a week, and you can only realistically pay them $10 an hour.

Now you may be thinking, "Who wants to work for $50 a week?" There is someone out there who would be thrilled to find a job like that. The mistake entrepreneurs make is to think that all people are seeking full-time jobs, and that all people expect top dollar. For example, Erin Moger has worked part time for Profit First Professionals from day one. She doesn't want to work more; she wants to raise her young family. My business partner Ron Saharyan and I are both humbled to know her and to work with her. Erin is an amazing team member. So we created a position that is a big win for her because it respects her time, and she serves our company, caring for our members in extraordinary ways. That's a big win for us.

The first hire I brought on, Jackie Ledowski, worked three hours a day, three days a week. It was perfect for what she wanted in her life at the time and she was perfect for what I needed. I was now able to transfer some administrative Doing to her—for nine hours a week at first—which allowed me to Design more.

A hire isn't restricted to full- or part-time employees. I have hired contractors, virtual team members, interns, and vendors. You can even make hires outside the traditional forms of employment, such as volunteers or family or volunteering family. I "hired" my mom and dad to help clean the office when I had my first company. The pay sucked for them (zero) and the benefits were worse (I would go to their house and eat all the leftovers). But they were great "hires" to reduce work, and yes, they are *great* parents. Think beyond traditional employment and consider anyone or anything that can take even a fraction of work off your plate.

The goal for early-stage hires (and every-stage hires, for that matter) is to free you up to focus more on Designing and less on Doing, and that can't happen soon enough. Remember, you need to make money without doing the work. Every dollar you make via your company's effort, and not your own, moves you closer and closer to becoming a Clockwork company.

WHOM SHOULD I HIRE?

The great irony is that you should not hire people based upon the skills on their résumés. The only thing you can give people is skills, and you want to give people the skills to do the work the way you do it. "Skill" jobs can be a trap. When you hire someone who has the skills already, it means they are walking in with the baggage of their past work. They will apply the skills you need their way, which is rarely the way you want or need the job done. This means there will be, best case, confusion and inconsistency, and worst case, the need to redo work.

You want to hire people with a great get-it-done attitude, high energy, and high intelligence; people who are a strong cultural fit and have a desire to do the work. All these are intangibles that can't be taught. Either they have them or they don't. So seek out people who have the intangibles you need, then give them the only thing that you really can: the skills.

Once you realize that you don't need a "senior specialist with ten years' experience in social media and product distribution," you could theoretically hire a teenager who has the right attitude, energy, and intelligence, and who is a good fit to do the same work. Well, that's not theory; that is exactly what we did. My office has a teenager who handles product distribution. Since she's a minor, I'll change her name to Alice. She may be a minor in age, but she is a majorly great employee. Alice works for a little above minimum wage—not because we are taking advantage of her, but because her experience and the job description dictate it. Oh, and she can't work until after school gets out at three o'clock, wants time off for sports and band, and needs to be able to walk to work or get a ride from her grandpa, which are all things that we gladly accommodate.

Remember, people don't pick jobs based on just pay and vacation. And if that is the only consideration those people are making, you don't want those people anyway. Yes, people want a good salary to live their lifestyle and take vacation and do other things, but good employees are also looking for something deeper. Fun, learning, impact, culture, and more.

When looking for new team members, seek diversity. The biggest mistake we make is hiring people we like. If we like them, it is usually because they are like us. We need people with different skills and points of view. Hire diversity. Don't hire people you like; hire people you respect.

Finally, be a trait-seeker. Look for employees with the traits and strengths you need. In your trait-seeking role you will want to determine whether this person needs to be super detail-oriented, or a great communicator, or analytical. Consider the different jobs you need completed at your office and the specific strengths those jobs need, and then hire for them.

Ever notice that when you run an ad for an open position, you get dozens or hundreds of applicants who are not really interested in the job? They are just applying for *any* job. Those people swamp your inbox with résumés, and if you try to interview them they respond with things like "What job is this again?" or "What is the pay and how much vacation do I get?" or "What do I need to do again?" I am not suggesting that these are bad people, but they surely are a bad fit for your company. And a big waste of your valuable time.

To find better candidates, create an ad that defines your culture and disqualifies the résumé spammers all in one shot. How do you pull off that little miracle? Create a looooong ad that describes your culture in detail, prepares potential employees for the fun and not-necessarily-fun job requirements, and embeds a little requirement in the ad itself. For example, near the end of the ad, require that an applicant respond with, "I'm pumped for this job" in the email subject line of their response. You will find that the vast majority of applicants won't do this, which means they did not read the ad and are not truly interested in the job, or they are spamming, or they aren't able to follow instructions (a critical ability). On clockwork.life, I share one of the best job ads I posted. You are welcome to copy, tweak, and paste it to attract your own part-time or full-time rock stars.

YOUR BIGGEST FEAR—TRUST

I need to get super real with you about something. Do me a favor, just peek around for a second and make sure no one else is listening in. We good? Good.

I think you may have a fear issue. Actually, I *know* you have a fear issue. Better said, you likely have a trust issue. The most common reason that businesses fail to grow and run like clockwork is not the system. Shoot, there are a lot of wildly helpful scaling systems out there, like Gino Wickman's *Traction*, Michael E. Gerber's *The E-Myth*, and Verne Harnish's *Scaling Up*. Yet most people who follow those systems, or the Clockwork system, or cherry-pick from all of them, still fail to scale.

Why? Because they can't trust other people to run the business. I mean, imagine bringing on a key employee who walks in to help with the business and then walks out with all your clients months later. This can and does happen. Imagine that new employee you entrust to take care of clients screwing up and losing you a key client forever. The risk feels too great to trust others. I could tell you to "buck up" and get over it, since you need to trust your people so that you can successfully remove yourself from the day-to-day. But that's like telling you to just buck up and run a marathon when you've never trained for it. The risk of injury is too great, and therefore you may back down and never do it.

So instead, we are going to do this slowly. Think about marriage. Chances are you don't just go up to a random person on the street and ask them to marry you. If you did that, you would probably get slapped. You don't just get married. More likely, you go on a date or two, or two hundred. You probably spend time learning about each other. Maybe you move in together for a while before tying the knot. There is a courtship—usually.

But when it comes to key hires or even business partners, decisions are often made way too quickly. You know a potential business partner for twenty-four hours and feel that is adequate to enter into an agreement to run a business together for life. You will literally spend more time with this partner than with your spouse, and yet spend so little time vetting them.

Move slowly with hires. Build the trust gradually but start immediately. The goal is for your new teammate to become fully autonomous, and to make that happen, start with low-risk transfers. Give them new work at a pace they can manage and measure their output as you do. As they can take on more, transfer bigger and bigger responsibilities to them. When you see indications that they may be overwhelmed, slow down or stop the transfer of new duties. Give a bit, measure a bit, give a bit more, measure a bit more. But no matter what, try to get them doing something on their own within the first week of employment. That will be a confidence builder for both of you.

Also, ensuring that your team is in alignment with your Big Promise and understands your QBR will help you build the trust you need to let go of responsibilities and begin to move people into the right positions.

EXERCISE: JOB TRAITS ANALYSIS

Understand that a company position, such as receptionist, salesperson, or something else, has a list of jobs/tasks required of that position. This list creates a round hole, yet most applicants are square pegs. Finding someone who has traits that allow them to excel in every job/task that the position requires is unlikely. You are better served evaluating the strong traits your current people and new applicants have, then matching those traits with the different jobs/tasks, regardless of position titles. For example, someone who has excellent phone skills may be great for some aspects of reception work, sales work, and customer service. At the same time, their disheveled presentation may make them unsuitable for other aspects of reception work, sales work, and customer-service work. Your goal: match people's best traits to the jobs and tasks that need those traits.

In this next exercise, you will conduct a Job Traits Analysis.

JOB TRAITS ANALYSIS

JOB/TASK	EXCEL TRAIT	IMPORTANCE QBR/PJ/H/M/L	CURRENT PERSON SERVING JOB	BEST PERSON SERVING JOB

Figure 10
A downloadable and printable version is available at clockwork.life.

1. In the Job/Task column, fill in all the jobs and tasks for a position in your company. Do this for all the positions you have in your company, including your own.

2. In the Excel Trait column, enter the primary behavior that would allow a person to excel at this job/task. For example, if a job/task is "Managing inbound calls from customers," the Excel Trait might be "Professional and confident voice" or "Empathetic and clear communication." Don't get into minutiae like "Ability to dial on keypad" or "Can transfer calls." Yes, that stuff is necessary, but what we are looking for here is not the skills required (you can train on skills). We are looking for inherent ability and enthusiasm that is difficult or impossible to teach. Just write down one trait. What is the one critical trait that moves that task forward the most successfully?

3. Importance: This column is for the impact it will have on the company. Mark each task as one of these five levels:

QBR, Primary Job, High, Medium, Low. QBR is the most critical level. Primary Job is their most important personal responsibility. High are the most important tasks that must be done as long as the Primary Job is done. Medium and Low are necessary but not critical functions.

4. Current Person Serving Job: List any people who currently do this job or task.

5. Then fill in Best Person Serving Job by listing the person (or people) who, based on the match-up with the trait, is best suited to doing this work. Start this matching process to the QBR, then to the Primary Job, then the High, the Medium, and finally the Low tasks. Remember, people are *not* their titles. People are their traits. For example, you are not seeking a receptionist. You are seeking "The Great Communicator," so identify who that person is and match them with the tasks and jobs that need a great communicator.

6. Then move people to the most critical tasks, starting with the most important first—the QBR. Match the person with a strength trait to the job that needs that trait. Move and observe. It will not be practical to move everyone to an optimized job/task. So always prioritize top down. Start with the QBR and end with the Low task.

   As such, we get rid of the traditional pyramid structure of organization charts, which focus on seniority and power/position. People need to "climb the ladder," and they often move into positions that don't make much use of their traits or abilities. A Clockwork company is not about the old pyramid structure; instead, it uses a web of connections, matching strength where strength is needed, resulting in a network structured like a brain.

ALIGN THEIR JOY WITH THEIR JOB

When Cordé Reed interviewed to join our team, I asked her, "What work would you love to do?"

"Oh my gosh," she said. "I've never been asked this question before. Are you being serious? Do you really want to know what I want to do?"

Yes. When people do what they love, they excel. Think about the hobbies or activities you enjoy the most. You can immerse yourself in doing them, right? You love fixing motorcycles, and you can fill up a whole weekend in your garage, happy as a clam. Or you love quilt-making and can be found stitching up a storm until midnight. When we love doing something, we'll invest a lot of time and energy into it. It gives us energy instead of drawing energy away from us.

Now imagine you have an entire team of employees who get energy from working at your company. Instead of finishing the workday drained and dragging, they feel empowered. Wouldn't that be magical? Don't you want your employees excited to come to work because they get to do what they love to do? You can have this—if you align their joy to their job. Match the tasks to the people with the talents. Match their work to their wants. That is a company people love to work for and help grow.

EXERCISE: TEAM BALANCING

For a business to stay afloat and grow, it must be actively Doing things that its clients value. The Designing work is about creating the best way to do things your clients value and have your company do those things on automatic.

Kyle Keegan owns a disaster (fire and flood) cleanup service, Team K Services, and he loves getting out there and helping people. He loves doing the work. He gets his hands dirty, literally, every week for at least a few hours. And he learns from the field how to make his company run better. The Big Promise he makes to his clients is an immediate answer to their number-one question: "What do I do now?" For a customer, often this is the first time they have ever experienced a disaster. And in many cases, Kyle's team is in communication with the client just hours after the disaster. His promise is to give them the right information, right then and there, so they can move forward. So the QBR he identified for his company is extremely fast and accurate estimates.

But Kyle realized that his time spent Doing was stalling company growth. He looked at his internal team to determine people's strongest traits and see whether anyone had the confident and empathetic communication skills to serve the QBR. Once he figured that out, he could shift more of this time to Design work and take his company to the next level. He found two ideal people for the role. With the new team members with the right communication traits identified, he balanced the time utilization of everyone (including himself). The QBR was protected and served by the two new folks, freeing up Kyle to focus more on Design time. To keep the business in balance, he leveraged his Time Analysis. You can, too.

Here's how you conduct your own team balancing:

1. As I shared previously, the optimal percentages-of-work balance for a company is 80/2/8/10. Eighty percent is Doing: getting tasks done that directly or ultimately serve the customer and bring value to them. Two percent is Deciding for others: making the necessary approvals

and helping employees with decision-making in unusual circumstances. Eight percent is Delegating the management of resources. To reiterate, Delegating is *not* making decisions for others; it means assigning ownership to others and providing the necessary leadership to bring about the desired outcome. Ten percent is Designing strategy. This is about making the other three levels—Doing, Deciding, and Delegating—more and more effective.

2. A single-employee company (just the owner) is the entire company. So their job/task breakdown should target 80/2/8/10.

3. When you have multiple employees, you want to balance the team to bring the average to 80/2/8/10. For example, your individual time may be 60 percent Doing, 4 percent Deciding, 16 percent Delegating, and 20 percent Designing. Assuming you have one other employee who works the same amount as you do, they will need to be 100 percent Doing in order to bring the aggregate of Doing for your company to 80 percent, as their 100 percent and your 60 percent average out to 80 percent. Similarly, Deciding would now be 2 percent for the company (the average of you both), 8 percent for Delegating, and 10 percent for Designing.

4. Use the 4D Time Analysis you did for yourself and your team to figure out the balance for your company. Put in each person. Weigh the amount of time they work for the company in relation to the total company. For example, if you work eighty hours a week (we need to fix that fast, by the way, because your working that much is not in the spirit of Clockwork) and another employee works eight hours a week, your work is weighted ten times more than the employee's.

5. Now look at what your people are doing as compared to what they want to do. Play with models where you move people around to leverage their strengths while keeping the company in that 80/2/8/10 zone. When you are ready to try out your new model, have trial runs and tests. Let people sample the new work to make sure it suits them. Shift deliberately but slowly and communicate throughout. Tell your team how you are trying to rebalance the work people do, so they are happier with the work and the efficiency increases. Prepare them for bumps and bruises in the transition. And ask for their active feedback on making the new balance even better.

FIND NEW WAYS TO CHALLENGE YOUR EMPLOYEES

When people master something, they get bored over time. Why do you think Mr. Miyagi in *The Karate Kid* took up the art of bonsai? Because he had already mastered karate, man. He needed something else to do. Sometimes people who are perpetually in mastery mode show up minimally and may start making mistakes. Because they aren't experiencing new learning or problemsolving, they become disengaged, or at least not fully engaged. Just like the super-smart kid in class who acted out because they were bored. Rebalance your team to keep challenges in front of your team that still leverage their skills and wants.

The last time I took a flight, I saw this happening at the by-theminute level. In the past, the TSA person staring at the baggage scanner screen would stare at bag after bag for hours on end. Their job was to scrutinize every detail, but the task repetition made them numb and they could easily miss, you know, something *really* important. Good on the TSA: they now rotate the team every twenty minutes or so. Employees move from luggage screening, to directing people through scanners, to the coveted (as in *not* coveted) pat-downs. They stay fresh because they don't stay stuck.

In our Run Like Clockwork program, we share the S-Curve of Learning concept created by Whitney Johnson, author of *Build an A-Team: Play to Their Strengths and Lead Them Up the Learning Curve.* A YouTube video about the book explains that the S-Curve of Learning is like a roller-coaster.[8] When an employee is at the bottom, they are total newbies with very little knowledge and experience. The ride up the roller-coaster—click, click, click, click, click—is the process of mastering the job. When they reach the top, it's awesome because it's gratifying. The view is pretty great from up there. But to be stuck at that level can get pretty boring pretty fast. And then there's the whole, what do I do if I have to go to the bathroom? Am I ever getting off this go-nowhere vomit comet? To start feeling excited again, they'll need to plummet to the bottom and start a new learning curve.

In Johnson's video, she reveals that the ideal mix for a balanced team is to have the majority learning, a few starting, and a few who have mastered it all. The majority who are learning are your producers, the masters can help the learners along, and the newbies are the ones who can challenge the entrenched ideas and ask, "Why do we do it this way?"

Balancing your team is a living process. Look at it every quarter. The goal is to get more and more of what they love to do on your employees' plates. It may not always be possible, but over time, the goal is to create a "dream job" for every member of your team. As this process evolves, your team will grow and change. In your quarterly review, make sure to consider how many of your employees are in learning mode and how many are in mastery mode.

Change is hard. I'm sure you don't need me to tell you that, but I'm bringing it up because after implementing the first five Clockwork steps, you will surely be feeling it. Even when business is booming, and even when you have more time to focus on Designing your business, change can be stressful—especially when you're changing the balance of your team. Your team will also feel that change, and they may feel insecure about their new positions, or worry that they may be eliminated entirely.

Remember, a balanced team isn't just a retention tool for your existing talent; it helps you recruit talent as well. Your company's commitment to helping your team love their work is hugely attractive to prospective employees.

For those people who will remain part of your team, give them reassurance. Listen to their concerns. Affirm their places on your team. Remember to take the time to breathe during this process. Yes, change is hard. It is also going to get you what you want: a business that runs itself.

FOR EMPLOYEES: CORA'S STORY

Cora loves Job Turf, and she loves her job, no matter what she's doing. But she really excelled at using the big equipment. She loved it and was great at it. Whenever she handled the large machines, they had fewer accidents. This wasn't a surprise to Cora. When she served in the military, she drove all different types of trucks. And she had a spotless record—no accidents in her near-decade of military truck driving.

So Cora approached Gordon and asked if she could do more

of the work she loved. He agreed and changed her Primary Job to working with the big equipment. This helped balance the team and take another step toward improving the company's productivity! Plus, Cora was thrilled. She had a job she loved, and now she had a dream Primary Job.

How can you help? Balance is about putting the right people in the right roles. It's also about *you* doing the right things in the right way. What do you love to do? What work do you avoid doing? Share with your manager the loves, likes, mehs, and hates of the work you do. Everyone has to do stuff at work that they don't like, sometimes for a long time. The goal is not to make you all warm and cozy. The goal is to lean into your strengths and give you chances to grow, and to constantly seek ways for you to do more of what you love.

 ## CLOCKWORK IN ACTION

1. Do an analysis to ensure that your company is at approximately 80 percent Doing. Make a note that when your company's resources expand or contract, it stays near that optimal 80 percent Doing.

2. Run an evaluation of your team to identify their strongest talents and traits. Then run an evaluation of the ten most important daily tasks your business must complete. Now match up the best traits of your people with the tasks that need those traits most.

    Balancing your team is an ongoing process, and it can't be accomplished in thirty minutes, or even a day. The exercises in this chapter will help you get there. Plan to focus on one company objective each week, and then evaluate the data to ensure the right people are in the right roles, doing the right things, in the right portions, right.

CHAPTER TEN

FIND AND FIX BOTTLENECKS

MASTER THE METHOD FOR ONGOING AND CONTINUOUS IMPROVEMENT IN ANY BUSINESS

Have you ever felt like you fix everything, yet nothing is working? If you are putting in lots of effort but you are not getting the results you want, the two usual suspects are: 1) you are working on the wrong thing, and 2) you are working on too many things at once.

Imagine a clogged drainpipe. If there are multiple blockages, you can only clear the pipe by fixing one block at a time, in sequence. You can't skip clog one and start on clog two. And even if you could magically do that, the first problem would remain and you wouldn't know if you cleared clog two. And you can't clear two clogs at the same time unless you take out segments of pipe and then rebuild the whole thing. Rebuilding your business is rarely a better choice than fixing a clog in your business. Clear one bottleneck at a time.

At the end of the day, every business is a manufacturer. Yours included. We start with raw goods (or in service-based businesses, raw ideas) and assemble them to deliver an end product. Manufacturers go through a sequence of steps to make those goods. In short, there is a lot to learn from manufacturers—in particular, manufacturing efficiency. I connected with Kevin Fox, the founder of Viable Vision, a company that specializes in manufacturing efficiency. As I spoke with him, he shared powerful stories about how to find the bottlenecks in a business—the points where the business slows down.

"With a metric," Kevin explained, "it doesn't need to be some fancy computer system reporting a flashing number to a flat-panel screen in the manager's office. In fact, I recommend simple measurements, things that you can see and evaluate in the moment without the need for calculations or computer algorithms. Something like the blue light measurement."

Metrics are used to identify blockages and problems that impede your business from running efficiently. Like when a doctor checks your pulse, if it is in normal range there is nothing to worry about. But when things aren't as they should be, use that indicator to investigate the problem more deeply. You want a snapshot of what is going on. Make your metrics simple to understand and they will act as the vital signs for your business's health.

Simple measurements. Reminds me of Occam's razor, the belief that simpler explanations are usually the preferable ones. Metrics are explanations of what is going on. Make them easy to understand and they will yield an easy-to-understand explanation of what is going on.

When Kevin said this, my mind instantly went to the Kmart blue light specials. Blue lights flashing and people flocking to the racks for the deals being offered. Turns out, I wasn't that far off. Kevin shared a story of a car bumper manufacturer that hired Viable Vision to improve the company's efficiency. Kevin and his team went to the manufacturer to seek out bottlenecks where things were waiting to get done. Sure enough, inventory was piling up right in front of the welding station, sitting there waiting. Your business's bottlenecks will reveal themselves in the same way. Right before the bottleneck, things will pile up and wait. Time just wastes away.

With the piled-up bumpers, Kevin looked at the step they were waiting for—to be welded. That was the bottleneck. He noticed that he rarely saw the distinctive blue light that welding torches produce. Then he simply observed. He noticed that the welders went to the stockpile, carried over the parts, put them in a jig, spot-welded them to hold the parts in position, and then and only then, fired up the welding torch to weld them all together. Then they cleaned off the parts, moved them to the completed section, and started the process all over again. All in all, the welders were spending about 10 percent of their time actually welding. So the blue light of the torches only happened—you guessed it—10 percent of the time.

The Primary Job of the welders is to weld. And it was clear from the lack of blue lights that their Primary Job was not being prioritized. In fact, they were doing their Primary Job only—you guessed it again—10 percent of the time.

To fix the problem, Kevin simply hired a few teenagers to serve as assemblers. Their job was to move parts and get them ready for the welders. The assemblers would carry the parts to the welders and put them in the jig. The assemblers would then move out any finished parts to the completed section. As the assemblers were doing this, the welders would do the spot-welds and then fire up the welding torch and get to work. Blue lights flashing. The assemblers, after moving the completed parts, would walk back to the parts waiting to be welded. They would assemble the parts in the jig (which had casters on it) and wheel the bumper components to the welder. By this time, the welders had just finished welding the other bumper. The assemblers would put the new jig in position and wheel out the completed bumper. The welders would start welding again, blue light flashing. A lot.

With this fix, bumpers now started to go through the former weakest link in the chain at lightning speed. The pile of parts was gone within days with parts rarely ever piling up again. And the entire business was able to put out bumpers faster than ever. The magic wasn't just in the solution, but in the metric. It was really simple—if Kevin saw blue light flashing constantly, that meant the bottleneck was flowing. But if the light stopped for any period of time, or flashed much less often, that indicated a problem.

Kevin, and subsequently the owner of the factory, had a ridiculously simple and yet wildly effective metric: are the blue lights flashing? You should aim to make your metrics as simple as possible, too. You want to measure if business is flowing well. That's it. When it's not, the job of the metric is to simply notify you that there is a problem. And if there is a problem, your job, chess master, is to investigate and fix it. Blue light flashing? All is good. Don't see the blue lights much? That is a signal for you to look for the problem.

A metric is usually a number. It can also be a binary (yes/no or on/off), health indicators (red=bad, yellow=okay, green=good), or it can be something else. But a metric is always measurable and comparable. A metric sets the expectations, and when the actual events that the metric is measuring are higher or lower than expected, it indicates that an investigation of the situation is appropriate, and a resolution may be required.

Think about you your car's dashboard. As you're driving, you have various gauges that you check to make sure everything is a-okay. In one two-second glance, you can tell if you're driving too fast, if your engine is overheating, or if you're running low on gas. These are all simple indicators of a problem, and that action is required.

If you're going too fast—which sounds like it may be your style, Speed Demon—you take your foot off the accelerator. If your engine is overheating, you can pull over and check your coolant levels. (Or if, like me, you are relatively clueless about cars, you pull over and jump out thinking your engine is on fire, then get roadside assistance to tell you it was just steam. True story.) If you're running low on gas, you can fill up at the next stop. Without the instruments on your dashboard, you might get pulled over for speeding, watch your engine smoke (for real), or find yourself stranded in the middle of nowhere.

The same is true in business. A dashboard with metrics will show you how critical parts of your business are doing. Then, if something is out of whack, you can quickly check on the health of your business and make tweaks if necessary. When all your dashboard metrics are indicating that all is well, you can focus on the future of your business and not worry about the day-to-day operation. That's a beautiful thing because this is when you're making money on autopilot. Yes, that's a real thing. I'm not talking about the "passive income" that so many late-night infomercials promise. I'm talking about running the business you love while spending a mere fraction of the time you currently spend doing the work in the business, bringing in more cash than you ever truly thought possible, and loving every minute of it.

WHEN YOUR QUEEN BEE ROLE IS CLEAR, METRICS WILL SET YOU FREE

Remember Lisé Kuecker's story? She opened Anytime Fitness franchises when her husband was deployed. Lisé started her first business in the second grade. She made coloring sheets for her classmates and sold them for $1 a book. Being an entrepreneur comes naturally to Lisé, and yet, when she first started out in the fitness industry, she had an all-too-familiar story. She had contracted with a Fortune 100 company to develop their Pilates and yoga programs, and despite long hours and successful outcomes, she rarely took home a paycheck. Then Lisé decided to take a leap of faith and buy three territories from a young fitness franchise, Anytime Fitness. This time, she didn't plan to work eighty hours a week. Nope. Once she had each location up and running, she planned to work as little as possible.

Lisé opened the first location with her six-month-old son trailing behind her in his walker. Then she opened two more. Then two more. As crazy as it sounds, she is a master of applying Parkinson's Law, which we discussed in Chapter One. She took on more and more business while her husband was deployed. And without the time to work, she had to make the business work for her. You know, just like clockwork.

As you may recall, all her locations were in different states than the one she was living in at the time, and even with that challenge (*cough*, opportunity, *cough*), Lisé made it work. She had a meticulous strategy that covered every aspect of running her business and a system for tracking progress—which I will explain in just a sec.

Within a few years, Lisé's five locations generated multiple seven figures in annual revenue—and she ran all the locations from her home, working no more than five hours per week. Yes, I am still amazed by that number! I might say it again. Maybe even right now. Lisé would typically spend about a month in a location getting it ready, but once it was up and running, she only spent *five hours a week* running *all five locations*. She and her husband sold their gyms, and now Lisé helps entrepreneurs grow their own businesses using the methods she developed and re-fined while running her franchises.

When Lisé and I spoke on the phone, she immediately shared how she set up her own dashboard so that she could run her business "on automatic." Lisé used . . . wait for it . . . wait for it . . . a dashboard *and* a drill down. The dashboard was a weekly spreadsheet that pulled data inputted by every single employee who had a sales role, in all five locations. Whether it was the gen-eral manager of a facility, a personal training manager, or a trainer who managed their own sales, they all inputted data every week that was funneled into the same report.

The weekly spreadsheet presented several key metrics related to gym memberships: new sales, renewals, cancellations, and any type of freezes put into place for members. The snapshot also tracked daily activity, such as how many appointments were made, how many phone calls were received, or how many walk-ins came in. Finally, it tracked each location's sales closing percent-age. It was easy to read and easy to pinpoint what worked and what didn't work—the exact goal of a dashboard.

"It was a powerful spreadsheet," Lisé told me. "But it only took five minutes to go over it, since it had master metrics (seven met-rics, to be exact) that gave the pulse. Then I could dig deep on any indicator of a problem. Additionally, my district manager would look at the weekly metrics and then, in our Monday morn-ing meeting, she would report on what she saw in those weekly numbers." So Lisé wasn't looking at her dashboard all week long; her district manager was tracking it. Lisé only looked at the sum-mary of the weekly dashboard for a few minutes each week. From that information, she could tell if she needed to make an im-provement somewhere.

"My Monday meeting was with six core team members—I still

do that today as a consultant for the businesses we sold. I would listen to their view of what was happening, and then provide them with guidance and encouragement. Depending on the time of year, I might do a second meeting, but never for more than half an hour. It's a simple numbers review. The numbers don't lie," Lisé explained. "During the meeting, the district manager will explain the circumstances behind the numbers. She might say, 'I know that number is down, but Brittany's husband was just deployed, so that's what's going on right now.'"

Lisé could then tell if a number was falling off due to a temporary situation, such as an employee dealing with the stress of her husband's deployment, or if the metrics indicated a bigger problem that needed to be addressed. The drill downs gave her even more detail to help make these determinations.

"At the end of the month, I got a mass metric sheet for my drill down. Beyond my dashboard that had the key indicators, each month I would dig deep into all the numbers," Lisé explained. "It was a very simple spreadsheet. One line was our projected goals for the entire year. The next line was last year's numbers for the same goals. And the next line was how we were doing in terms of meeting those goals right now. We could tell where we came from, where we thought we were going, where we expected to go next month, and how we were really doing at that time.

"I could look at last year's attrition numbers for July, for example, and then compare them to July this year and determine what we need to tweak to get that metric closer to where we wanted it to be," Lisé continued. "When you are making goals and projections for your business, many of the shifts are circumstantial— especially as your team grows. You may lose an employee, or something may drop off. The numbers can shift rapidly, and this dashboard allowed me to see the whole picture."

Remember, Lisé was only at the actual gym location in the beginning, but it was during those formative weeks that she would make sure that everyone knew the QBR and how to deliver on it. "I had a big vision for what I wanted the gyms to look like, and I understood that I had to inspire that vision in my team," Lisé said. She also made sure she communicated the gym's QBR to existing members, and to people in the community. And, no surprise, she hired based on the QBR. A gym manager who can run a tight ship but is a jerk is not helpful. A gym manager who will do whatever they can to deliver extraordinary customer service but struggles at times with keeping things running smoothly is okay. The QBR always comes first.

Would Lisé have been able to run her businesses—from another state—working only five hours a week (after the initial location setup) if she wasn't clear about her QBR? If she hadn't trained her team to deliver on that QBR? And if her customers didn't feel the benefits of that QBR? And if she didn't have a strong dashboard to keep her apprised throughout? No way. Furthermore, it was Lisé's passion for changing the obesity rate that kept her motivated, and the success stories she heard from members kept her fulfilled, despite her distance from the locations.

ATTRACT, CONVERT, DELIVER, AND COLLECT

Like the links of a chain, these are the four elements in every business, but not necessarily always in the same order. They are Attract, Convert, Deliver, and Collect. Simply called the ACDC. Spelled like the band (without the lightning bolt slash), and just as badass.

Whether you are a business coach, or you own a car wash, or

anything in between, your business must complete four significant steps to stay up and running. The business coach brings in a prospect (Attract), turns them into a customer (Convert), provides them with coaching services (Deliver), and gets paid for the work they do (Collect). A car wash has someone drive up to the business (Attract), ask for a level of washing service (Convert), pay for the service (Collect), and drive into the wash to have the car cleaned (Deliver). Your business gets leads (Attract) that become paying (Collect) clients (Convert), and you provide them with your service or product (Deliver).

THE ACDC MODEL

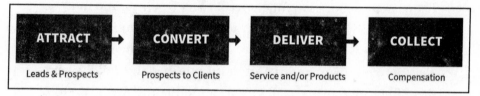

Figure 11

1. **Attract.** Every business needs to attract prospects, or leads, which are inquiries into your product or service. Leads feed your sales. No leads and your sales will dry up because you have no one to sell to.
2. **Convert.** The goal of the sales activity is to *convert* a lead into a paying customer. You may have all the leads in the world, but if you can't convert them into sales, your business is going to die starving for work.
3. **Deliver.** This refers to the processes and services necessary to properly deliver on what you sold to the customer. If you don't deliver on what the customer buys, they will seek a way out—sometimes cancelling their order,

sometimes seeking a refund, possibly spreading the word about how you stink. Can't deliver? You can't stay in business.

4. **Collect.** If the customer doesn't deliver on their promise to pay you, you are in trouble. If you don't collect the money for the work you do or can't keep the money (because the customer takes it back or you blow it), your business is going to die starving for cash.

THE ACDC MODEL

These are the four core functions of every business. You must do them all well. And as we get on to playing the famous game all good business leaders play, "bottleneck whack-a-mole," you will constantly evaluate and fix all the things big and small within these four areas. Almost all businesses follow the ACDC predictable path of sustainability, in the same sequence.

However, there are a few unique cases. For example, some businesses do work "on spec," meaning that the deliverable is completed before the prospect becomes a customer. In this case, the flow would be ADCC.

Collecting cash can be seen as a little bit of a wild card. You, for example, may collect it before you even start the work (the deliverable). But even if you have collected the money before you do the work, it is not really yours until after you deliver on your promise to your client. If you don't, the customer might request their money back. You know, by suing you. That is why I put the categories in this sequence, and why you need at least one metric for each category. This is how you can see the flow of clients through your business.

Let me show you my own dashboard for Profit First Professionals.

1. **Attract.** Your metric for attracting leads may be how many people have completed a specific action. For an online training program, it could be how many people are giving their email address to you in exchange for your free giveaway. For a B2B (business to business), it could be how many people ask for a proposal. For Profit First Professionals (PFP), it's how many people have filled out our initial application form on our website.* If we get three people a day completing that form, that translates to a little more than one thousand applications a year (three leads a day times 365 days). When they fill it out and submit it, we acknowledge it as a lead. When fewer people are filling out a form, that triggers a question. The metric doesn't say that our form isn't working, but that could be the issue. It tells us that we have *some* kind of issue, because fewer people are filling out the form. This leads us to investigate and resolve the problem. Just as when your check engine light comes on, you know that you need to get a diagnostic check. It could be nothing (a loose wire) or it could be big (a busted transmission). When we see our metric fall short of our expectation of three per day, our question is, "Why aren't more people filling out our form?" The answer could be because our website is down, or because people are calling us instead,

---

* We subsequently have improved the process by requiring a small deposit. Prospects now self-select. People who are seriously interested and have done their research move to the front of the line with their deposits. People who are just kicking the tires never leave a deposit and are deprioritized in our Convert process.

or because we have an issue with the QBR (the messenger of Profit First Professionals) and nothing is trickling out on the other side, which means we need to find and fix a bottleneck.

2. **Convert.** Our metric for converting leads into sales is the number of people who join us as new members within three months of originating as a lead. It's a simple percentage: We want a 33 percent conversion rate, which will bring in approximately 360 new members a year. That being said, not all prospects are made the same (you know what I am talking about). Some leads are ideal, some are total tire kickers, others are too early in their business to be a fit, and so on. Some qualitative discussions that come up during our quarterly meetings are how to message better, how to bring in better-qualified leads, and how to sell better so we can more quickly separate the ideal fits from the misfits. The metrics are simply dashboard indicators of performance, but we (and you should) dig deeper to make even more impactful decisions. The way this metric works, we know that if we talk to one hundred people in a month and only ten become members (10 percent instead of 33 percent), something may be askew. Likewise, if eighty become members (as glorious as that sounds), something else may be askew. The metric simply tells you whether something is different from our expectations. When that happens, you need to investigate.* Well outside our 33

---

* Sometimes the gauge in any of these metrics will stay the same, yet there still is a problem. Your sales conversion rate stays at 33 percent, but you are only making one sale a month. That means the problem is likely leads, where, sure enough, there are only three leads that month. But it could be worse. You might have all the leads you expect, and all the conversions, but the new clients might be impossible to retain. A problem like this might reveal itself in a retention metric (showing turnover), but

percent conversion goal? We ask ourselves, "What's going on with sales? Did we introduce a new pricing structure that didn't work? Did we hire a new sales team member? Is the quality of leads changing?" We also look back up the chain. Before conversions is leads, so if we have a red flag with conversions, we ask, "Do we have a slowdown in the leads metric, too?" If so, the problem is likely leads, so we investigate there first.

3. **Deliver.** Do you deliver on what the customer expects (or better)? For some businesses, the best indicator of nailing the deliverables is that customers come back again and again (retention). Another is when customers rave about their experience, therefore gaining additional exposure by word of mouth. Maybe, if you have different standards, it is the lack of complaints. For example, think of a rest stop on a highway. Surely it has happened, but I think that people rarely post, "I just took the most glorious whiz at the most remarkable rest stop ever" or "You have just got to see these urinal cakes. Out. Of. This. World!" If people have anything to say about a rest stop, it's usually a complaint. So the fewer complaints, the better.

At PFP, our deliverables are measured in completed milestones. One of those milestones is certification. This is because I know that once a person gets certified in Profit First, they have completed a sequence of training through PFP and have been adequately trained to pass

---

the problem might be the lead quality. Meaning, sometimes the problem reveals itself elsewhere (retention), but the cause is not there (in this case, leads). Take a lesson from roof repairs. Even though the water leak is coming into your home at the wall, the hole in the roof can be somewhere totally different. Occasionally, problems travel around before they reveal themselves.

that test. I know that if people get the certificate, they have mastered the process in their business and are ready to serve clients. Our metric is how many people have completed their certification within six months of signing up. We want that metric to be 97 percent. While we would love to have 100 percent as our metric, that is not realistic (unforeseen circumstances do happen, such as life events). And aiming for 100 percent means that we would be in a constant red-flag situation. Oh no, we are not at 100 percent again, what happened? Since it is unachievable, we will never get there, which means we will begin to ignore it.

The lesson here is, don't make your metrics dream numbers; make them realistic indicators. As I write this, that metric for our member certification is at about 90 percent. That's lower than the target 97 percent, and I know that means that members are possibly not engaged in some way. Are we falling short on our support to them or have they lost interest? I need to figure it out, since I am sure that at least that missing 7 percent will be less engaged, or less prepared, or need extra attention to catch up.

4. **Collect.** Repeat after me: cash is the lifeblood of my business. Again. Cash is the lifeblood of my business. Cash is the most important yet most overlooked part of every small business. You could not have a single good client, your services could be horrible, and you could be clueless about how to generate leads, but if you have wads of cash, your business will survive. In our organization, we look for the percentage of members who miss a payment during any given month. If that is over 3 percent,

we have an issue. Any time we can make it lower (and we found that offering an annual payment program did), we are feeding our business the money it needs to sustain itself. How is cash flowing (or not flowing) through your business? Determine the metric that you can use to measure its health. Your business's life depends on it.

5. **Queen Bee Role.** The Big Promise for Profit First Professionals is that we are the best method to transition accountants, bookkeepers, and coaches from compliance work (plugging in numbers for their clients) to advisory work (helping their clients with strategic direction for profit). The QBR is the one-on-one coaching from our guide team. Becoming certified in Profit First is one key part, but working in a brand-new capacity with your clients, as an advisor, is difficult when you have never done it before. It is like transitioning from playing soccer to coaching it. Different skills.

The metric for the QBR is simple: it is our members doing the implementations with clients. Our guide team gives our members (clients) specific directions on how to do the consultative work with Profit First. Our members are directed on how to do calls with existing clients, how to discuss Profit First, how to do full profit assessments and rollouts. But unless they get the experience under their belt, it is all just theory. So our team tracks member implementations. Because when you do, you improve.

As our organization grows, so does the QBR activity. We have more guides guiding. And some of our member organizations have grown to the point where they have a team of certified Profit First Professionals working within their company. They are using the same QBR metric to track internally how much implementation activity their Profit First employees are doing. The demand on the QBR is growing, and we know that because the QBR is being tracked. And that means our impact is growing. But if the QBR metric indicates a problem, we are right back to fixing that.

The four core areas—Attract, Convert, Deliver, and Collect (ACDC)—become the gauges on your dashboard, along with the QBR. What you need to do first is identify how you measure progress (or the lack thereof) in each of these five spots, and what your goal is for each. When implementing metrics, don't go overboard, because more than five can be overwhelming. Too many dials and too many instruments make it difficult for you to notice when something isn't working, which defeats the purpose of having a dashboard.

Imagine a security guard on the night shift. The guard can stare at six different screens and easily spot the slightest movement. But give that guard six hundred screens and you can be sure that he will miss something. In every movie where that bad guy gets past the security guard watching the monitors, it's because the guard has too many freaking monitors or got distracted by the "suspicious noise" of that metal object the bad guy just threw down the hallway. (It always works like a charm.) A dashboard allows you to be the security guard for your business, so the fewer metrics you have to monitor, the better. And for God's sake, don't fall for the "noise down the hallway" trick—it's always a trap.

WHEN YOUR BUSINESS RUNS *TOO* EFFICIENTLY

When Andrew Johnson and his siblings took over their family business, O-Ring Sales & Service Inc., a physical goods distribution company in Lenexa, Kansas, they set an optimization goal that they called "15-15-15." That translated to running the company with a team of fifteen, using only 15,000 square feet of warehouse space, and generating $15 million in annual revenue. To reach those goals, they would have to be extremely efficient in every aspect of their business.

"It became an arms race for internal efficiencies," Andrew told me when I interviewed him for this book.

And that race worked well. Actually, too well. When O-Ring Sales & Service received an order, a picker would take a basket, walk the aisles, and pick items to ship. Because Andrew and his siblings had set their 15-15-15 goal, they came up with strategies and inventions that they might not have considered if they had not imposed those constraints. They created a new shopping cart with a picking system—made from a car battery, a mini-computer and screen, and a scanning wand. They got so much faster that the limit was how fast the carts (ahem, people) could move.

Every day, they checked their metrics. They pushed harder. They dug deeper. They were almost there. They had seventeen employees, were using about 18,000 square feet of warehouse space, and were bringing in $14 million. And then the cracks started to show.

The pickers pushing the carts were at their limits. They could only move so fast, so as they tried to keep up with the newly optimized system, they got overwhelmed. They made mistakes. They needed breaks, but the optimization goal wouldn't allow that. Maxed out, they exploded at each other.

"I was willing to get over to the warehouse and start cracking the whip harder, but I realized that to get to 15-15-15 and maintain it would have such a cost to human capital," Andrew said. "People will lose their minds. Employees will quit. It would be very caustic. We needed a more measured approach because people are our greatest assets. If we lost great people because we're maniacal maniacs, singularly focused on getting to some lofty number, then we are stupid. They are the ones going insane because we are the ones who are insane."

Andrew and his siblings realized that efficiency may drive profit, but it can go too far. People can be the grease of the gears, and if you lose good people, no matter how fast your gears are spinning, they will burn up and grind to a halt. Great systems with people who don't do a great job, or no people at all, fail. Ironically, marginal systems with great people can still squeak by.

ONE DIAL AT A TIME

It is easy to assume that a business will have multiple bottlenecks at any given time, but by the nature of bottlenecks, there can only be one. Imagine an hourglass, with the one choke point in the middle. Now add three more choke points of different sizes. The sand will pile up at the narrowest choke point, regardless of where it is. That is the one bottleneck for everything else. And if every choke point is the exact same size (which practically never happens in real life), the bottleneck is the first one in the sequence. Once a bottleneck is opened up, the next-slowest spot that reveals itself is the new bottleneck. There is always only one. It just moves.

Fixing a bottleneck is "easy," right? Just push harder. You're busting your ass out there, burning a bucket of candles at both ends, so you damn well better get results. The reality is that effort only works well when focused on the right thing. I know a guy who put a ton of effort into the wrong things, and very often into multiple wrong things at the same time. (I'm not naming names, but it might rhyme with Pike Pichalowicz.) Many entrepreneurs fall into the same trap. This is why I wrote *Fix This Next*, to help business owners identify the one *right* thing they need to address next.

To find your "one right thing," go through each of the metrics associated with ACDC. Ask yourself what you expect for each metric and what you have to do to fix the one that is currently the biggest impediment to the entire system.

My lawnmower stopped working the summer I started writing the first edition of this book. It began sputtering randomly and instead of cutting the grass, it was lightly fanning it—moving the grass from one side to the other. Off to the shed I went to repair this beast once and for all, and I immediately committed the cardinal sin. I tried to fix all the possible causes at once. I cleaned the carburetor, replaced the air filter, changed the oil, sharpened the blade, and refueled it, all at one time. Then I tried to start the engine. This time, it ran worse.

Because none of my efforts had fixed the problem, I readied myself for extreme engine repair. I gave it new belts and new spark plugs and flushed the engine with a cleaner. Sure enough, it didn't work. Finally, after two days of working on the mower, I brought it into a shop. Thirty minutes later it was fixed. The problem? The carburetor was damaged, presumably by me. (I won't confirm or deny jamming the cover back into place when it wouldn't #$@!% close properly.) The original problem was likely a clogged air filter. But even though I fixed that, I "fixed" other things at the same time, which actually caused a new problem, which I mistakenly concluded was the same as the original problem.

The point is, when you work on multiple things at once to fix one problem, you may actually fix and unfix the problem all in one shot, not realizing that you actually had fixed it and what the cause was. The solution is to work on one piece at a time and see if that fixes the problem. Start with the most likely issue, test it, and then move to the next likely issue.

The dashboard of your business is a good indicator of what to investigate and possibly fix next. At times things will fail, and when that happens you need to turn (fix) one dial at a time.

Take sales, for example. Let's say you notice that you have a big sales drop-off. You notice that lead flow has not changed much at all, and, if anything, has increased, but the sales team is selling way less. You hired a new salesperson who is coming up to speed, and you see that their sales are far lower than you expected. So you set out to fix it. But you try to turn too many dials at once: you give them a new sales script to follow. You give them more leads than the rest of the team so they can cut their teeth faster. Instead of one of your experienced people giving sales training, you now have two working with the new guy in the hope that they will gain even more knowledge. With all the fixes in place, sales are sure to increase. But they drop further. Why? Is it the script? Is this person handling too many leads at once? Or maybe the salesperson is too intimidated when two people are watching over their shoulder.

Rewind and start again. This time, turn one dial at a time. Sales are slower since the new guy started. You conclude that the two things are probably related. You go to the obvious thing, the script, and just turn that dial. You change the script to an easier version. Then you observe. Sales don't move up or down. Now you go back to the prior sales script, setting the dial back to its original setting, and then move the next dial. Thinking it has something to do with the training, you try having two salespeople work with the new guy. As before, sales don't increase, but in fact drop sharp and fast. Interesting. You found a dial that is negatively affecting sales. Now you investigate this oddity.

When you go back to just one salesperson mentoring the new guy, sales go up but stay lower than your historical average. Then you try the crazy idea of eliminating the role of sales mentor, and sales go back to normal. Weird. Now you know exactly what is causing your problem, and you do a deep investigation. You discover that your sales mentors, when working with the new salesperson, were putting off their own sales calls. Prospects were calling the mentors and waiting and waiting for a response. So you move the mentoring work to after-hours and improve it with the use of some technology—recording calls. Now your best salespeople are closing deals, and then going over the recordings of those calls with the new salesperson after-hours. And guess what? Sales skyrocket.

Sometimes, when you spot a problem on your dashboard in one category, the problem can be emanating from another. For example, the challenge with collections is that some people get paid before they actually do the work. That's great, but if your business has a cash-flow issue, is it really a collections issue? When you look at your dashboard, you might see that your sales are down and your leads metrics are right on point. What could that mean? Perhaps because wannabe customers are required to pay up front, no one is buying. The fix? Testing one dial at a time. Try removing the up-front payment requirement and see what happens. If things go back to normal, you found the cause. But if it doesn't fix it, then—and this is the key—put the up-front payment requirement back and go for the next fix. You have to test each dial independently to find the cause.

If multiple things can affect an outcome, changing those things at the same time can cloud the solution. Use the technique of A/B testing. Try A and then try B and then compare. Yes, you could get more sophisticated in your testing, but the moment you put yourself in the position of being unsure of cause and effect, you will impede your ability to fix the problem with confidence. Turn the dials in sequence until you find the cause, and only after you do the single dial turns, consider multiple dial turns where a contingency may be in place requiring multiple dials to be turned to fix it.

That last line is a particularly important one. Businesses are complex beasts. It is possible that the cause and effect do not have a one-to-one relationship. It could be that multiple components are affecting an outcome at the same time. But it is really time-consuming to find solutions by trying a mix of fixes simultaneously. Start with the usual suspects and the easiest tests first. If the obvious, easy, fast, and cheap fixes don't bring about the solution, you will be forced to do multiple dial turns.

Moving one dial at a time for one problem at a time seems very time-consuming. So the question that begs to be asked is, "Can you ever fix more than one thing at once?" When analyzing a specific situation where multiple dials could potentially influence the outcome, most often the answer is no. You must move one dial at a time to fix one problem. But when your company is working on independent problems, and the dials address different outcomes, you can turn multiple dials at the same time. Always prioritize the most important bottleneck, and only address other independent bottlenecks at the same time if you have the capacity to do so.

For example, I may determine that the most important current bottleneck is a Convert problem, so I want to try turning the dial of revisiting past prospects who didn't convert. I may also have a Deliver bottleneck that has customers waiting to talk with an implementation specialist, so I want to try turning the dial of doing group sessions for implementation instead of one-on-one. Those are distinct dials that affect distinct outcomes, so I can try both simultaneously. That's a specific opportunity we had in my business, and we had enough people and capacity to turn both of those dials at the same time. And each one improved its specific outcome.

The other situation where you can turn multiple dials is when you have a known problem and a known solution. This is the old been-there-done-that situation. Our bank recently stopped doing an automatic transfer associated with our Profit First implementation. This happens every so often. In the past, this meant that the password had expired and the processing bank failed the transaction. Then, perhaps as a precautionary measure, or because there's a bug in the system, it disconnects the transfer accounts and locks the account. So the dials to be turned are: set a new password, unlock the account, and relink the account. Oh, and the fourth move, which is for my assistant, Erin Chazotte, to wait on hold for eternity and, when she gets through, to tell the manager that this is the fifth time in just as many years we have had to call in for this problem. Because asking didn't seem to fix it, on the last call Erin (who doesn't mince words) asked for the mailing address of the bank president so they could be "gifted" a copy of *Clockwork* and read this story specifically.

I know this may seem like a lot of dial turnin', and you may question your ability to recognize when some aspects of your business need to be tweaked, but you've got this. You *do*.

In 2018, my father had a health issue that scared the living bejeezus out of our family. As he was rushed to the hospital, he was immediately put on certain machines to measure critical vital signs. His pulse, blood pressure, and temperature were monitored. While none of those were his immediate problem, they are critical to life and therefore were monitored. His "bottleneck" was diagnosed by its symptoms: extreme weakness, dehydration, hallucinations. The belief was that it could be a stroke or a urinary tract infection (which manifests in the elderly with symptoms like those he was experiencing). The test showed a urinary tract infection and he was put on antibiotics. Metrics were put in place and his health recovered slowly but surely. And the metrics showed that his health improved as the urinary tract infection went away. Two weeks later, we all celebrated my pop's ninetieth birthday, with the big guy blowing out the candles with one sturdy exhalation. If the metrics had not been in place, I can only imagine the horrible consequences.

With a clearly defined QBR and a team focused on ensuring that the QBR is delivered consistently, without fail, you can monitor the health of your business using a dashboard made up of simple metrics. You must have numbers that tell you the normal expectations for the four core parts of your business: Attracting (leads), Converting (sales), Delivering (your promise), and Collecting (their promise). The numbers don't lie. But they don't tell you the whole story, either. They simply flag an opportunity to fix or amplify something. With the metric flag raised, take action and investigate. You can finally fully step away from your business and manage by the numbers. And you can still experience joy and fulfillment as you grow your business. Even if you only work a few hours a week.

FOR EMPLOYEES: CORA'S STORY

Cora works in the D of ACDC. She works with the big equipment now, but she is still responsible for the integration of home and nature. While her activities have changed, the impact of her work is the same, and that affects the A and the C. So she is regularly meeting with the sales team, telling them the new techniques they can use and the new stuff they can do. With this knowledge, the sales team is better equipped to sell benefits to Job Turf's customers. So even though she does not work on the Attract or Convert elements of the company, she influences them by sharing the company's newest capabilities.

Cora also actively listens. The marketing and sales teams share what they are doing so she can enhance the delivery of work. During one session, a sales rep mentioned that a client asked if Job Turf uses a hydro-excavation system. Which they did not. Cora jumped on the opportunity to research hydro-excavation and submitted a report to Calvin and Gordon for consideration. She thinks it may be the most environmentally sound method for large digging projects and could replace the spade on the skid steer. This free flow of communication up and down the ACDC chain ensures that the Big Promise is kept, and that the business is always improving.

How can you help? First, know which element of ACDC your Primary Job falls into. Sometimes it's obvious. If you're a salesperson, you work in the Convert stage. Other times, it may not be as clear. For example, if you write copy for the packaging for your company's products. Since your goal is to get the attention of retail shoppers, you may wonder if your work falls under Attract. That copy is also designed to get them to buy, so maybe your work is in Convert. Then again, the copy also includes instructions about how to use the products, so one could argue that your work is also in the Deliver element. Maybe the answer is all three, but only one can be the most important. When you're confused, have a conversation—a lesson I learned from my mom. To get clarity about which ACDC element you serve, talk with your manager.

Once you are clear about where your work fits in the ACDC chain, connect with people who serve other parts of the chain and show them how you operate. When you understand each other's workflow and management, you can help each other produce better results.

When you know the area (or areas) you serve within the ACDC chain, monitor the flow. Do things slow down or speed up? What do you notice when these changes happen? Is there something that can be changed to improve efficiency? Ask yourself these questions as you do your work. Then work with leadership to see if you can institute improvements. Hey, if you actively make the company better, maybe you are making yourself more valuable. Just sayin'.

 ## CLOCKWORK IN ACTION

Take twenty minutes right now and determine the core metrics you want to use to create your own dashboard. Remember to keep it simple; it's too hard to track too many things. Set your smartphone alarm or timer for twenty minutes, and just get started identifying those core metrics—those few things that best measure the health of your business.

The ideal metrics to create always include a way to measure QBR performance as well as the bottleneck(s) you have identified with the ACDC. What are the key things you think you can do to increase the flow through your ACDC? Identify those metrics and measure the progress over time. Where do you think your business is at the most risk when there is a problem in the ACDC? What dimensions of the business are you trying to improve? Determine metrics to help you monitor those things.

Still struggling or want to bring in an expert to help you fully design a business that runs itself, one that *runs like clockwork*? If you want to learn how we can help you, go to runlikeclockwork.com.

CHAPTER ELEVEN

TAKE THE FOUR-WEEK VACATION

COMMIT TO THE ONE ACTION THAT WILL ENSURE YOUR BUSINESS PERMANENTLY RUNS ITSELF

Two years from now my family and I will be living in Italy. We will be sipping on limoncellos from our apartment balcony overlooking Rome."

When Greg Redington made that announcement to our mastermind group during our perfunctory pre-meeting personal updates, it caught everyone's attention. It wasn't what we expected to hear. When one of us asks, "Anything cool going on?" the replies are typically one of the famous three: "Nah, nothing new," "All is good," or "I've got this weird pain in my [fill in the blank]." But Italy? Huh? WTF?

At first, we thought Greg was joking, that he was just making a flippant comment. When we realized he was serious, we were all taken aback.

"Greg, do you mean *Italy* Italy? Like the boot-shaped country? Or are you talking about that new Little Italy neighborhood popping up in your town?" I asked, still confused about the prospect of Greg leaving his booming business in New Jersey to head to another country permanently. Or at least permanently enough that he was going to declare Rome as his new hometown and the Pantheon as his favorite stop for a morning cup o' joe.

Greg is the founder of REDCOM Design & Construction LLC, a commercial construction management firm serving New York and New Jersey. He had grown his business into a substantial company, earning $25 million in annual revenue. He enjoyed the work tremendously, but the business was still dependent on him. Greg wanted more out of life and more time *in* his life. He wanted to be released from serving the QBR.

Greg's gift is meticulousness. You see it in the way he dresses, the home he keeps, even the way he talks. He is specific. He is detailed. He is exacting. REDCOM has built its reputation on that meticulousness. In an industry where construction errors, redos, and on-the-fly changes are commonplace, REDCOM's Big Promise is that they do the project right from start to finish. They build magnificent structures perfectly the first time, every time. You know, like the Pantheon, but in New Jersey. But up until this point, Greg was serving the QBR of detailed, daily checkups during construction. As the final step of designing his business to run itself, he had to step out of serving it. And he wanted to do it in grand fashion, by living out a long-held dream.

When my fellow masterminds pushed Greg for more details, he explained that he had wanted to move his family to Rome, Italy, for a year. To do that, he committed to the final stage of establishing a Clockwork business. He removed himself from his business, to a point where it had to stand on its own. And the result was astonishing. Greg returned from Italy after two years to a business that was now double its size, earning $50 million in annual revenue, and with double the team.

That's what I'm working toward, and what I call on you to work toward. Not the number, but the freedom where you can leave the business and still have it drive forward. You've already made significant headway in that direction. You've Aligned your company around serving your Top Clients, your Big Promise, and your QBR. You've Integrated that clarity into the day-to-day operations of your business so that everyone serves and protects the QBR and then focuses on their Primary Job; you and your team have a more optimal 4D Mix and have Trashed, Transferred, Trimmed, or Treasured tasks; and you have Captured systems so that anyone can step in to do almost any task. And in this Accelerate phase, you've balanced your team and identified and fixed your bottlenecks. Hopefully, you've already started to see improvements in business efficiency. You've calmed your mind and developed systems. Heck, just by reading this book all the way through you're further along than most entrepreneurs. Now it is time to do the ultimate Accelerate move: schedule your intentional disruption, the four-week vacation. Remember, this is not just you getting a much-needed break from your business. It is your business getting a much-needed break from *you*.

You can do this. I promise you, you can. And sure, maybe some people will think you're joking when you tell them your plan. You may get pushback from your friends, who may be jealous because, for whatever reason, they are not able to take a four-week vacation. You may get strong pushback from your family, who may be nervous about money. You may get pushback from your colleagues, who don't believe that taking a four-week vacation is possible or deserved for business owners. And you will surely get pushback from that good ol' naysaying pal of yours, the voice in your head that says ugly things like "you can't do this" and "this won't work." It's okay. In my experience, pushback from others and your inner critic is usually a sign that you're doing something that challenges the preprogrammed, drone-like mindset that asserts things need to be the way they always have been. Of course, you'll want to address your family's concerns about money so that they can enjoy the vacation (*cough,* read *Profit First, cough cough*), but ignore the rest. You've worked the system, and now you're going to reap the rewards.

You may fear taking a four-week vacation because you aren't sure what you'll do with yourself. You're so conditioned to use every free moment for Doing, you may not even remember what it's like to have down time. If you aren't working, who are you? The reality is, part of you will still be working on your business. Finally, you'll have the space to think. After you remove yourself physically and digitally from your company, and after you've had enough rest, your mind will naturally start to strategize. Those five-minute shower inspiration moments will turn into four weeks of big ideas. Even if all you do with your four weeks off is sit in your backyard and watch the squirrels, you and your business will be better for it. After all, if your business can hold its own—and even experience growth—with you out of the picture, how much easier will it be to run your business when you get back? (Answer: Heaps. Tons. Loads easier.)

You don't need to leave that vacation behind, either. Greg didn't. After two years of living in Rome, it was tough for him to leave Italy. So when he returned to his company, he made sure he brought a little bit of Italy back with him. No, not a limoncello. Greg brought back a Fiat Cinquecento. The fabled minicar is parked inside his office's "hangar" for display and quick drives. On a warm spring day, he'll take it for a little drive. Not all over town, of course, just in Little Italy.

And what about working in his business? Was Greg happy to return to serving the QBR? Actually, yes. That is the power of Clockwork. You aren't forced to leave your business; you are *freed* to leave. This means you are free to do what your heart sings out to do. Greg thrives on overseeing detailed construction projects by checking in on the daily progress at sites. When he returned from his dream of living in Italy, he did only the work he wanted to do. Greg has become a specialty player for his company. He no longer swoops in to "fix things." The company is running well on its own, and he is free to do the work he does best and loves best. And the results are even more magnificent.

WHY A FOUR-WEEK VACATION?

As I explained earlier in the book, almost all companies go through a full business cycle within four weeks. This means that most businesses have activity within all four of the ACDC stages of an organization: Attract, Convert, Deliver, Collect. If you look at your company over the last month, it is likely there was some effort made to attract clients. Perhaps you had another client give you a referral, or you ran an ad, or you spoke at a conference, or you sent out an announcement, or you had visitors at your website, or a combination of all of the above. It is also likely that during the past four weeks your business made an effort to convert prospects into new clients. Maybe you had a sales call, or your website has an active "buy now" option, or an automated email campaign asked for the sale. In short, you tried (and hopefully have been able) to persuade someone to buy from you. During the last four weeks, you probably worked on a project for a client, or created a product, or shipped goods; you tried to deliver something in part or in whole per a request of a client. And throughout the last four weeks, you managed the cash flow; you probably paid some money out and (hopefully) brought some more in.

In a four-week cycle, most businesses will also experience internal issues or challenges, big or small—an interpersonal conflict on your team, a friggin' pandemic, a technology breakdown, someone forgetting to do something, or someone remembering to do something but, unfortunately, it's the wrong thing. And during those four weeks you'll also probably deal with external problems, such as disgruntled customers or a competitor's new product launch or a banking error or a vendor failing to deliver on a promise.

At our company, every employee takes a four-week (consecutive) vacation every year. As the owner, at first, I was terrified to be without a key employee for that length of time. Until I saw the results. Everyone on the team has everyone's back. We are stronger and leaner than our competitors. And my already loyal and amazing team are even more invested in the company's success.

When you—or anyone on your team—are removed from the business for four weeks, it is likely that the vast majority of things your company faces on a daily basis will happen, so you must find a way for the work to get done and the problems to be solved in your absence. When you are gone for only a few days, your team can often delay the resolution of problems until you return. But if you are gone for a few weeks, the business is forced to support itself. And when it can support itself for four weeks, you know you have achieved a Clockwork business. You can put the certified stamp of Clockwork approval on your company's door, and now you have the freedom to get out of Dodge permanently, if you like.

Warning: booking a four-week vacation in the next year can result in panic attacks, nausea, and mumbling to yourself. It can feel so scary that you just don't do it. That is why you run abbreviated test vacations. Maybe you start with a scheduled three-day break, then a week, then two weeks, and so on.

Let's put your business to the test and get you out of the office and to destination "outta-here."

YES, YOUR TEAM CAN HANDLE IT

How many times have you left for a vacation—even a weekend getaway—and made sure your team had a way to contact you in case of an emergency? Probably every time you go anywhere for longer than a few days. Or hours. Or just to the bathroom. When you do that, you're telling your team that they can't (and shouldn't) handle the emergency on their own. And if you believe that, it's because you haven't prepared them. You haven't clockworked your business.

A few days into Leslie Liondas's first one-week test vacation, Winter Storm Uri blew through Texas. Her CPA firm in Jackson was right in the heart of it. That tragic storm caused the Texas power grid crisis that left most of the state without power for days. With Leslie and her business partner both away and unplugged, that left their team to try to figure out how to run payroll for dozens of clients—without power.

"We're south of Houston on the Gulf," Leslie told me. "We never see snow."

The freak blizzard of February 2021 wreaked havoc on Texas and neighboring states. Everything shut down and many people went into panic mode. Nobody got work done. But because they'd been clockworking their business for years, Leslie's five employees knew exactly what to do. Even the marketing person sprang into action.

As a result of the power grid failure, Texas experienced rolling blackouts. When a two-hour window of electricity opened up, the marketer drove to the office and processed as much payroll as she could before the power shut off again. One team member managed to get a big client's payroll handled *from her car.*

"Our clients never saw any glitch in our systems," Leslie said.

"We didn't even get a phone call asking, 'Hey, is my payroll going to be run?' They just assumed we would take care of it and everything would be great."

As it turned out, other CPA firms in the area struggled to fulfill their obligations to clients—and some people did not get paid. Some payroll agency owners had to figure out how to deliver services themselves because their teams either couldn't get into the office or had to stay with their children. Leslie's employees also had kids *and* struggled to get to the office, but they worked together to solve the problem.

Leslie said, "They actually felt more empowered because they handled it, and they handled it together. It seemed to bring them closer because they went through it together."

If you've clockworked your team, trust them to handle not just the day-to-day operations, but emergencies, too. Even the worst ice storm in Texas history can't bring them down.

GO ON VACATION—FOR REAL

For years I pondered how to get out of my own businesses. No matter if I was Doing the work, Deciding for others about the work, Delegating the work, or Designing the work, I always felt trapped by the business. I was sure that I "just had to be there." As I shared in Chapter One, even on the few occasions that I took a vacation, I didn't really "vacate"—I may have physically left, but I stayed connected. I would contact the office multiple times during the day. I would check email constantly. I would "sneak away" to make client calls, to write proposals, to just work. Then one day I accidentally learned how to take a *real* vacation, one that disconnects you from your business so that it needs to live on its own.

I went to Maine.

Now, there are plenty of places to visit in Maine that will allow you to stay connected to your business. The place we chose to visit—not so much. I booked a vacation at an all-inclusive camp in the Lakes and Mountains region of Maine, called Grant's Kennebago Camps. I fit the planning for the vacation into my busy work schedule, so in my haste I didn't fully examine the camp's website. I saw the "all-inclusive meals" part. I saw the beautiful lake. I saw pictures of families boating and having fun, all with big smiles on their faces.

What escaped my attention was that, in those pictures, mom and dad and their kiddos were wearing camouflage.

When we arrived at the camp, we quickly realized I had booked our family vacation at a hunting and fishing camp. And the only "family" part about the camp was that the campers were hunting families of deer.

We were totally disconnected from the outside world—no cell, no TV, no nothing. The only radio station we could find was broadcasting out of Canada. In French.

The first day, I was in detox from constant connection. *Will the business die without me?* The second day, I began to analyze my options. *I could drive into town every day to check in.* The nearest town was an hour away, and I was seriously contemplating a two-hour round-trip commute to check in with work. *Or I could just enjoy the time with my family. All of it.* By the third day, I was at peace and loved the vacation.

I'm sure you're not surprised—the business didn't die. Did my team have problems? Sure. Did they fix the problems on their own? Some of them, yes. For those problems they couldn't solve, they bought time so I could fix them when I returned. They did a great job managing our customers' expectations, which meant that, even though they did have problems, the customers knew their problems were being addressed.

We ended up having the time of our lives. We skipped rocks, hiked, and boated around the lake. We spotted geese and mooses! Or is it meese and gooses? The vacation was so powerful that right then and there we declared the moose our family mascot. It is powerful and serene, even though the impression at first glance is that it is a little bit goofy, which is very much our family creed.

Today I reflect back on that life-defining vacation and remember everything with such joy. Including the hysterical "bat attack" and "leech assault" and "lobster reanimation" stories that Krista and I will gladly share with you over dinner. We recall every single detail of those stories and more. The daily work I missed? I don't recall anything about it. In fact, I can't remember a single business initiative I had going on then. But I do remember a light-bulb moment. As I sat in a rocking chair watching the sunset, it struck me that the traditional pyramid organization chart used by most companies is the root of poor decision-making, even though it is intended to be the opposite. In the years since, I have played with and tested a new concept that I will share in future work.

When I wrote the first edition of this book, I was planning my four-week vacation, and at the top of my mind was how to ensure a disconnection. I had to guard against my own weakness for finding excuses to "check in" and ruining the test. When you think about where you want to go on your vacation, and what you want to experience, take into account how connected you want to be. The first time I visited Australia, I was in a different, upside-down time zone from my team, and so I felt completely disconnected—even though I had email and could video-call and text. And boy, did I use that technology to screw things up and annoy my team. Will you need to force the disconnection by choosing a place with limited options for you to check in with work? Maybe. It certainly helps.

Design your vacation around the type of experience you and

your loved ones would like to have, with the intent of being disconnected. Enjoying yourself while away will help you keep your mind off the business, and the inability to connect will protect you from caving in to the temptation to "check in" and F everything up.

You need to plan your four-week vacation now, even if you are a single-practitioner business, because even a single-practitioner business can find ways to have at least partial independence from the owner doing all the work. You can empower vendors. You can automate processes and deliverables. The technology exists and the subcontractors are out there to bring large amounts of independence to any size business.

Some single-practitioner businesses get confused with a one-person operation. That is not necessarily true, nor should it be. A single-practitioner business means that the owner is actively involved in every facet of the business, but it does not mean they do everything. The use of vendors, such as a web designer or graphic designer, is delegation. If you have a cell phone, you are delegating a system to manage communication for you.

No matter how isolated you believe you are, you are utilizing others without a conscious awareness. Now you can make that delegation conscious. Ask yourself what things you do that a vendor could do. What next thing can you take off your plate and have a virtual assistant do for you?

Start transferring stuff off your plate. If you have no clue where to start, hire a part-time personal assistant, someone to help you with any aspect of your life that will create more time for your business. If your assistant helps you schedule your doctor appointments, or picks up your kids from school, or just gets you coffee—that is all time freed up for you to serve your company better. It doesn't matter how small (or big) your business is or how much revenue you do or don't make. Anyone and everyone can significantly benefit in building a business by hiring a personal assistant. Even if all you can afford is a few hours a week.

And if you happen to be a personal assistant yourself, you still need to hire a personal assistant. You can't be an assistant to yourself. That's not how Clockwork works.

The four-week vacation does not need to be something extravagant. You can do it anywhere you want and within a budget that you can afford. You just need to achieve certain goals:

1. Physically disconnect from the office.
2. Virtually disconnect from the office. There is a way to do this, even if there is cell reception and Wi-Fi where you are. Hint: ask a colleague to change the passwords on all your business apps. You can change them back when you return to work.
3. Let the business run for the entire time without you connecting. You can go to Maine (awesome) or you can go to your mother-in-law's (let's just say that it may not rank up there with Maine). But there is a budget-friendly way to do this. Your business needs you to do this so it can grow. *You* need to do this so *you* can grow.

OPERATION VACATION

When planning your four-week vacation, start by picking a date that is eighteen to twenty-four months from today. Yes, you can do it faster and split in six months. Or super fast and just split tomorrow. But that likely won't give you time to prepare. If you plan your four-week vacation more than a year out, you'll have a chance to live and work through that same four-week span on the calendar year, which is crucial to effective planning.

Once you commit to your vacation, you will likely notice an immediate shift in your mind. First you'll have the "Oh, shit, what have I done?" moment. That's normal. You'll get over that within forty-eight hours. Then you will notice that your focus is no longer on the super short term, or simply what is urgent now. Thoughts such as "How do I get through today?" will shift to "How can I make this happen without me?" or "What needs to change so that this aspect of my business can run without dependency on me?"

To make your life easier, I have broken down the tasks you need to complete at various milestones. This will help you stay the course so you can actually *get* to Rome, or Maine, or Rome, Maine (yes, it exists), or wherever you want to hang for twenty-eight days.

EIGHTEEN MONTHS OUT—DECLARE IT

1. Put your vacation dates on the calendar. Block off four consecutive weeks. Do this *now*, as you read this. Don't delay. Your freedom and your company's success depend on it.
2. Tell your family, your loved ones, the people who will hold you accountable, about your vacation—especially if they are coming with you! They will hold your feet to the fire.
3. If you haven't done this yet, declare yourself the shareholder of your small business. Use your new title forevermore and start acting accordingly. In the beginning of the book, I asked you to email me and put in the subject

line, "I'm a shareholder!" If you haven't done that yet, do it now (my email is Mike@MikeMichalowicz.com). And no matter what, going forward anytime someone asks you what you do, respond with "I'm a shareholder of a small business." It may be awkward in the beginning, but we comply with how we identify. The shift will happen and you will, by definition, do less and design more.

SEVENTEEN MONTHS OUT—RUN A TIME ANALYSIS

1. Run a Time Analysis of your work. Track and analyze your time for at least one "typical" week. Complete all other Clockwork exercises for yourself.

FOURTEEN MONTHS OUT—TELL YOUR TEAM

1. Tell your team about your commitment to your four-week vacation. Explain why you are doing this and the outcome you are hoping to achieve. Tell them you trust them to "run the ship." Explain the benefit to the business of not having dependency on the owner.
2. Invite them to ask questions and share concerns. Empower them to achieve the outcome. (Remember the Delegating phase of business growth?)
3. Ask them for support. Make it clear to them that you don't expect them to work harder. Tell them the goal is to automate the business as much as possible. And the goal is never to defer or delay, because that does not address problems. The goal is for the problems to present themselves, and to be addressed without you.

    a. If I may suggest, give each employee a copy of *Clockwork, Revised and Expanded* to read. As you've noticed, there is a section in each chapter dedicated specifically to the employee of a Clockwork company. They should still read (or listen to) the entire book to better understand the system, how it works, and their role in this shift to awesome organizational efficiency.

4. Establish better cross-communication among team members.

    a. Have a clear line of responsibility for each role in the business (who is the person responsible for ensuring that the job is done and done right?), and have a backup person for each role if the primary person is unable to cover.

    b. Get a daily huddle going. You can do this in person or virtually, but it is a must. Review key performance metrics for the company. Have each person share the big thing they accomplished the day before, then share the big thing they are doing today and why it is important. Then give shout-outs to other employees and share a personal update. A recording of one of my company's daily huddles is available at clockwork.life.

TWELVE MONTHS OUT—CUT DOWN ON DOING

1. Have a meeting with your team to determine what you need to stop Doing. Write up an action plan to Trash, Transfer, Trim, and Treasure all your actions, including your QBR work.

2. Now that they've had two months to read up on the Clockwork system, have a discussion. What are their concerns, if any? What are they most excited about implementing first? What are their ideas? Should your team have regular Clockwork discussions and status check-ins?

3. If you haven't already, have your team go through all the Clockwork exercises.

4. Within the next two months, commit to cutting down your Doing workload to under 80 percent of your time. Trash, Transfer, Trim, and Treasure. You may already be below 80 percent, and that is great. If that's the case, try to cut another 10 percent of Doing work off your plate and push your time toward Designing.

5. Commit to putting in substitutes for the QBR so that you are not the only one serving it.

6. Visualize your four-week vacation and how it will affect your business. What issues do you anticipate coming up while you're away? How smoothly will your business run without you?

7. If you haven't done so already, book your vacation. Make reservations, make deposits, buy tickets, tell the mom-in-law to start cooking because you're coming, order the materials for that big home project—whatever you need to do to make a full commitment. There's no turning back now, pal!

8. You can get professional help with organizational efficiency, too. Whereas some people join a gym and work out of their own volition, others have much greater success when they get the guidance (and accountability) of a trainer. You can go to runlikeclockwork.com to get a "trainer" to guide your business to run like, you know, clockwork.

TEN MONTHS OUT—DEEPER CUTS TO DOING

1. Run a fresh Time Analysis on yourself. Confirm you are under 80 percent Doing or better.
2. Meet with your team to cut your Doing time to less than 40 percent. As much as possible, allocate your freed-up time to Designing.

EIGHT MONTHS OUT—MEASURE PROGRESS AND ESTABLISH BACKUPS

1. Run a Time Analysis on yourself, again. Confirm you are at less than 40 percent Doing.
2. Commit to achieving 0 percent Doing time within the next sixty days.
3. Meet with your team to plan and measure progress.
4. Identify backups and redundancy for each person.

SIX MONTHS OUT—RUN A TEST

1. Run a one-week vacation test. Head out of town to a place with no internet connection. Or do a virtual disconnect and stay home. Just don't go to the office and don't connect remotely. Expect withdrawal symptoms, including headaches, random crying fits, and more mumbling to yourself. But also expect moments of clarity, moments of thinking about your business as a business, not a fire station.
2. Have a team meeting on your first day back. Review what worked and what didn't. Make improvements and fixes.

3. Confirm plans for your four-week vacation.

4. Commit to reducing your Deciding and Delegating time to 5 percent and increasing your Designing time to 95 percent, by two months out.

FOUR MONTHS OUT—RUN MORE TESTS

1. Week One, run another one-week vacation test. No connection for seven days. You will be disconnected but your brain will be on the business (at times). This is you turning into a true shareholder. Expect some break-through thoughts on ways to strategically improve your business.

2. Week Two, come back for a week. Meet with your team to debrief and fix the roadblocks before your four-week vacation.

3. Week Three, run another one-week vacation. No connection. You will surely be thinking about the business. Conceptualize strategies and systems that you can implement. When you get to your four-weeker, you will be ready for profound thoughts (like master yogi–type stuff).

4. Week Four, meet again to debrief and fix.

TWO MONTHS OUT—PLAN FULL DISCONNECT

1. Run another Time Analysis on yourself over a two-week period. Confirm that you are at 0 percent Doing. If not, establish a plan to get there immediately.

2. Plan a full disconnect with your team. Who will be responsible for monitoring your email, social media

outlets, and other communication platforms? When you leave, they'll have to change your passwords and not give them to you until you return. That way they can manage your accounts and you can't access them. Two birds. One stone.

3. Who will take your cell phone? If you will be near a land-line (do they even exist anymore?), give that number to your team. Or you can get a four-week, prepaid cell for emergencies.

4. Who will have your itinerary so that if a true emergency happens, they know where you are and how to contact you? This is in case of dying—personal or business.

5. Commit to 99 percent Design time. There is no such thing as 100 percent Design time since, ultimately, you will have to share insights with your team, thereby Delegating work and Deciding for others. But the goal is for that time to be minimal.

ONE MONTH OUT—ACT AS AN OBSERVER

1. Act as an observer of your business. Be tough on yourself. Make sure you are not Doing or Deciding. Be the shareholder who comes to the office to observe the operation (even if the observation is done virtually). Look to understand how things work, but don't seek to fix them. Seek to understand the connection of everything within your company.

2. Delegate the outcomes for any remaining work.

3. Look for any loose ends that you need to tie up. Don't tie them up; instead, document that you have loose ends. That is a problem because a loose end is something that

wasn't Trashed, Transferred, or Trimmed. Give those loose ends to someone else.

4. Get anyone who is going on the four-weeker with you pumped. It is only four weeks until your four weeks!

ONE WEEK OUT—TAKE A VACATION AT WORK

1. Take a vacation, so to speak, at the office. The goal here is to have no Doing work at all. You shouldn't have a deadline for anything except self-imposed stuff. This is where you have moved to focus on what is important, not what is urgent. In fact, you shouldn't even be aware of what is urgent at this point. Your team should be handling everything but the most serious emergency.

2. If you have anything besides Design work that consumes your time, Delegate it to your team. This includes any task that you've secretly been hoarding for yourself. You know, the thing that, even after all this streamlining, you still think only you can do. Yes, I'm looking at you. I know you. I know you like I know my twin (if I had one). We're cut from the same cloth, my friend. Time to let go of that one last thing.

THE DAY BEFORE OPERATION VACATION

1. Send your team a written message, or step it up a notch and make a video. Express your gratitude for the work they do. Thank them for their leadership and taking on this challenge. Point out the growth you all will experience. And then hand them the reins. Maybe you

commemorate it by giving the team the "key(s) to the business," similar to when someone is given the keys to the city.

2. Have your assistant—or whomever you delegated to check your accounts—change the passwords on your email, business-related social media, and any other accounts so that only they can see them.

3. Get your ass in the car. You have a vacation to get to!

WHILE YOU ARE AWAY

1. **Contemplate.** I am not good at meditating in the traditional sense. Sitting criss-cross applesauce while saying *om* is just uncomfortable in so many ways for me. But I do find that I get lost in moments, or daydream. I don't know when these things will happen, but I do know when they don't happen: when I am focused on work. But if I just chill, hike, bike, sit in a coffee shop, sit in a sauna, take a long shower—those magic moments of pure genius happen. *Let them happen.*

2. **Have a notepad at the ready.** Always. I have a little spiral notebook that fits in my pocket, and a pen. And my phone has a voice recorder that I use to record thoughts and ideas. Just because you're off work for four weeks doesn't mean you can't record business insights or goals that you can review when you get back.

3. **Make meaningful connections.** When we're grinding, one of the first things to move down the priority list is time with our loved ones, friends, and even total strangers who may have something to share with us. We move too fast for meaningful connections. Now that you're

away, make it a point to listen to those you love, to stop and talk to a fellow tourist, vendor, or busker on the street.

4. **Take pictures.** You'll probably do this anyway, but the reason I'm adding this obvious task to your list is because you need at least one memorable picture that illustrates your four-week vacation experience. Why? Because when you get back, you're going to frame it and hang it in your office as a visual reminder of all that you accomplished—and as inspiration for your next trip.

WHEN YOU RETURN

1. Have a debrief meeting scheduled for the day after you return to the office, then one a week for the next four weeks. You are going to debrief, improve, review, improve, review, improve . . .

2. In your meetings, evaluate what worked and what didn't. What went as you expected? What surprise challenges came up? What did you forget to handle before you left? What areas need improvements? The four-week vacation will magnify what you didn't plan for or expect. Set out to fix and improve those things.

3. Schedule your next four-week vacation for twelve months from now. This will be a regular thing. And then perhaps you want to go for the big one: the fifty-two-week vacation. Or maybe the ultimate: the forever vacation.

You will notice that nowhere throughout this process did I say, "Notify your clients that you will be away for four weeks." The ultimate success is when your customers say, "I didn't realize you were away." Of course, if you are in a business where your absence would put your customers at risk, you should tell them. For example, if you are a doctor, you may have a patient reach out with an emergency. Or if you have fifty accounting clients and will be away during the last four weeks of tax season (that would be bad-ass if you committed to that), you might want to give them notice and explain how you plan to address it. I prefer not to notify clients, and I don't set up an "I'm on vacation" autoresponder, but you should use your professional discretion.

WHEN FOUR WEEKS STRETCHES INTO MONTHS

We can't prevent life events from happening. Sometimes, a crisis forces us to take a break from our business. And sometimes that break is much longer than four weeks. When Alex Beadon's grandmother got cancer, she dropped everything to ensure that she got the best medical care possible in her home country of Trinidad. The founder of Beadon International, a company that helps entrepreneurs grow their Instagram following and teaches them how to do a six-figure launch, Alex had begun the Clockwork process the year before. Much of her focus had been on capturing her own ideas and systems so her team could do the work without her. Because she had taken those steps, she was able to move to Trinidad and focus entirely on Granny.

"I completely switched off from my business—for months," Alex told me when I interviewed her for this book. "I'd check in every few weeks, but basically, I was done."

Alex has a great team. She explained that had she not clockworked her company, it would have survived when she left to help her granny, but the back end would have been "a mess." And she would have had to juggle work and caregiving, which is like having three jobs—because we all know being an entrepreneur is not a forty-hours-a-week gig.

"Being there for Granny made a real difference," she added. "She was more comfortable on her journey and got the medical care she needed."

It warms my heart to know that Clockwork makes it possible for business owners to be there for the people they love. But you don't have to wait for a medical issue or crisis to come up to take a longer break from your company. You can do it simply because you want to do it. Your business should be serving you, not the reverse. So take the time you need to for whatever you want, with no regrets. You might want to take a long parental leave if you have a new child. You may want to take a sabbatical to do a big project or learn a new skill. Or maybe you want to go on a spiritual quest. When you Clockwork your business, you can truly experience the freedom to live life on your own terms. And isn't that one of the reasons you started your company in the first place?

Jessi and Marie of North Star, whom you first met in Chapter Four, had put off taking a vacation for years. After implementing Clockwork, they were able to take their first four-week vacation. They scheduled it for the same time so they could truly test their business and free up their team to run the company. And because they wanted to plot out their next co-written novel.

In a follow-up call after they got back from the trip, Jessi told me, "The first two days we felt liberated. Then panic set in. Then we got distracted by all the fun things we had scheduled. We honestly didn't talk that much about work, even though we were together the whole time."

Jessi and Marie had a lot of confidence in their team. They

had run a lot of one- and two-week mini vacations leading up to it, had always kept a list of things that broke, and had put in place a standard operating procedure (SOP) each time.

"We knew that our team knew the drill," Jessi said. "They knew what to do."

Jessi explained that as excited as they were, their team was even more pumped. "We let them know a year in advance, and they knew they were working toward this, and they knew it was because we wanted to empower them to make decisions."

Jessi and Marie came back to the office to find that everything had been running well, their team had handled all issues effectively, and they even had new clients, people they'd never heard of before.

"It was one of my favorite victories," Jessi said.

You can Clockwork your business—even if you think you are the only person who can do the work.

You can Clockwork your business—even if you think you don't have time to take off one day, much less four weeks.

You can Clockwork your business—even if you're worried that you won't know what to do with yourself while you're away.

Just start. Just start today.

FOR EMPLOYEES: CORA'S STORY

At Job Turf, every employee takes a four-week vacation. Everyone. It is a great benefit for employees, but it may just be a greater benefit for the company itself.

By the time Cora wrapped up her first year at Job Turf, she had already planned her four-week vacation, a road trip to visit ten members of her former military squad. In preparation for her departure, she cross-trained other employees to back her up.

Gordon knew how to work the machinery, but so did Jamal and Kim, because Cora trained them.

On her road trip, Cora saw something cool at a military base: an electric bulldozer, which was quiet and produced no exhaust fumes. When she returned to work, she mentioned it to Gordon, and together they hatched a plan. Today, Job Turf is on track to be the first private company to utilize the new electric bulldozer. Less air pollution and less noise pollution.

How can you help? The best employees are not concerned about being irreplaceable; they are eager to show other people how to do their Primary Job and other tasks. While preparing for your four-week vacation, or a vacation of any length, capture all your systems so anyone on your team can do the work for you. When you are on your vacation, let them do it. Disconnect fully from the company and enjoy yourself. Open your mind to discovering new ways to improve yourself and your company while you explore life. When you return to work, make a note of any problems that came up. These are the areas you need to systematize next.

CLOCKWORK IN ACTION

I get it. I'm asking you to do something that at this time in your life may seem impossible. How are you going to plan for a four-week vacation when you're operating on four *hours* of sleep every day? I want to inspire you to make this commitment, of course, but I know from experience that it's more important that you make a commitment you will actually honor. So start small. Start so small that you have no excuse for an excuse.

Over the years, I've heard from countless entrepreneurs and business owners who follow Profit First—almost. Many people don't follow the whole system. They do the minimum required—they set aside a small percentage for profit with each deposit. Even this one tiny change has had a dramatic effect on their businesses. So much so that many people whisper about their successes to me, as if they can't believe that simply setting aside profit first could work such magic on their business's growth and bottom line.

So now, even though I want you to plan for this vacation so that you can design your business to run itself, I am asking you to lower the bar. Keep it simple. Start by committing to three small changes for your business:

1. Call yourself a shareholder.
2. Declare your company's QBR.
3. Take 1 percent Design time.

A small amount of Design time can help you implement the other steps in this book, or it can help you come up with your next great product idea or a solution to a problem. Similarly, simply being *aware* of your QBR will change the way you operate on a day-to-day basis. And what you label yourself as, so you become. When you consistently call yourself a shareholder, you will consistently behave that way.

Three changes. That's it. You can do it. When you get good at these three things, you can take on more. This book will be here when you're ready to go "full Clockwork." And I'll be here for you, no matter what.

CHAPTER TWELVE

PUTTING IT ALL TOGETHER

FOLLOW THE JOURNEY OF ONE BUSINESS OWNER AS THEY CLOCKWORK THEIR COMPANY

Now that you've learned the three Clockwork phases, I'll show you how they work together to not only streamline your business, but to also trigger massive growth. To do that, I've written a fictional story that shows the entire Clockwork process applied to a company I wish did exist, Outlandish Dish.

Outlandish Dish is a culinary tourism company specializing in European excursions for English-speaking foodies primarily from Australia, Canada, the United Kingdom, and the United States. On their three-day "quick study" trips and fourteen-day "immersion" adventures, guests experience authentic local cuisine in different countries. They meet the chefs, learn the history of the food, and meet local farmers and artisans who create specialty items.

The owner, Roberto Nolletto, is an Italian expat who moved to Paris, where Outlandish Dish is headquartered. He oversees the company, runs its marquee trip four times a year, and develops new programs. Roberto started the business because he loved experiencing different food and cultures so much that he was doing his own trips and bringing friends. Eating a meal with

Roberto and listening to the stories and history had his friends lining up to go with him, so he decided to launch Outlandish Dish and make a business out of his passion.

The company was built around Roberto's experience as a child. Both his parents were in the military back when it was still compulsory. Their assignments had them traveling throughout Europe, with Roberto in tow, during his teenage years. It was difficult for him to make friends at the schools because Roberto was rarely there long enough to fit in. But the cafés and restaurants throughout Europe were different. The locals and travelers alike reveled in connecting with each other. If you were new, you were welcome. And connections formed fast through shared stories. Roberto didn't know it at the time, but the essence of his Big BANG was formed during those years. He realized that a stranger was simply a friend you hadn't met yet, and that he could make "the world of strangers into a family of friends." Even though he hadn't settled on the words, the reason he structured the trips the way he did was because of the joy he got from connecting strangers to one another.

A typical trip may start with dining in Geneva on the fabled cheese dishes, traveling through Germany to try their wursts (which, ironically, are their bests), enjoying the most incredible breads and pastas from Italy, and finishing in France with a feast of wine, pastries, and world-class entrées. The final night of each trip includes a cooking experience: under the guidance of a world-renowned chef, guests prepare a meal, dine, and party the night away. These events have landed Outlandish Dish rave reviews and international press.

The problem is, even though the United States and Canada are the company's biggest market, they struggle to pull customers from there. They do heavy marketing in both countries, yet only 20 percent of their customers are North Americans; 80 percent of their customer base comes from Australia and the UK.

Roberto wants Outlandish Dish to run (and scale) like clockwork, but the company is stuck. They generate $3.5 million in annual revenue, but the company is only marginally profitable. They employ twenty-five people, including Roberto: fourteen additional tour guides, one website developer, one marketer, two salespeople, three tour planners, one admin, and two bookkeepers. Roberto doesn't think he can afford to make new hires, but at the same time, his team is maxed out. He believes he needs more tour guides and more people to help market more effectively in the United States. Roberto helps with the marketing, scouts new tours, and leads the marquee fourteen-day tours. He can't work any more hours, and he is exhausted.

Roberto wants to start the Clockwork process, but he has been dragging his feet. Ironically, he hasn't taken a break from work in twenty years. All his wife wants for their anniversary is to go on a trip with him, alone, so he books one week on a tiny island in the Bahamas. He finds it hilarious to plan his own vacation, since he does this professionally. And he's nervous about taking time away from his business, especially because he hasn't found a solution to the problems his company faces.

A monster storm knocks out the phone and Wi-Fi on the island for a few days. Seemingly, the Clockwork gods are trying to send a message to Roberto. One that puts him in pure anxiety mode. When he comes back from his trip, he expects Disasterville. He expects client calamities and planning problems galore, since those are the issues he deals with on a weekly basis. Although his team did leave a few issues for him to resolve, for the most part, they managed well without him. They even came up with a creative solution to an itinerary change and had a group travel by ferry when a puddle jumper was grounded due to strong winds. He realizes it's well past time to start clockworking his business.

PHASE ONE: ALIGN

As he begins the Clockwork phases, Roberto first reviews the post-trip survey responses from his most successful trips and the thank-you cards he's received from happy customers. Most of them mention him.

"We loved getting to know you, Roberto!"

"We had so much fun at dinner with Roberto."

"Roberto's stories were the highlight of highlights!"

He notes that all the guests who raved about his ability to connect with them became lifers. More than half the guests have come back over the years, many for a decade or more. He is such a good storyteller that people get excited about their adventure before the trip begins, stay excited while they are there, and talk excitedly about their trip after they get home. If Roberto doesn't do the tours himself, the "repeat rate" of guests plummets to less than 20 percent. Roberto determines that his company's Big Promise is "Travel adventures with your new oldest friend."

Next, Roberto does a Crush/Cringe Analysis on his guests. His Crush customers are the people who go with the flow, don't squabble about the price, and return again and again. His Cringe customers are the folks who are super high-maintenance, try to get a discount for everything, and are shocked that they can't get hamburgers and hot dogs at every restaurant.

When Roberto compares his stack of survey responses and thank-you cards with his Crush list, he realizes that the lists are almost identical. Now he knows that his Big Promise speaks to his Crush customers.

Then he considers his QBR, the main activity that supports his Big Promise. He realizes that if he had skipped the Big Promise exercise, he would have assumed that their unique travel itineraries were the QBR. Or maybe access to local cuisine, sans the hot dogs. But now he understands that his company's QBR is connecting with guests as if they were lifelong friends.

Next, Roberto starts to look at ways that he can focus on the QBR (and Trash, Transfer, or Trim the other work he does). But he has a problem. How can Roberto build intimate connections with guests unless he is the guide for all the trips? Impossible, right? Or maybe . . .

One night his new in-house booker, Mariette, says, "The main way you connect with guests is through storytelling. Why don't we have you drop in on a trip near the beginning, and then again on the final big night? Instead of running a trip for two weeks, you can connect with the guests on the trip for a day or two. And, since almost all our tours pass through Paris, our home base, many of these story times will have you out of the office for just four or five hours. That way, you don't have to run any of the trips by yourself, and you take a step back from the long hours. You'll be freed up to think about other stuff."

Roberto likes the idea but is skeptical. He knows that connecting with guests is the QBR, but he finds it hard to believe that showing up only at the beginning and end of a trip will have a big impact.

Roberto is right. That small tweak to the approach doesn't have a big impact. It has a massive one.

When he shows up for the mingling and dining parts of the trips, he is on fire. He isn't drained from travel, so he's able to be fully present. He regales the guests with stories, and they hang on every word. He spends one-on-one time with each guest. He gives insider tips on things to do on their own. And because Roberto isn't tied up for two weeks running the marquee adventures, he can now visit with every tour group, including those on the three-day trips.

Raves pour in. People who take the three-day trip now start

booking the fourteen-day trip. People want more adventures. They want more stories with their meals. More intimate time with Roberto. And now, instead of 50 percent of just the marquee trip guests repeating trips, every trip is getting a 50 percent rebooking rate. Within a year, sales increase to $4.5 million. Outlandish Dish is no longer *one* of many culinary tourism companies—it is *the* culinary tourism company. It increases prices and margins.

PHASE TWO: INTEGRATE

Two problems remain. The first is that the team is still only twenty-five people, but with everyone focused on protecting the QBR (Roberto's baby, for now), the demand has taxed the tour guide team and they need to make a new hire. The other is that sales from the US market continue to be a dribble.

Roberto does the Time Analysis to first address the challenge of his overloaded team. He evaluates the Time Analysis and discovers that his company is heavy in the Deciding, Delegating, and Designing phases, almost 40 percent. He is shocked because his tour guides are constantly saying how busy they are (Doing). And with Roberto no longer running any tours himself, he was sure that the only thing tour guides were doing was facilitating tours.

But looking into it further, the percentages start to make sense. Roberto realizes that his three tour planners are contributing to the skewed 4D Mix. Tour planners carry out many administrative tasks, and their jobs are heavy on Deciding (making decisions for tour guides), Delegating (assigning resources and responsibilities to tour guides), and Designing (formulating a variety of new tours or tour modifications). As a result, these tour planners are also overloaded and stressed. Since the popular tours represent most of the demand, three tour planners working on new trips is too many. It is clear that doing more work doesn't yield more results.

Instead of creating new tours, Roberto chooses to do more of what has been working. He decides to keep the most successful existing tours and freshen them up every year with new restaurants and new chefs, but the rest can stay the same: same cities, same sites, same hotels, same transportation. This change significantly frees up his tour planners, since they can plan multiple years out with the hotels, transportation companies, and certain sites. This, in turn, reduces all the associated Deciding, Delegating, and Designing.

PHASE THREE: AMPLIFY

Next, Roberto sets up his metrics dashboard. To be sure his QBR is working, he sets the metric of at least 50 percent of guests booking another trip after their tour is complete.

During a break from tours, Roberto and his employees sort out their Primary Jobs, note the ways in which they each support the QBR, and determine who oversees each metric on the dashboard. Then, they consider what each of them will need to Trash, Transfer, Trim, and Treasure in order to ensure that they are only doing their Primary Jobs and supporting the QBR.

With the goal of supporting the tour guides, who also need relief, Roberto does the Job Traits Analysis for his team. The key job trait for a tour guide is customer care. Roberto loves the saying: "No one cares about how much you know until they know how much you care." Knowledge of the area is important, addressing the problems that spring up as things move along is important, but nothing is as important as caring for the customer.

Evaluating the results of the Job Traits Analysis, Roberto

notices that Janet, one of his three tour planners, is extraordinary at customer care. An American expat who moved to Paris to care for her grandmother in her final days, Janet fell in love with the city, and with all of Europe. In her work as a planner, her care for people shines. For example, she is known for sending gifts to the chefs and vendors she meets while scouting for tours, and for staying in touch with them even if they don't become part of a trip. While she's never run a tour, she has the key trait that positions her for great success.

Roberto tests Janet's tour guide abilities, first as a shadow guide and then with her own solo trip. She does well, so he officially moves her into the position. Within a few months, she becomes one of their highest-rated guides.

Janet's success inspires Roberto to Capture systems for connecting with guests through storytelling. In short videos, he creates a library of tips that any guide can use to get similar results: get personal details about guests, particularly their lineage and where they live currently; when telling stories, show how where they are touring is connected to the guests personally (making the guests themselves part of the story); and show how to time storytelling, mingling time, and alone time.

One of the scouts, Sankara, produces videos as his side-hustle. Every time he gets a chance to make a video, he does. Roberto asks him to share recordings of some of the best stories so he can include them in the video library for tour guides.

Outlandish Dish still has a twenty-five-person team, and with a focus on improving successful tours rather than creating new ones, Roberto realizes that two scouts is too many. He looks at their traits. Roberto remembers a suggestion Mariette made at one point. She thought videos would help to break into the US market, but Roberto couldn't fathom assigning that task to someone when most of his team was working overtime to meet demand.

He asks Janet about this idea, and she tells him that Americans watch more video on social media than they watch on television.

Roberto matches the new job of tour videographer to Sankara's talent. Within two days, Sankara films the first video with Roberto and Janet. Targeted toward the US market, the video features Janet talking about the life-changing experiences Outlandish Dish provides. Then she introduces Roberto, who talks about how the continents were connected at one time and invites Americans to come to Europe to connect again. He shares stories of laughter and tears with his past American guests and invites the new guests to visit so that he can personally pour their wine on arrival.

The videos crush it online. Roberto is a massive hit; his charisma and charm are unmatched. Soon, Outlandish Dish has a rush of American tourists booking trips.

With all the new customers, Roberto and his team pay special attention to tracking ACDC on their dashboard. Scaling has caused some issues in the Collect stage, a problem they've never had before. With so much of their previous revenue based on returning customers and their referrals, they rarely had to chase down final payments before the trip began. And they have more last-minute cancellations than they ever had before. He suspects the problem is financial. The team evaluates solutions and decides that they need to secure a larger deposit up-front in order to weed out impulse buyers who don't have the funds to pay for the trip.

For his next four-week vacation, Roberto decides to stay home so he can plant a garden. He's always wanted to convert his backyard into an oasis for butterflies and birds, and he has an idea for a vegetable garden full of ingredients for his wife's favorite dishes. He figures that once he has the garden in, keeping up with it will be a good use of his Downtime.

He's planting tomato seeds and thinking about the salads he'll make once the fruit grows when he remembers the exquisite olive oil he tasted at Azienda Agricola Il Brolo, a small olive oil vineyard in Brescia, Italy, about two hours outside of Milan. The tour bus had to make an emergency stop to get medical attention for a guest; Il Brolo was the closet facility. Then it hits him: "Wait! I could include farms and vineyards on my tour!" Roberto's idea leads to the creation of the most popular culinary tours his company has ever created.

Because everyone is in the right job, doing the right things, in the right portions, right; because the entire team is protecting the QBR; and because Roberto has enough time to focus on Designing his company, Outlandish Dish grows by leaps and bounds.

Americans start talking about the company, and then the unexpected magic happens: a major US network contacts Roberto about doing a show on European culinary tours. His natural storytelling ability serves him well, and once the show airs, he becomes a celebrity. Demand for his business skyrockets—well past $10 million in annual revenue.

Roberto is not done yet. His final step is to remove himself from directly serving the QBR. And wouldn't you know it? Janet shares the same trait Roberto is known for. She becomes the lead storyteller, especially on tours for Americans. Roberto enjoys his new career in television, and his team runs Outlandish Dish like clockwork. Done.

The ending to this story may seem like a fairy tale, but any dream you have for your business, any goal you hope to achieve with your company, any contribution you hope to make to the world, is possible when you are not hampered by work you shouldn't be doing, and when your team is running like clockwork.

CHAPTER THIRTEEN

PUSHBACK
(AND WHAT TO DO ABOUT IT)

NAVIGATE THROUGH RESISTANCE,
CHALLENGES, AND STAGNATION

On a speaking tour in Perth, Australia, I initiated the necessary disconnect from my business for a four-week vacation—and promptly panicked. I was working on the first version of this book at the time and I was in the midst of testing the Clockwork process on my own business. (I think this is what makes my work somewhat atypical among authors or consultants. When I research a concept, I first test it on my own businesses, often for years, before I start to write about it. And then, during the documenting and writing stages, I continue to test the system on other businesses and test tweaks on mine. It is a very iterative process.)

After enjoying the smorgasbord breakfast, including world-class pastries, at the iconic albeit old-fashioned Miss Maud Hotel in Perth, I sipped on coffee and opened my laptop right there at the table. I had thought of a tweak to the system after having a conversation with Australian entrepreneur Leticia Mooney earlier in the week. Once I had made that improvement, I was done with the core of the book and had nothing left to do. I considered a second round at the smorgasbord, but that would only result in a larger tire around the waistline. What could I do? I checked email. Nothing. Refreshed. Still nothing. If you've ever experienced the stress of an overflowing inbox, it doesn't come anywhere near the terror I felt looking at an empty one. At that moment I had a realization. I thought I had finally moved past the biggest barrier to ensuring my businesses ran on their own— my ego. But, alas, I had not.

In Perth, I was literally on the other side of the world—almost directly opposite on the globe from my home in New Jersey. The time difference between the two places is twelve hours, so my day was their night and vice versa. This meant that my team slept while I worked the day away in Australia. And while they were awake and getting things done in Jersey, I was asleep and dreaming of shrimp on the barbie. With the extreme time difference, if my team needed anything, they couldn't immediately get ahold of me, nor could I get ahold of them.

After a couple of days of this, I began to feel as though the world didn't need me. It was the ultimate disconnect. The difference between freedom and not being needed was stark. Really, it was a bucket of cold water to the face. I always wanted to be free of my business, but no one calling me, not even to ask for my credit card to pay for the office pizza party? Well, jeez, that was tough to accept. My team wasn't just running the business, they were running it without me. I had spent years designing a company that could run on its own and now I had *proof* that I'd pulled it off. The realization that I was not needed? That just tore into my soul.

Sitting at my table for one, the downward spiral of thoughts kicked in. I was alone in Australia, locked in solitary confinement by a wall of Danishes and apple turnovers, and no one at my office even cared. Cue the panic! Would they even notice if I went on a walkabout in the outback and never came back?

As I mentioned in an earlier chapter, the only thing a human being faced with their own dispensability would do: I reinserted myself into the business. I started sending emails with questions and requests. I made busywork for myself and others. I started throwing wrenches into the well-oiled machine we created. As soon as my team in Jersey woke up, they saw dozens of emails from me, all of which made them slow down, start stumbling on tasks, and seek my input on how to proceed. It instantly made my schedule in Australia that much more demanding. Brilliant, right? If you think even for a second that my decision was smart, just picture me. There I am, sitting with a plate of food in front of me, surrounded by Australian grandmas (who apparently like to frequent the hotel), barking out commands in voicemails to my team, and as a result, hampering my own company.

And in case you forgot, I had just written a draft of *this book*. Which advocated the four-week vacation. And I couldn't even hack it for four days. Upon reflection many months later, I realized that I had been going through withdrawal. In a way, I was addicted to my business, to the *doing*, and you can't ease your way out of addiction. You have to go cold turkey. I had prepared for my time away. I had built the systems to support my time away. But my mind had not caught up to it.

Let's be clear on this: I've never claimed to be the sharpest tool in the shed. A tool, maybe. Okay, I was definitely a tool. This was not about my brains—this was about my ego. This was about human nature. You may have experienced a similar need to remain relevant in your own business, or in other aspects of your life. Maybe when you sent your kids off to college. I know my wife and I felt that. All of a sudden, a house of commotion became an empty warehouse of "now what?" First, you get the amazing "this is the first day of my new life" feeling of relief when they walk out the door. Then, when dinner time rolls around, and there's no one yelling, "What's for dinner, Ma?" the realization that you're not needed takes your breath away. It's painful! So you pick up the phone and call them, getting all up in their business in an effort to make yourself indispensable. I had already lost two of my kids to college and had one on the verge of going. My ego couldn't take losing my last child—my business. By reinserting myself into the company, I was trying to pull my "adult child" back into the house with me. It wasn't good for my team, and it wasn't good for me.

The truth is, our kids still need us after they go off to college, and our team still needs us when they're running the business on their own. They just need us *in a different way.*

Dealing with your own bruised ego is just one of the ways you—and others in your organization—may resist the streamlining process I've detailed in this book. Don't marginalize this. In my personal experience, and the experience of the majority of business owners who implemented Clockwork, the *biggest* impediment to our progress was ourselves. When you want to get out of the weeds, get out. Don't say you want out of the day-to-day and then stay in the day-to-day. Get out. Don't say you want to work less and then work more to work less. Get out first, then observe from the outside and fix things from there. Don't let your ego keep you in.

One technique I used was to stop calling myself the superhero for my business. First, I had to learn to channel my ego. Instead of seeing myself as a superhero for my business, able to swoop in and fix any problem, I see myself as the "super visionary," a role to which I attach even more significance. This is a role that requires me to do visionary work, out of the business. Learn about the world, take ideas from the outside, and introduce them to the inside team. "Super visionary" changes my behavior so that I act like a shareholder of the business—*and* it feeds my fat ego.

When you start implementing the Clockwork system, you may experience blowback or resistance from your team, partners, colleagues, friends, family—and, in particular, yourself. Expect it. Plan for it. And above all, be patient with yourself and others. Change is hard, partner. We're only human beings. And human beings are notorious for being awfully human.

IT FEELS CONTRARY TO WHAT WILL WORK

The greatest irony is that while building systems is hard work, it is not busywork. You won't be typing away all the time. You won't be meeting with people all the time. You won't be busy. You will be focusing on the hardest work of all—thinking.

Thinking about your business—*Designing* your business— takes a lot of energy and concentration. So, because we're humans, the natural instinct is to distract ourselves by doing the work. It may sound crazy that hard work is easier than hard thinking, but it is.

Just like if you had two options: 1) Try to dig a ditch in fifteen minutes, or 2) Try to solve a Rubik's Cube in fifteen minutes. The ditch, even as hard as it is physically for many people, will be easier to complete. Since we are almost guaranteed to see a result with the ditch, many people will turn to that. Or try the Rubik's Cube for just a few minutes and get frustrated that the #$@!% yellow center square is still on the #$@!% other side from all the other #$@!% yellow pieces. So then we throw the cube down, run outside, and dig the ditch. Thinking takes a lot of energy, a lot of patience, and a lot of concentration.

Also, when we are "thinking" and not "doing," it feels as though we are not bringing a benefit to our business because we often don't get immediate results from thinking. We want the instant gratification of checking tasks off a list, filling a quota, delivering services, or reaching a goal.

The truth is, the thinker is getting *serious* stuff done. They even dedicated a statue to him—you know, *The Thinker*—because he has figured out that the goal is not to do stuff but to think about how to get stuff done. Getting stuff done is not the goal. The goal is to have the *company* get stuff done. Instead of doing the work, you need to be *thinking* about the work, and whom you can get to do it.

Don't fool yourself into believing that just because you're sitting there with your chin resting on your fist—naked—you are not working. Heck, everyone knows the best ideas come when you're in the shower! Why? Because you are not doing work—no email, no calls, none of that. You are doing the most important work: thinking. I now seek out saunas whenever I'm traveling because they are like showers on steroids (I can't do anything in there, including moving). I just sit, sweat, and think, and sure enough I get my best work done in them.

Want to know how to design a business that runs itself? Ask yourself big, powerful questions and let your mind work on them. And remember, just because you're naked doesn't mean it's not work!

PUSHBACK FROM PARTNERS

I can't tell you how many times my Profit First Professionals business partner said, "You aren't doing enough for the business. We need more of you." I get why Ron felt this way. He was still caught up in the "do everything" mentality. Everything is important. Everything is critical. Everything is urgent. Ron would say, "You used to run circles around this place. I've never seen someone work so hard. Now you are never around." Which, you and I know, is because of the move from the Doing to the Designing phase. But to the outside world—or even your business partner—it may look as if you have just abandoned the business.

Ron has a heart of gold. I admire him, and I know how much he cares for our business, and for our clients, and for our mission of eradicating entrepreneurial poverty. He takes everything to heart, and he wants everyone to have an extraordinary experience. I trust him more than anyone in the business world.

When we started to streamline Profit First Professionals (PFP), we used one of our quarterly meetings to explain to all our employees what I did to serve the QBR, and how they were supporting it. I explained that Profit First was a concept I had created eight years before the business even existed, including it in my first book and subsequently expanding on it in an article I wrote for *The Wall Street Journal*. It was the time I had to work on the concept and improve it that made it a reality. I explained that my job now was making strategic decisions. Planning the big moves. Spreading the word and finding others who could spread the word. When we started PFP, I had to do it all. It was just me and Ron, after all, and we were both needed for the Doing. Now I was needed as a Designer.

Ron and I met privately. I asked for more help getting the day-to-day off my plate, and he was not happy about it. We had a lot of tough, heated conversations in which he asserted that I had to spend more time working *in* the business and less time writing and speaking. As I said earlier, our QBR is spreading the message of eradicating entrepreneurial poverty, so what he was asking me for would not help us grow our business—it would actually restrict it. But for Ron, who was busy all day every day, my plan seemed counterintuitive.

His understandable pushback against my efforts to make PFP run without me (and him) came to a head when we hired a new employee, Billie Anne. She was quite capable with tech, which thrilled me because up until that point, I was the only person in-house who had the skill set to work on technology. With more experience in this space than the other five full-timers at our office combined, I was the obvious choice to head up our app development work. But because I was focused on trying to serve the QBR, and because I still hadn't removed myself from managing other projects, I only got around to working on our tech project sporadically.

At the time, we were developing software that would be essential for PFP members. I had been leading the project for five months but had only managed to get the software to the point where it was functional but not usable. The indicator was obvious: our members weren't using it.

I met with Ron, gave him an update about the project, and said, "I want to give this to Billie Anne. She can handle it."

Ron was adamant that I stay the course. He said, "When you take something on, Mike, it's your responsibility to see it through. You've got to work harder. Push through."

What Ron was saying wasn't wrong. It was consistent with his experience, but that experience was not consistent with operational efficiency; instead, it was consistent with the brute force approach of "just be more productive." I blame it on lacrosse.

Growing up, Ron and I were on the same lacrosse team in high school. Ron was a better player than I was (and still is, I recently discovered when he schooled me in a face-off at an alumni game). Everyone on the team has to pull their weight, plus some. Ron, an avid lacrosse player, knew the golden rule of lacrosse all too well: when any player is down or not playing well, the team captains have to play harder. You don't seek to do less, you toughen up and do more and more and more. Of course, a lacrosse game is a sprint. The entire playing time is one hour. Business is a marathon, the entire "game" being played over years, decades, or a lifetime.

"We're not the players on the lacrosse team, Ron," I told him. "We're the team owners. We have to act like owners, and since we haven't hired the coaches yet, you need to serve that role as I push forward on our QBR. We need to coach our team, our employees, and give them the strategy to win. We're off the field now."

I think he heard what I said but it didn't land. That meeting didn't end well. So, out of respect for Ron, I stayed on as lead for the tech project. What I *did* do was run a test, with Ron's permission. I had Billie Anne help me with one tiny piece of the project, which she knocked out in no time. Then I went back to Ron, told him I got one piece done with Billie Anne's help, and showed him the results.

Ron said, "Wow! She's fast. Let's do that again," and he agreed to let Billie Anne take on more and more of the tasks. Now she's leading the project. Over the course of three weeks, I convinced him, by showing him Billie Anne's results, that it would be better if I pulled out of the project. More important, he convinced himself.

Ron is smart and thirsts to learn, but just like you and me, he is comfortable with the familiar. He worked harder on the field than any other lacrosse player, me included. He worked harder at work than any of his colleagues, hence his success. But now he had to let go of the comfort of hard work and start supporting choreographed work. Sometimes your biggest resistance, if it doesn't come from you, will come from your business partners or executive team. They are human and need guidance with change.

Take small steps toward organizational efficiency, and prove through tests that everyone on your executive team needs to move toward Designing and away from Doing.

With my time freed up from working on the software project, I had time to meet with international partners and negotiate international contracts for PFP. Under the leadership of Femke Hogema, we opened a new location in the Netherlands and brought on thirty members with little effort. We then launched a location in Australia with Laura Elkaslassy, and she is already proving that she can serve the community (and grow our organization) in extraordinary ways. Then Ron started managing our international growth, adding a location in Germany under the leadership of Benita Königbauer. As I write this, he has just finished up the plans for our location in the United Kingdom. Next up: Mexico, or Japan, or Kenya, or somewhere else. They are in the works, and the QBR is always the priority.

You will be challenged by partners who are still playing like team captains—not coaches or owners. It's not because they are wrong, or bad. It's because they are doing what they have always done. Work with your partners. Meet them halfway, and then halfway again, until they finally see the benefits of organizational efficiency.

I took a quick day trip to Chicago and met up with my long-time friend Rich Manders. His company, Freescale Coaching, has been so successful in bringing efficiency, growth, and profitability to companies that prospects are putting down $50,000* deposits to have the privilege of getting his coaching a year or more from now. Yes, he is that good.

We were walking down Michigan Avenue to a group meeting

---

* In the original *Clockwork*, Rich collected $10,000 deposits. But the demand for his work only increased. Now companies must put down $50,000 deposits a full year in advance to even be considered.

we were attending, and I asked Rich, "With all your success help-ing companies grow, what would you say is the most common and biggest roadblock businesses need to get past?" I fully expected something about finances, marketing, and/or the product mix.

Rich looked at me and said, "That's easy. It's always a lack of communication and clarity among the executive team. Always."

Clockwork is not a system for you. It is a system for your entire company. Everyone needs to know it. Everyone needs to be on the same page. Everyone needs to begin moving the leadership from Doing to Designing.

Even after Billie Anne's project ended, Ron's default position was "Mike should be doing more in the business." He equated *time* with contribution. After I had my revelation about why I couldn't let go in Australia, I realized that *impact* is the most sig-nificant contribution, not time. This really hit home with Ron one day after I did a $20,000 sales call.

Ron said, "That's amazing. Why don't you do calls all day? We'll bring in millions."

"Because I'm the spokesperson for Profit First, which is why I *can* secure a $20,000 deal on a call," I explained. "If I'm doing calls all day instead of being in my spokesperson role—speaking, writing, etc.—that will lessen the impact and those $20,000 calls will be a thing of the past."

In that moment it clicked with Ron. He got that impact was more valuable than time. And now he teaches it.

PUSHBACK FROM EVERYONE ELSE

As you move into the Design role and shift your business to the optimal 4D Mix, you will likely get pushback from other people—your team, your vendors, your fellow shareholders (if you have them), and even your customers. Pushback from these groups is easier to deal with than the pushback from active partners because, ultimately, you're in charge. You're not sharing the decision-making with someone who has equal decision-making authority.

Pushback does not mean that you are on the wrong track, nor does it mean that you have to barrel through conflicts without a second thought. Expect to meet resistance along the way and strategize in advance. This will help you manage it. Ultimately, pushback comes from a place of fear and insecurity. Clear communication goes a long way in mitigating some of those feelings, as do managing expectations, listening to questions and concerns, and providing reassurance.

Some people feel strongly about tradition, legacy, and company culture. Listening to their feedback will help you to make the transition to a Clockwork business smooth and successful. After all, you can't anticipate every mistake or wrong turn, but the people who work with you can certainly help you spot them.

When Ruth Soukup, of Living Well Spending Less, began working with Adrienne Dorison on deploying Clockwork in her business, she identified the company's QBR as product design. They create products that help women simplify their lives, and their business growth depends on improving on those deliverables and creating new offerings.

Ruth is the primary person serving her company's QBR. She authored a *New York Times* bestselling book, *Living Well, Spending Less*, and creates planners and other helpful tools. It won't surprise you to learn that Ruth discovered she was wearing too many hats, and that she needed to let her team take on some of her duties. She and Adrienne set a goal of freeing up three "coffee shop" days a week—time when Ruth could focus on Design and on expanding her vision for the company. It soon became clear that in order to meet this and other goals, she would have to add people to her team. Ruth brought on a new CMO (chief marketing officer) and a creative director, which helped immensely.

As Ruth told Adrienne, "Giving me three days of 'focus time' has forced every department to adjust to support that goal. They track how many times I meet that goal, which is one of their metrics. We're not there yet, but we're getting there. Everyone is working well together and stepping up to do what needs to get done."

Ruth went on to explain that, for the first time in the history of her company, she was not stressed out during a major product launch. And since she began applying Clockwork to her business, she has had zero employee turnover.

Ruth also addressed the way her team handled conflict and put a system in place for acknowledging concerns and finding solutions. For example, up until then, Ruth had been the only person focused on revenue and cash flow. When she tasked her team with meeting specific revenue goals, she initially met some resistance. It wasn't that they didn't want to focus on revenue; it was just a new way of looking at their roles in the company.

"I can't even tell you how amazing it is," Ruth added. "When we started this process, our fourth quarter sucked. We had just added a lot of people and we had two poor-performing months. My team came to me and assured me we were doing the right thing, and to trust that they could handle it. They took the reins, created a new product in four days, and crushed it."

With the team supporting Ruth's goals and specific solutions and outcomes, the company had record earnings the next quarter. Ruth said, "The more I see their efforts, the more I am willing to trust my team. I am so grateful they fight for what they believe in, for margin, and for me, because they know that's important."

As your business begins to tick along beautifully, you will meet with resistance from the usual suspects—your team and your partners—and from people you don't expect. Your family may question your new freedom and express concern about potential cash-flow problems. Your colleagues and friends may wonder why you turned in your workaholic badge and give you a hard time about your new way of running your business. No matter who pushes back against the way you now run your business, remember that they, just like you, are only human. They'll get there. And so will you. The proof's in the pudding, as they say: a profitable business that is designed to run itself.

 ## CLOCKWORK IN ACTION

Start having active conversations about your vision and plan for your business. Talk with and listen to your partners, colleagues, vendors, clients, and family. Open, active dialogue greases many wheels as you transition a business to running itself. Action is everything, so start the conversation now. Stop measuring hours and start measuring impact.

CLOSING

Lin-Manuel Miranda didn't have time for vacations. Getting a musical off the ground is a grueling, yearslong process and you need to do just about anything to see it succeed. Sounds a bit like the life of an entrepreneur. And, as is true for some business owners, the life of a theatrical composer often requires working another job to support yourself. For Miranda, that meant writing political jingles while he brought his first musical to life.

After he finished the off-Broadway run of his first musical, *In the Heights*, and before work on the Broadway run began, Miranda's wife insisted that they take a real vacation. They went to Mexico. Nowadays, if you put *me* on a white sandy beach next to a bar, you're going to get a heck of a lot of frolicking. I'm talking drip sandcastles, pathetic attempts at surfing while trying to look cool, and writing stuff in the sand that makes my wife roll her eyes and say, "*Michael.*" (She only uses my full name when she's mad at me.) Miranda, well, he took a different approach to rest and relaxation: he read an 818-page book. Potato, po-tah-to. You do you, Lin.

You may have heard of the book, by the way. It was Ron Chernow's award-winning biography of a certain founding father, Alexander Hamilton. And in a hammock on a beach, Miranda got the spark of an idea that would become one of the most culturally significant and successful Broadway musicals of all time—*Hamilton.*

Now, to be clear, he wasn't working on vacation like I once did and like so many of my beach-house neighbors do every summer at the Jersey Shore. The dude was just doing a super nerdy thing and got inspired. He got inspired because his Doing brain was at rest. He didn't have *anything to do.* He wasn't chained to his work, filled with the next obligation, the next task, and the next crisis. As Tim Kreider wrote in his article "The 'Busy' Trap" in *The New York Times,* "The space and quiet that idleness provides is a necessary condition for standing back from life and seeing it whole, for making unexpected connections and waiting for the wild summer lightning strikes of inspiration—it is, paradoxically, necessary to getting any work done."[9]

We need breaks from our business. And our business needs breaks from us. Period. *And,* sometimes, while on those getaways, we are gifted with a little gem that turns into a multimillion-dollar cultural phenomenon. When the Doing brain is at rest, the Designing brain activates.

Great ideas come to you in the shower because your work brain shuts down and your wonderment brain turns on. With a vacation—a real vacation—you have a multiday or multiweek shower break for your brain. It is ironic, but when you work less, your brain works more. Differently. Exploring, creating, and designing.

"It's no accident that the best idea I've ever had in my life—

perhaps maybe the best one I'll ever have in my life—came to me on vacation," Miranda told *HuffPost* president and editor in chief Arianna Huffington in a live-streamed interview.[10] "The moment my brain got a moment's rest, *Hamilton* walked into it."

Will you get a *Hamilton*-level idea on your next vacation? I don't know. What I *do* know is that you are far less likely to get any great ideas if you don't let your business run like clockwork. I also know that, if you know your business is running like clockwork while you sip that margarita, you are far more likely to feel totally and completely free. And it's when you are at rest and free from worry that the best stuff comes to you. The best stuff for your life and for your business.

You now know how to make that happen. You're no longer unsure how to free yourself from the endless hamster wheel of business ownership. You know the Big Promise your business is making to your clients. You know how to align your business, your employees, and even your clients and customers with your vision. You know your QBR and how to protect it. You've got your 4Ds and your metrics down cold, and you and your balanced team will be able to Trash, Transfer, Trim, and Treasure with the best of them. You know how to spot bottlenecks and how to re-move them. You're behaving like a shareholder now because you are calling yourself a shareholder. You've got this.

Yes. *You've got this.*

Maybe you won't get that once-in-a-lifetime idea on your next vacation. But what if you do? What if it's major? What if a break from doing work and thinking about work makes the impossible suddenly possible, or even probable? What if your light-bulb mo-ment saves you buckets of money, or makes things easier for your team? What if you think of a new product or service that could solve a major problem for your clients? Your industry? The world?

What if you're just one vacation away from a ridiculously

brilliant idea that could make all your biggest dreams come true? And what if you are one vacation away from being who you envisioned you would be?

"The lessons I try to hang on from *Hamilton* are—it was one of the best ideas I ever had and it happened while I was on vacation, so take more vacations," Miranda told the Press Association.[11]

Vacations work. They help you and they help your business. And even if you started reading this book just hoping you could figure out how to take a Sunday off once in a while, you are now equipped to take a real one. Maybe you'll start with one week, then work your way up to two, then four. Maybe you'll end up taking multiple four-week vacations every year, like I do now. The point is, you now have the means to pull that off. And your business will thank you for it.

No matter what you have or don't have, no matter what challenges you face or what mistakes you make, no matter *what*, you can grow a business that runs itself. Before you cracked this book, you may not have known how to do that. Now you're armed with a system that's doable. One that tens of thousands of entrepreneurs have successfully done before you. And now you will join the army of shareholders who have designed their business to run itself.

I know this system works. And I believe in you.

I can't wait to see your vacation pictures from Maine. Or Spain. Or Antarctica. Or simply your own backyard. Or wherever you plan to spend your four-week vacation. And I can't wait to hear about the ideas you came up with while you were chilling by the sea.

It starts with a four-week vacation, so book it now. Oh, the places *your business* will go.

ACKNOWLEDGMENTS

I remember the first time I heard Leonard Cohen sing "Hallelu-jah." It was beautiful. Years later, I heard the rendition by Jeff Buckley. This time, I wept. I had no idea that an already beautiful song could be improved so dramatically. I feel the same way about this new version of *Clockwork*.

Writing *Clockwork, Revised and Expanded* has been an extraordinary project. While the core system hasn't changed, everything else has. Our crew worked relentlessly to make this book easier to absorb and faster to implement so you could get far greater results. While I have the joy of being the front man of this book, creating it has been a group effort. Let me introduce you to the band.

On drums is Anjanette "AJ" Harper. If I am the soul of my books, she is the heart. Every one of my books has been a collaborative writing effort between myself and AJ. She is a relentless stickler for quality in writing and clarity in communication. *Clockwork, Revised and Expanded* has been one of the most demanding projects we have done together. And it was worth it. The result is a Jeff Buckley rendition of the original. This book is the best of me and it is the best of Anjanette. Thank you, AJ.

Our soundboard producers are Noah Schwartzberg and Kimberly Melium. They listened for what you, the reader, would hear.

They noted where you might get stuck or confused, and then proposed fixes. They are more than editors; they are also our roadies. They were always one step ahead of me on this project, making it easier to just do what I do: write. Thank you, Noah and Kimberly.

On lead guitar is Liz Dobrinska. I have worked with Liz for more than ten years. Every website, every graphic, even the original cover of *Clockwork*, was created by Liz. Her ability to take my ideas and bring them to life blows me away every time. Thank you, Liz.

On backup vocals are Izzy Capodanno, Cordé Reed, Erin Chazotte, Amy Cartelli, Jeremy Smith, Jenna Lorenz, Adayla Michalowicz, and Edgar Amutavi. This team of wonderful humans is the essence of our operation. They make sure that, when one of my books is available for sale, the world hears about it. Just like the best backup vocalists, they do their part with a big smile while swaying their arms and snapping their fingers in perfect synchronization. Thank you, team Michalo-verse.

On bass is Adrienne Dorison. The bass is the instrument that ties all of the other sounds together. Adrienne did that for this book. She made good ideas better. She smoothed out clunky concepts. She introduced new techniques. She grew runlikeclockwork .com specifically to deliver support to the countless entrepreneurs who seek it. And she did all that while taking multiple four-week vacations, often during her company's busiest time of the year. She does what she teaches others to do. I can't imagine partnering with anyone more capable. Thank you, Adrienne.

On cowbell is Kelsey Ayres. I will never be able to fully express how grateful I am to be working with Kelsey. She is more than the president of our company. She is a remarkable friend. And she just happens to be the kindest soul to have ever walked this planet. I am humbled to work with you, Kelsey. I am forever grateful for your tireless efforts in serving entrepreneurs with our work. Thank you, Kelsey. We need more cowbell.

Last but not least is my greatest fan (she's kind of a groupie)— my wife, Krista. From the bottom of my heart, I thank you and our children for supporting my dream of writing books that will eradicate entrepreneurial poverty. I love you and the kids more than I can ever express. Thank you for our journey together. I live you (that's not a typo).

Hallelujah! I love this book. For me, it is the best rendition of *Clockwork*. I hope you feel the same.

GLOSSARY OF KEY TERMS

ACDC. The four major stages in the flow of business are: Attracting prospects, Converting prospects into clients, Delivering the promised offering to clients, and Collecting payment in return. Most businesses flow in the ACDC sequence, but it is not necessary. Some businesses, for example, collect payment before delivering services. And others may deliver a service before the prospect becomes a client.

Big BANG. A Big Beautiful Audacious Noble Goal that drives you to succeed in your business. This is an enhancement to Jim Collins's definition of a company's BHAG (Big Hairy Audacious Goal). For small businesses, the addition of Beautiful and Noble is necessary. Beauty is what is attractive to the business owner, and Nobility is what purposefully motivates the business owner. A company that is both attractive and of service to the shareholder(s) is one that brings fulfillment throughout the journey to the audacious goal.

Big Promise. The main thing you want your business to be known for among your prospects and clients. This is what you stake your company's reputation on.

The Clockwork Phases. Align, Integrate, and Accelerate are the three major phases of Clockwork, and within each phase are steps to take. The Align phase is the prework necessary to bring efficiencies to the business or an element of the business. The Integrate phase is the foundational work for business efficiencies and the application of discoveries/improvements achieved in the Align phase. And the Accelerate phase is the scaling work that achieves more results with less effort. The Clockwork Phases are not "one and done," but are activities that will forever be present and acted upon in a business abiding by the Clockwork system.

The Fifth D. In addition to the 4D activities, Downtime is the necessary time for people to recover and recharge.

The Four Ds (4Ds). The four types of activities, and four phases of work, that any individual in a company will spend their time engaged in. They will either be Doing the work, Deciding about the work for others, Delegating the work to others, or Designing how the work gets done. In many cases, individuals will be doing a combination of the 4Ds.

Four-Week Vacation. Most businesses experience all their critical activities within a four-week period. Therefore if you, as a leader of the business, remove yourself from the company for a four-week period, your business will be forced to run itself. By making a commitment to a four-week vacation, you will immediately be in the mindset of setting up your company to run itself.

Grant's Kennebago Camps. It is a bit of a tradition for our family now. None of us hunt or fish (or wear camo, for that matter), so we are always the oddballs. But now it is part of us. If you ever go and we run into you, please ask my wife to share the "bat attack," "leech assault," and "lobster reanimation" stories. They are family faves.

Miss Maud Hotel. A must-visit institution in Perth, Australia. They recently rebranded from the Miss Maud Hotel to the European Hotel. Go for the smorgasbord and try the apple turnovers. They're to die for.

Operation Vacation. A movement of *Clockwork* readers (and others) who are allocating time for themselves first and building their business around it. Similar to the Profit First method of first allocating profit, then reverse-engineering the business to ensure that profit happens.

The Optimal 4D Mix. The optimal mix for a company is 80 percent Doing, 2 percent Deciding, 8 percent Delegating, and 10 percent Designing. This is not the optimal mix for the entrepreneur or business owner, and not necessarily the optimal mix for employees; it is the optimal mix for the entire business (which is made up of the work contribution of many individuals).

Parkinson's Law. The theory that people expand their consumption of a resource to meet its supply. For example, the more time that is allocated for a project, the longer it will take to complete.

Primary Job. This is the most critical activity that an employee does in the scope of their work. It needs to be prioritized over any other work.

Profit First Method. This is the process of allocating a predetermined percentage of your company's income directly to a profit account before anything else is done with the money. The profit allocation occurs before paying bills. The entire process is documented in my book *Profit First*.

QBR. The Queen Bee Role. This is the one core function of your business that is most important to your Big Promise. It is the heart of an organization, and the company's success hinges on it.

Solopreneur. A person who exclusively owns and operates their business.

Survival Trap. The Survival Trap is the never-ending cycle of reacting to the urgent at the cost of disregarding the important. This makes business survival a day-to-day emergency. Building a Clockwork business gets you out of the Survival Trap.

Time Analysis. This is the process of tracking how a person (either you or someone you work with) typically spends their time at work. Use this tool to discover how much time you devote to each of the 4Ds.

Top Client. The best client(s) of your business, as determined by you. Typically, this is the client who pays you the most and with whom you most enjoy working. The process of identifying and cloning your Top Client is documented in my book *The Pumpkin Plan*.

Trash, Transfer, Trim, and Treasure. Take one of these first three steps to remove work that distracts an individual from serving the QBR or doing their Primary Job. This process typically moves Doing and Deciding work to "lower-level" employees and elevates Designing and Delegating to "higher-level" employees. The fourth step, Treasure, is for work that brings joy to the person performing the task. Treasured work amplifies joy and therefore improves performance. Seek to align the work individuals treasure with the jobs that need that work done.

AUTHOR'S NOTE

I hope you have enjoyed reading *Clockwork, Revised and Expanded*. It is my deepest desire to help you achieve the business you envision. I hope this book has taken you one significant step closer to just that.

It has for me. You see, I don't consider myself a creator of ideas, as much as a curator. I collect ideas, strategies, and stories and assemble them to gain knowledge for myself and impart wisdom to others. Throughout the process I learn and, hopefully, expand. This book did that for me.

You may have noticed that I dedicated this book to Jason Barker. We are not friends or family. We don't know each other outside of a few email exchanges. Yet he transformed *my* life. His story shifted something in me, and I committed to taking an annual trip with my college buddies. And that is what I did.

I organized an annual trip with my freshman-year roommate and two hall-mates. This picture is from our most recent trip, when we visited our original dormitory and went to the stadium to watch our beloved Hokies play Notre Dame.

What about you? What are you going to do that matters most? What memories will you forever cherish because you made your business run without you?

You deserve the life you envisioned when you built your business. Today is the day you make it a reality. No more delays. No more excuses. No more waiting.

Mike

NOTES

1. Julian E. Lange et al., "United States Report 2017," Global Entrepreneurship Monitor (2018), https://www.babson.edu/media/babson/site-assets/content-assets/academics/centers-and-institutes/the-arthur-m-blank-center-for-entrepreneurship/global-research/GEM_USA_2017.

2. Katherine Gustafson, "What Percentage of Businesses Fail and How to Improve Your Chances of Success," LendingTree, last modified August 7, 2020, https://www.lendingtree.com/business/small/failure-rate.

3. Mary Oliver, "The Summer Day," in *House of Light* (Boston: Beacon Press, 1990), 18–19.

4. Brian Michael Jenkins and Bruce R. Butterworth, "Does 'See Something, Say Something' Work?" Mineta Transportation Institute Publications (2018), https://transweb.sjsu.edu/sites/default/files/SP-1118_SeeSomethingSaySomething.pdf.

5. "Frequently Asked Questions," US Small Business Administration Office of Advocacy, last modified October 2020, https://cdn.advocacy.sba.gov/wp-content/uploads/2020/11/05122043/Small-Business-FAQ-2020.pdf.

6. Ferris Jabr, "Why Your Brain Needs More Downtime," *Scientific American*, October 15, 2013, https://www.scientificamerican.com/article/mental-downtime.

7. Sara Blakely, "Billionaire Sara Blakely Says Secret to Success Is Failure," interview by Robert Frank, CNBC, October 16, 2013, http://www.cnbc.com/2013/10/16/billionaire-sara-blakely-says-secret-to-success-is-failure.

8. Book Video Club, "'Build an A Team' by Whitney Johnson—Company Culture," November 29, 2018, YouTube video, 2:53, https://www.youtube.com/watch?v=ZN8l0ZJzi4Q.

9. Tim Kreider, "The 'Busy' Trap," *Opinionator* (blog), *New York Times,* June 30, 2012, https://opinionator.blogs.nytimes.com/2012/06/30/the-busy-trap.

10. Arianna Huffington, "Lin-Manuel Miranda Chats Before the Rockefeller Foundation's Insight Dialogues," June 23, 2016, Facebook video, 25:42, https://www.facebook.com/watch/live/?ref=watch_permalink&v=10154240062808279.

11. "Lin-Manuel Miranda: Hamilton Taught Me to Take More Holidays," *Belfast Telegraph,* December 22, 2018, https://www.belfasttelegraph.co.uk/entertainment/film-tv/news/lin-manuel-miranda-hamilton-taught-me-to-take-more-holidays-37650944.html.

INDEX

Page numbers in italics refer to charts or worksheets.

INDEX

DISCOVER MORE BOOKS!

Want to make more money?

Want to spend less time working?

Want to market better than ever?

Want to grow your business fast & strong?

Want to do the right things for your business?

Want to build your first company?

Want to be an industry leader?

Want to teach your kids money management for life?

DESIGN YOUR BUSINESS
TO RUN ITSELF!

Download the *free resources* and join our *workshops* at:

CLOCKWORK.LIFE

CLOCKWORK.LIFE

- *Free resources and tools*
- *Access to workshops + training*
- *Ensure you do Clockwork right*